Setting the Table

Setting the Table

Women in Theological Conversation

Edited by
Rita Nakashima Brock,
Claudia Camp, and Serene Jones
of the Forrest-Moss Institute

Chalice Press
St. Louis, Missouri

Biblical quotations, unless otherwise noted, are from the *New Revised Standard Version Bible*, copyright 1989, Division of Christian Education of the National Council of the Churches of Christ in the USA. Used by permission.

Cover design: Lynne Condellone
Art Director: Michael Domínguez

1 2 3 4 5 6 7 8 9 10   99 98 97 96 95

Library of Congress Cataloging-in-Publication Data

Setting the table: women in theological conversation / edited
  by Rita Nakashima Brock, Claudia Camp, and Serene Jones.
        p.   cm.
  Includes bibliographical references.
  ISBN 0-8272-3433-3
  1. Feminist theology. 2. Christian Church (Disciples of Christ)—
Doctrines. I. Brock, Rita Nakashima. II. Camp, Claudia V., 1951- .
III. Jones, Serene, 1959- .
BT83.55.S447   1995
230'.082—dc20   95-36895
                                                        CIP

Printed in the United States of America

Contents

SECTION III—CHRISTIAN LIFE

STUDY GUIDE

Preface

Perhaps you are a woman who shares our experience of attending meeting after meeting, year after year, in rooms filled predominantly by men. Then suddenly, one year, that critical mass of women appears, enough of us that when we find each other we are no longer a handful, but a group, enough to make a difference. Such was the case for women scholars of the Christian Church (Disciples of Christ) attending the denominational breakfast at our national professional meeting in the fall of 1990.

Coinciding with this event were a series of conversations, inspired by Rita Nakashima Brock, about the need for a new introduction to feminist theology. Classroom experience witnessed to the need for a book that could present both the history of and recent developments in the discipline for an entry-level audience in colleges, seminaries, and church education settings. Our church experience also cried out for an introduction that would be marked in some discernible, yet not exclusivistic, way by the values and concerns of the Disciples tradition. Taking the Disciples' nonhierarchical structure as a point of departure, we envisioned a collectively written book that would join many voices. We envisioned as well a book that, true to our ecumenical heritage, could speak to an audience interested in North American Protestant thought in general and its "low church" aspects in particular.

Beginning with that breakfast meeting, *Setting the Table: Women in Theological Conversation* emerged, true to its name, in conversations around many tables. In 1991, with the support of the Disciples' Division of Higher Education, the women who had watched each other across that crowded room the preceding year gathered for our own breakfast to begin discussion of "the book." Realizing that a collectively written volume required much more time together than was available in the press of a professional meeting, we agreed to meet at the Disciples Divinity House at the University of Chicago the following summer and, as it turned out, during the next two summers as well. There, through the facilitation of Disciples House Dean Kristine Culp, our minds and bodies were well fed, whether around the House's glass-topped library table or around the one in Kris's kitchen, laden with the vegetables and herbs from her garden.

As the book began to take shape, however, so did a larger vision, one of an ongoing institutional "table" that would continue to nurture the work of women scholars who seek to make a contribution to the church. In forming the Forrest-Moss Institute, Disciples women have taken as our model the denomination's earlier Campbell Institute, formed in 1896 to encourage both scholarship and "spiritual maturity" among Disciples. Albertina Allen Forrest, the only woman charter member and the first secretary of the Institute, lends us her name, as does Luella St. Clair Moss, the first of only four women to serve as president of a Disciples college (Columbia College in Missouri).

It should not be surprising that during half a decade of gathering around tables, much more has emerged from our conversations than is represented by the pages of this book and the ongoing Forrest-Moss Institute. What has emerged as well is a sense of community among the authors. In good Disciples fashion, we began each meeting around a table where a powerful experience of communion occurred. We spent an hour or two sharing the stories of our lives: we spoke about sick children, the passing of loved ones, and the changing of relationships; we spoke as well about vacations, job exhaustion, and tenure decisions; about horses and music; about racism and the ongoing struggle for justice in our nation; and we spoke too about writing books, going to church, dealing with sexism, and being women scholars in an academy where our numbers are still small. In these conversations, it became increasingly clear to us that each perspective represented at the table was and still remains profoundly unique, that our differences are myriad. In a similar fashion, this book represents not one single or unified perspective on feminist theology, but many. As expressions of our varied life stories and perspectives, our essays represent our differences and, at times, our disagreements. For the authors, these differences have been a source of both community and growth as well as a cause for celebration. We hope the array of perspectives presented here will serve the reader similarly.

Alongside our differences, it is important that we acknowledge also the many deep resonances and commonalities that have sounded in our voices over the years when, sitting around that table, we have spoken of our daily lives and the ways that our faith continually disposes us to live in the world. While these resonances have many sources, we have been particularly struck by how much we share based on our common grounding in the Disciples tradition and in Disciples' communities. Sometimes these resonances were softly present and hence hard to identify directly, as in the case of that gentle feeling of being theologically "at home" when speaking with one another about our faith perspectives. Similarly, we reflected often on our common experience of being shaped by a tradition that is low church in its polity and yet highly liturgical with regard to its weekly practice of communion, and we slowly discovered together that as Disciples, we stand uniquely positioned to speak theologically to traditions ranging from Baptist to Episcopal and Roman Catholic. At other times, the similarities between us were more obvious, such as our shared sense of being called to a Christian fellowship that is deeply ecumenical in spirit, our collective "looseness" on issues of doctrinal/creedal correctness, our firm rootedness in the scriptural story, our discomfort with rigid ecclesial and social hierarchies, and our abiding love for the local church. In our conversations, one could also hear subtle echoes of older voices, voices from our Disciples past, which came through in our shared sense of frontier, of open spaces, of struggle, and of possibility. It may be that in this last sense of voice we most clearly exhibited the "culture" of our Disciples heritage. We hope that this sensibility comes through in these essays as well and is able to evoke in the reader an excitement akin to our own.

In addition to these words about the history behind and the voices within this book, the authors wish to recognize the many people who have helped to "set the table" for this book over the past four years. We thank David Polk and Chalice Press for supporting this project from the time of its inception as an idea to its final publication. We appreciate the support of Dean Kristine Culp and the Disciples Divinity House at the University of Chicago for literally setting the table for the book by providing us with a place to meet and other in-kind financial support. Similarly, Texas Christian University, Hamline University, and our other work-related institutions have generously supported this project in varied ways. We have benefited as well from the continued support of John Imbler, Curt Jones, and the Christian Church (Disciples of Christ) Division of Higher Education. We further wish to thank Ursula Pfafflin and Karen-Marie Yust for their much appreciated contributions to the project. In addition to the authors represented here, there are a number of women scholars teaching in Disciples-related institutions around the country whose voices do not appear directly in this volume but who nonetheless have contributed to this project through the continued offering of their scholarly insights and their lively feminist spirits. To our families, our close friends, our students, our church communities, and our sister theologians everywhere, we hope you catch a glimpse of the myriad contributions your lives have made to our writings. We have "set the table" of this book for you especially, as but a small thanks for the empowering communion you offer us daily.

About the Authors

Rita Nakashima Brock holds the Endowed Chair in Humanities at Hamline University where she teaches in the Religion and Women's Studies departments. When she isn't teaching, she writes feminist theology, speaks in churches, and tries to stay warm during the Minnesota winters. She is a member of the Board of Directors of the Christian Church (Disciples of Christ) Division of Overseas Ministries. In her (scarce) spare time, she cooks for friends and family, reads novels, plays with her cats, walks when it isn't snowing, and skis when it snows enough.

Claudia V. Camp is associate professor of religion at Texas Christian University, specializing in Hebrew Bible. She has written extensively on the female imagery for Wisdom in the Bible, including a book, *Wisdom and the Feminine in the Book of Proverbs*, and on feminist biblical interpretation. She is active in her church's community work and organizations, and has one daughter.

Kristine A. Culp is dean of the Disciples Divinity House of the University of Chicago and senior lecturer in theology at the Divinity School, the University of Chicago. Her chapter is based on research for a book she is writing on feminist ecclesiology. Among the places where her research has found practical expression is in her work as co-chair of the Vision Panel, a task force appointed to review the mission and structure of the Christian Church (Disciples of Christ). She keeps a splendid garden that fed the authors of this book during our summer meetings.

Serene Jones is assistant professor of systematic theology at Yale University Divinity School, is an ordained minister in the Christian Church (Disciples of Christ) and the United Church of Christ. She is a fifth-generation Disciple and is the author of *John Calvin and the Rhetoric of Piety* and *Feminist Theory and Feminist Theology*. She spends her summers on a farm in Connecticut, and she loves to ride horses and fly-fish. She reads mysteries when she has time.

Belva Brown Jordan is assistant professor of field education at Lancaster Theological Seminary and an ordained minister in the Christian Church (Disciples of Christ). She has also been the director of youth ministries and of multicultural education for the Disciples denomination. She is the daughter of two ordained Disciples ministers. In her spare time, she tries to maintain her sense of connection to the universe by hiking, swimming, and other physical activities. Her teenage daughter, Tonee, is about to spend a year abroad in Brazil.

Nadia Lahutsky is associate professor of religion at Texas Christian University, where she teaches courses in Christian history, women and religion, and world religions. She is an elder at South Hills Christian Church in Fort Worth, Texas, where she and her husband and six-year-old daughter worship. Her favorite church job is baking bread for communion.

Jane McAvoy is professor of religious studies at Hiram College and an ordained minister of the Christian Church (Disciples of Christ). She recently edited a collection of communion resources entitled *Table Talk: Resources for the Communion Meal.* In her spare time, Jane enjoys playing the saxophone in a jazz band and in a sax quartet.

Bonnie J. Miller-McLemore is associate professor of pastoral theology and counseling at The Divinity School of Vanderbilt University, Nashville, Tennessee, an ordained minister of the Christian Church (Disciples of Christ), and the mother of three small children. She is author of *Also a Mother: Work and Family as Theological Dilemma; Death, Sin and the Moral Life*, and has just completed *The American Family Debate and Religion*, which includes articles on feminism, gender, family, and pastoral care.

Kay Bessler Northcutt is an ordained minister living in Tulsa, Oklahoma. Devoted to the work of spiritual formation, Kay is a retreat leader, preacher, educator, pianist, daughter, aunt, godmother, sister, wife, cousin, niece, and friend. A feminist and a homemaker, Kay is a great cook and voracious reader. She also knows how to quilt and do minor car repairs. Mostly, she prays and writes.

Nancy Claire Pittman is an ordained minister in the Christian Church (Disciples of Christ) and currently serves as lecturer in New Testament at Tainan Theological College and Seminary, Tainan, Taiwan. Her commission for service with the Presbyterian Church in Taiwan was jointly approved by the Division of Overseas Ministries of the Christian Church (Disciples of Christ) and the United Church Board for World Ministries of the United Church of Christ.

Sondra Stalcup is an ordained minister in the Christian Church (Disciples of Christ) and a Ph.D. candidate in systematic theology at Southern Methodist University, completing a dissertation on contemporary christologies. She is an active ecumenist and frequent preacher, speaker, and retreat leader with a passion for women's concerns stemming from her days as president of the Southwest Region's Christian Women's Fellowship. She is a poet, collector of art pottery, and, most important, mother of Rachel and Stephen.

Marti J. Steussy is an ordained minister of the Christian Church (Disciples of Christ). She received her Ph.D. in Hebrew Bible from Vanderbilt University in 1992. She and her husband, Nic, live with their two children in Indianapolis, where Marti teaches at Christian Theological Seminary. She is writing a book about King David. Her nonacademic interests include weaving, horses, and writing science fiction novels.

Elizabeth Lee Thomsen is an ordained minister in the Christian Church (Disciples of Christ) currently living in New Mexico. She recently received her Ph.D. from Berkeley's Graduate Theological Union in New Testament studies and is looking for a teaching job. She has a twenty-three-year-old son and gardens in her spare time.

Mary Donovan Turner is assistant professor of homiletics at Pacific School of Religion and an ordained minister in the Christian Church (Disciples of Christ). She has been a parish minister in Georgia, and she and her husband, Lamar, and two children—Chris, 18, and Erin, 9—have found adapting to life in El Cerrito, California, a challenging and engaging experience.

A Glossary of Terms

Anchorite: one of two types of religious women in the Middle Ages who dedicated themselves to God. One type, *nuns*, lived in communities and hermitages; the other, *anchoresses* (such as Julian), lived an enclosed life in solitude. Julian lived in a cell adjoining the Church of St. Julian in Conisford at Norwich and devoted her life to prayer.

Androcentric, androcentrism: ideas and points of view that assume that maleness or men, their concepts, behaviors, and lives, are the norm for all human beings.

Christian feminist: a person who, in response to the Christian gospel's claim that in Christ all are equal and women are made in God's image, is committed to working for justice and equality of rights for women.

Christology: thought and speech about the Christ, including asking who the Christ is and what confessing Jesus as the Christ means to us. More narrowly and technically: the field of critical inquiry that asks about the conditions necessary for any subject to be "the Christ" and asserts that Jesus is the Christ.

Critical scholarship: study that uses the best available background information and tries to avoid sloppy thinking and hidden assumptions; not necessarily "critical" in the sense of "fault-finding."

Enlightenment: a European intellectual movement, beginning in the eighteenth century, that emphasized the use of reason to examine reality, encouraged a spirit of skepticism, and used objective research and rational thinking to test claims to truth.

Epistemological: having to do with the nature of knowing and knowledge; the study of how we know what we know, for example, through rational thinking, through our senses, or through intuition.

Epistolary: contained in the epistles, that is, the letters, such as Romans or 1 John.

Exegesis: careful study of a text (usually biblical) to decide what it meant in its ancient context.

Exegete: one attempting to explain or interpret a text, particularly a biblical text.

Existentialist: concerning reflections on the meaning of human existence; concerned especially with our deepest questions as human creatures, with our ultimate concerns about the meaning of our lives and how we are to live, based on our understanding of how we were created or meant to be.

Feminism: refers to both the social movement for women's equality and the intellectual movement that uses gender as a primary way of analyzing and understanding human society and ideas.

Feminist: a person committed to working for equal status and rights of women; someone who believes in and is committed to nurturing and promoting the inherent equality of women and men, girls and boys, in every aspect of our lives together on this planet. Men are referred to as either pro-feminist or feminist.

Feminist hermeneutics: see **Hermeneutics.**

First-wave feminism: applied to the first major feminist movement of the twentieth century focusing especially around the struggle for women's suffrage, which was won in 1920.

Hermeneutics, feminist hermeneutics: the theory and process of interpretation of texts. It is necessary because meaning does not simply "jump off the page"; rather, readers go through a process of achieving understanding that involves both intellectual reasoning and emotional response to what is written. Hermeneuticians not only "do interpretation" but also reflect on the process by which they arrive at their understandings, including awareness that biases and preconceptions on the part of the interpreter affect the outcome. Feminist hermeneutics is done with particular attention to the role of gender in the creation and interpretation of texts.

Heterosexism: ideas and points of view that assume that heterosexual behaviors and lives are the norm or the only way for all human beings to be.

Homiletics: the art of writing and preaching sermons; the study of preaching.

Homophobia: attitudes, norms, and social systems that create fear and hostility toward gay and lesbian people because of negative prejudices and stereotypes about homosexuals.

Iconoclastic: from *icon* (image) and *clastic* (to break); refers to the attacking of established beliefs or institutions, especially religious beliefs. (See **Idolatry.**)

Ideology, ideological criticism: the system of ideas that justifies, and thereby helps maintain, a given social system with its particular set of institutions and power relations. Gender ideology—ideas about female and male nature, abilities, relationships, and authority—is one aspect of a larger ideological system. Feminist ideological critics seek to make explicit what are often the hidden assumptions of gender ideology and show how these influence our thinking about both humans and God.

Idolatry: worshiping any created thing as the Creator. Common examples are worshiping money, or a person, as God. (See **Iconoclastic**.)

Inclusive language: language that includes references to both genders—for example, replacing the generic use of "he" with "he or she" or "they." (See **Nonsexist language**.)

Lectionary: a three-year cycle of biblical texts to be read in worship throughout the year. An Old Testament reading, a psalm, a reading from the epistles, and a reading from the Gospels are designated for each week and for other important days in the life of the church.

Literary criticism: an umbrella term for a wide range of approaches to studying literary texts. Literary approaches are important to feminist biblical scholars because of the awareness that virtually all biblical material about women was written by men, and may be more indicative of male values and projections than of female reality. Feminist literary critics study how female images are used to construct female identity, as well as to convey larger messages about the beliefs and cultural values of a patriarchal society. (See **Patriarchy**.)

Mujerista: taken from *mujer*, the Spanish word for woman; refers to Hispanic feminists and a developing field in theology that uses the history and life experiences of Hispanic women.

Mystic: one who has had a direct experience of the Divine.

Mythopoetic: having to do with the making of myths; used especially to indicate that the Bible is not solely or essentially "historic" in the modern sense of that word.

Narrative: the "story" element of a text, told by a narrator; the plot or sequence of events.

Nonsexist language: language that removes references to one specific gender; for example, the replacing of the word *mankind* with *humankind*. (See **Inclusive language**.)

Paradigm: a pattern, example, or model used to illustrate an idea.

Pastoral care: expressions and acts of concern [performed by those in the faith community] for members of the faith community and members of the wider community, including attentiveness to personal, interpersonal, and spiritual well-being through life experiences and crises of illness, death and grieving, life transitions, family conflict, aging, and so forth.

Pastoral theology: the theological discipline or the intellectual and practical activity of engaging and reflecting on the practices and traditions of care and moral guidance within religious communities.

Patriarchy: literally "rule by the fathers," referring to the male-dominant ruling structure of most cultures for about the last three or four thousand years, i.e., the sociopolitical, religious, economic, familial systems in various cultures on the planet that are male-oriented and male-ordered as to law, custom, belief, and decision-making. Also includes other relations of the domination/subordination structure, e.g., masters/slaves, ruling class/working class, imperialism, colonialism, racism, religious bigotry, heterosexism, and so forth, so that all such skewed hierarchical structures may sometimes be included in the term "patriarchal."

Process thought, process theology, or process philosophy: an understanding of life or a theory of reality in which the "really real" is not matter and substance, but social process, interaction, relationality, and change. In other words, both the structure of reality and the definition of reality are the very *process* of relating one to another, from the tiniest particle to human beings, and which also includes God's relatedness to us and to all creatures.

Reformation: the period beginning in the late fifteenth century when the Roman Catholic Church experienced movements of dissent that led to splinter groups founding their own churches, such as the Lutheran and Reformed traditions and other groups such as the Baptists, Mennonites, and Quakers; also referred to as the Protestant Reformation.

Second-wave feminism: describes the feminist activism that emerged in the 1960s and includes a revival of some issues begun in the First Wave (q.v.).

Sexism: attitudes and social systems that prejudge all women based on stereotyped assumptions about women's proper roles, behaviors, intelligence, etc.

Social history: as used by feminists, an approach that seeks to gain information about the lives of women in earlier times. This search is often difficult because historical records tend to focus on the deeds and words of powerful men. Feminist social historians seek more widely for information about social institutions and roles to gain insight into informal power and authority relations. They also examine archeological data that suggest how ordinary people lived, and cross-cultural data from which to draw inferences about ancient life through comparison with known societies.

Strata (as in "middle strata," "upper strata," and "working-class strata"): similar to the term "class"—the economic status of a particular group of people—but more distinctly referring to a less rigid or narrow grouping of people. The term includes people's political and social status.

Theism: from the Greek word *theos*, which means "God"; the understanding of ultimate reality that includes deities or one deity or "God"—as in Christianity, Judaism, and Islam—as *the* strictly ultimate reality, the ground or source and end of all things.

Torah: Hebrew for "teaching," sometimes translated "law," usually referring to the first five books of the Bible. Jewish people sometimes use the term more generally to mean "scripture" or "God's teaching."

Verdancy: green, young life, fresh.

Victorian: historical period associated with Queen Victoria of England (1837-1901) and often used to describe attitudes of middle-class respectability and prudery.

Womanist: an African-American feminist; also refers to a developing field in theology that uses the history and life experiences of African-American women.

Introduction

1

What Is a Feminist?

Strategies for Change and Transformations of Consciousness

Rita Nakashima Brock

At the 1994 Quadrennial gathering of the International Christian Women's Fellowship of the Christian Church (Disciples of Christ), a processional of women clergy opened one of the worship services. Many of the several thousand women watching the processional were thrilled, felt chills, and wept in gratitude for the hundreds of ordained women who marched in their vestments and received a standing ovation. Few social movements in Western history have had as much impact on ordinary life and the Protestant church as feminism, the movement for justice and equality for women. Women's lives have changed dramatically, as has the leadership of our churches. That processional of women clergy and the reaction of their supporters are visible signs of the magnitude of change in women's lives. That change is also evident in women's work in theology, which has created new understandings of God, Christ, salvation, the Bible, preaching, pastoral counseling, and worship. Rooted in the Christian good news, we have unset the old theological table and reset it to welcome women at a time when many feminists have come to associate Christianity with bad news.

This feminist movement arrived to these shores from Europe through the Quakers and other progressive religious groups. In addition, Enlightenment ideas such as scientific rationality and the development of democratic ideas helped feminists argue, on the basis of their intelligence and morality, that their humanity transcended biological destiny. While Native American and African-American women often had more equality than their white sisters in their own ethnic communities, the dominant culture's racism and imperialism prevented the mainstream white culture from learning from these traditions.

Women's activity for justice in the dominant European-based culture has swelled and waned through U.S. history, depending on the historical forces of the time and the social and legal circumstances of women's lives. Abigail Adams warned her husband, John, that if women were not included as full citizens in the U.S. Constitution, there would be great trouble in the land. We might be tempted to claim her as a wise prophet, given what has happened to women and families since.

There has been a persistent struggle waged by many women and men, not only for equal rights, but also to humanize and make women's lives safe.[1] For example, in the early nineteenth century the popular health movement, which had a high women's participation rate, emphasized nutrition and self-help health care, and women fought alcohol abuse because of its impact on families. Women in Chicago organized a shelter for battered women and volunteered to sit in courtrooms during rape trials so women testifying against their rapists could look into friendly, supportive women's faces. (Ehrenreich) Women such as Matilda Joslyn Gage and Elizabeth Cady Stanton criticized religious authorities for subordinating women and argued, on religious grounds, that women were equal. Stanton went so far as to challenge the use of the Bible against women, a challenge described by Elizabeth Thomsen in her essay in Section I. Many women, such as the Grimke sisters, developed their feminist consciousness from working in the antislavery movement and were severely disappointed when their citizenship rights were separated from those of black men and denied.

The twentieth century has seen two major waves of feminist activity, one that carried over from the nineteenth century and receded with the Depression, and the second that surged in the 1960s following the publication of Betty Friedan's *The Feminine Mystique* and Simone de Beauvoir's *The Second Sex*. First-wave feminism resulted in women's suffrage and in access to birth control for women, both of which cannot be underestimated for the impact they have had.

---

[1] Men have a history of their own in supporting women's rights. For example, Frederick Douglas, an ex-slave, attended the first women's rights convention at Seneca Falls, NY. See Kimmel in the list of works cited.

Feminists have changed laws that made women the property of their husbands and fathers, and we now serve at almost all levels of government. Access to safe and affordable birth control has extended women's lives and changed our life stages and patterns. Women continue to bear and raise children and face the challenges of mothering, as Bonnie Miller-McLemore makes evident in her essay in Section III, but many women have become more intentional about the choice to mother. In the past, many mothers died before their youngest child had reached adulthood. Now the vast majority of women spend the largest part of their adult lives alone or married in a home without children present, sometimes while caring for aging parents. Sometimes for financial reasons and sometimes out of a desire for self-fulfillment and independence, more and more women work for pay outside the home, joining a history of immigrant and African-American women who have worked outside their homes since their arrival in North America. The increase in women's paid work outside the home has affected the numbers of volunteers available to churches, which have often counted on the time and unpaid work of its women members. Understanding women's lives in the Christian church means understanding how the feminist movement has touched women in churches, in seminaries, and in pulpits. The essays in Section III of this book address some of those changes.

Despite its commitments to humanize women's lives and its considerable contributions to life in the U.S. and Canada, feminism remains one of the most misunderstood social movements of our time. It is as nearly misunderstood in the public mind and media as religion. Stereotypes label feminists as man-hating (and woman-hating), bra-burning, angry women. The public is encouraged to believe that feminists believe all women are victims and that anyone who advocates women's rights and cares about what happens to women must automatically be anti-male and anti-family. Such stereotypes belittle one of the most important social movements in the history of Western culture and of Christianity. This social, political, and intellectual movement has transformed the lives of many women. Yet the enormous legacy of intelligent, compassionate, creative, committed women throughout American and Canadian history has had to be relearned by every new generation of women because so many women's accomplishments are ignored and forgotten. The social and cultural biases are obviously very strong against seeing women as achievers, fully and equally human, and deserving of all rights of citizenship.

While feminists are often blamed for every ill that faces society, it is probably more helpful and accurate to understand the women's movement as a process that reflects how women have responded to the social forces that shape our lives. Women did not invent the industrial revolution, science, medicine, urbanization, racism, homophobia, and American individualism, but we have had to cope with the consequences, which have been devastating to some women. And we have, as well, participated in the development of these social forces. The history of women's responses to the social forces of our times reaches back to biblical times with women such as Hagar, Deborah, Tamar, Ruth, and Naomi. Each of us, as we struggle in our own places, stands as part of a rich and powerful legacy.

Just as stereotypes about feminism and feminists are inadequate and inaccurate, any attempt to define feminism for all women who call themselves feminists would leave out a great deal. In fact, a more helpful approach is to talk of many women's movements, some based in the lives of African-American women and the antislavery movement, or in the lives of Hispanic or Native American women, or in the coalition between labor unions and women workers, or in the work of lesbians in solidarity with gay men, as well as the more visible white, middle-class movement. This introduction will not articulate all of these, but will look at how the women's movement, in its most visible forms, has impacted the work and theology of the mainline Protestant church, which is the focus of this book.

Feminist thinking began with women's awareness of a mismatch between our lives and the social, cultural, and religious expectations, stereotypes, and attitudes imposed on us. As women talked to other women about that mismatch, collective reflections developed about our experiences in a male-dominated society. Christine de Pizan, a fifteenth-century French woman who made an independent living for herself and her daughter by writing, describes her own conversations with women in her gentle argument for the dignity and worth of women, *Book of the City of Ladies*. (Anderson) Feminist reflections on women's lives had to be developed by women's friendships because, unlike oppressed and marginalized groups who are separated into neighborhoods and subcultures, women live at all levels of society. We love, nurture, teach, and/or live with those who sometimes abuse or oppress us. Realizing the frustrations, pain, and suffering of our lives and doing something about them are difficult in isolation, especially when no one in particular in our lives is causing us harm or means us ill.

The experiences of women, even in patriarchal societies, are very diverse. Hence, how women understand, think about, and cope with our status and roles under male-dominance are also quite diverse. Our conversations are determined by our friendships and conversation partners, and in so racially and economically divided a society as ours, our conversations have had clear limits. Christian women in

Africa or Asia think about their lives and status differently than do North American women; they also reach different conclusions and employ different strategies for change. Often, conversations and friendships among women that cross economic, racial, and other social barriers are infrequent. When they occur, cross-cultural con- versations among Christian women, while often difficult and politi- cally charged, have helped us all find better means for change. The increase in such conversations have also helped us build networks of solidarity and support for unleashing women's work for justice.

The following five ways of creating change represent how domi- nant, middle-class North American feminist movements have arrived at strategies. Each of the strategies is effective in certain contexts and for particular purposes, and a feminist may employ one or more, depending on the situation. We are calling the five strategies the Just Like a Man Strategy, the Add Women and Stir Strategy, the Women as Victims Strategy, the Women-Centered Strategy, and the Include Everyone Strategy. They represent how some women, who have been part of second-wave feminism, think about change and how that thinking has impacted theology.[2] Nancy Pittman's essay in Section I illustrates how different strategies work in reading the biblical text.

These strategies are based on states of consciousness within the dominant feminist movement, states that developed over time, but not necessarily in a hierarchical sequence. The states are presented below in sequence to give order to them and also to show how the transformation of consciousness happened for many feminists. The states and strategies indicate how trends in some feminists' thinking developed from the mid-1960s to the 1990s, but operating out of one state of consciousness does not mean leaving others behind. Being able to integrate them means being able to use them effectively. Al- though no particular strategy is superior to the others, the associ- ated states of consciousness emerge from transformation and growth in some cases. From stage four, stages one to three look different, and at level four, one usually does not yet understand what level five sees. The authors hope this laying out of states and strategies is helpful to those struggling to understand a very complex and pow- erful movement that is reshaping the Christian church.

In second-wave feminism, women began to enter professions and institutions that had earlier been closed off to all but an exceptional few. The surge of women into traditional male occupations happened

---

[2] Peggy McIntosh, listed at the end of this introduction, developed this schema of five phases to describe the process of integration of feminist re- search into the traditional academic curriculum. The schema has been some- what modified here.

because an increasing number of women began to attend college in the 1960s, when rising affluence, the growth of state university systems and readily available financial aid made higher education accessible to children born after World War II. Birth control and legalized abortion also freed women from fears of early parenting responsibilities, and women began to delay marriage. In addition, many of us had our political consciousness awakened by participation in the civil rights and anti-Vietnam War movements.

The number of women attending college and seminary and entering traditional male occupations has continued to increase, as is obvious now in churches, with the rapidly growing number of women pastors. The presence of more and more women in many previously male-defined occupations, such as the military, ministry, politics, or police work, may give us a false sense of complacency about equality, false because discrimination against women still exists in salary inequities, in promotion decisions, in maternity and elder care policies, in the awarding of senior pastorates, and in gender expectations and roles. In addition, domestic violence and lack of good, affordable child care still impact women's lives disproportionately because so many working women also perform the lion's share of domestic chores (despite media hype about some "Mr. Moms" and public perceptions to the contrary). Men who participate substantially in child care or raise children on their own have noticed also how much the world of work is not structured to enable anyone to both pursue meaningful full-time work and raise a family.

Of course, the five strategies and states described below outline only one sequence by which women develop a feminist consciousness. The experiences of women who work in female-dominated professions have their own patterns of consciousness and growing awareness. In addition, women of color, working-class women, lesbians, and poor women have experienced other forms of discrimination besides that based on gender. In addition, women who worked in the civil rights movement have tended to view injustices as linked together. The following patterns summarize the dominant context of feminist thinking through which many women, including some of the authors of this book, began to name our frustrations and articulate our awareness of oppression.

Just Like a Man

Women who entered college in the late 1960s or early 1970s grew up in woman-less (and woman=less) churches. A woman-less church is not one without women, but one in which the leadership is predominantly male—pastors, elders, deacons, church officers, theologians, and church executives. In addition, sermon illustrations, biblical stories, religious language, and images of God are oriented around the worlds, values, and experiences of men, such as competitive sports or the military. The few biblical stories mentioned about women tended to emphasize women's traditional, and usually subservient, roles and behavior.

Unfortunately, many educated women did not notice a problem—because they were busy proving they were equal to the men in the world. They liked being told by professors that they could think just like a man. This state of consciousness might be called "the woman who wasn't there." Many women did not want to be the best female anything, but the best person, the best actor or doctor, not the best actress or doctoress. In order to gain professional respect and equal access to the ladder of success, this strategy involves doing things "just like a man."

This strategy makes some sense because the farther a woman wants to go in a predominantly male subject and/or profession, the more she finds herself in an all-male environment, modeling herself on men. To succeed, she must fit in, which may limit her ability to notice the absence of other women. Or, if fitting in has been a tight squeeze, she may resent the presence of other women because she is reminded of her difference from the men around her. Equality gained by this strategy is often a lonely and difficult form of success. Pioneers in many fields, theology included, had few choices for women making gains outside fitting in. Women in such circumstances may feel forced to remain single or to deal with the demands of their families in jobs designed for those who have "wives" at home to take care of children. In addition, women often take on the stresses and health problems created by the demands of intense competition, in addition to conflicts between work and home. Nancy Mairs describes this loneliness and difficulty in her autobiography, *Ordinary Time*.

> When…a fellow creative writing student "told me one day that he didn't enjoy reading women authors and another day that the class had been good because no women were there," I kept silent "for fear that I'll get shrugged off as a bitchy feminist and do more harm than good." Harm to whom? The man who had just told me that the best thing about me was my absence?…To the extent that I adulterated my gender, I could disguise its force in my life. I was a woman, sure, but since when did that keep a good man down? This bravado, brittle and about one millimeter thick, masked terror instead of lancing it. In the roles that most unambiguously marked me a woman—wife, mother—I felt "sick and empty and scared." If anything threatened to punch my man-mask, beneath which lay only a vast cipher, as gaping

and greedy as a black hole, I ducked and dodged....Slowly and painfully...the mask cracked. (95-96)

The women wearing their "man-masks" had no way to name the problem, until something triggered an awareness of the absence of women or the inadequacy of the traditional female models to address their needs. The first awareness that something was wrong sometimes came when a woman noticed that she did not fit entirely, as Mairs became aware above, or that jokes about women weren't so funny anymore, or that she made half what her less-gifted and less-hardworking colleague made. Some women were stunned when they realized many men they worked with in the civil rights movement did not care about justice for women of any color. For other women, awareness came through more personal ways, through coming to see the limitations of a difficult marriage or struggling to live up to feminine ideals of behavior and appearance. Still other women met a feminist and talked to her or read a feminist book, such as Friedan's. The courage of a few women who faced the ambiguity of their lives and who told the truth about that ambiguity opened up moments of truth for many others. The ensuing conversations where the truths of our lives can be told continue to empower us all.

The philosopher Sara Ruddick describes her awakening after a long love affair with "Reason" that led her into a career in philosophy and ethics. Her love of rationality led her to learn to think abstractly, from principles and ideas detached from her embodied, emotionally complicated life. At first the detachment of "Reason" from the particularities of time and place and personal idiosyncrasies reassured her because it allowed her to avoid facing the personal conflicts in her life, including her loves and passions. But such detachment ultimately failed her:

Then I had children and another 'irrational' passion, a grittier, more troubling one but equally consuming....Increasingly I felt a fraud and also disloyal to the other mere women-and-mothers with whom I spent much of my time. (7-8)

Ruddick also found that "Reason" failed her work for desegregation, in which concrete action was necessary. While Ruddick's dilemma was not new—nineteenth-century educated feminists also struggled with conflicting demands—the lack of information about women in the past has resulted in women in this century having to reinvent the wheel, as it were. Ruddick says, "Reason was failing me—as a lover, mother, and citizen" (8). Using her experiences as a woman, Ruddick rethought "Reason," rather than reject it wholesale, and reached a breakthrough in which she used a redefined reason to strengthen her passions and to connect love to knowledge—

to bind reason to life as concretely, incarnately lived. In other words, rather than finding fault with her life as a woman, she found fault with the traditional ideals of reason and reconceived it.

Such feminist moments, such breakthroughs, brought a whole new world of awareness to women—the first step in a long journey. Women began to notice the absence of their sisters everywhere outside the domestic world, and women in theology began to want to transform the woman-less church, for example, as Mary Daly did in *The Church and the Second Sex.*

Add Women and Stir

The Just Like a Man strategy produced for many women a hunger for the presence of other women. As women entered seminary and graduate school, many wanted to know about all the women in the Bible and in Christian history. These pioneering feminists were stunned to learn there had been women pastors and theologians, powerful church women leaders throughout the Christian tradition who had somehow been erased or ignored (the amount of erasure is so extensive that some women call it the "eraser theory of history"). This hunger for women has generated an enormous amount of research on women, as feminists discovered women who had achievements just as great as any man's—or greater. The stage of consciousness that accompanies this strategy might be called "women are equal to and just as capable as men."

Out of this concern for women's equality, feminist research has balanced our picture of the church and added to our knowledge of who has contributed to its successes. Adding women into the recipe of history and restirring the pot has created a whole new cuisine and a much richer mix. This research also inspired feminists to aspire to and to achieve more as we discovered successful role models from both the past and the present. For example, the historian Jane Douglas (the first woman to earn a Ph.D. at Harvard Divinity School) showed that women were crucial to the success of the Calvinist Protestant Reformation in Europe in the sixteenth century. Feminist research proved a woman often achieved a great deal in the church, regardless of what church authorities said. For example, in the late nineteenth and early twentieth centuries a number of Protestant women formed their own mission societies to send women abroad to preach and minister when their own home churches refused to accept their gifts and ordain them. Finding all these lost women made feminists hungry for fairness and equality, as well as for the comforting presence of other women. Mary Donovan Turner's essay on preaching in Section III illustrates the value of knowing women in the past who could do what we today struggle to learn.

There was a problem, however, that emerged as this phase of active research on women flourished. No matter how hard we searched and no matter how far we looked, there were not enough women to balance the male-dominated picture. Women did not achieve visibly in equal numbers to men, and the women achievers often had to overcome enormous obstacles. Regardless of how much feminists studied the Bible and history, there was a shortage of women in the ranks of heroes and leaders. And looking at heroes and leaders turned us away from the deeds and work of most women in the world. *Still*, equality has not been achieved in church leadership. We have to ask why.

The dearth of women might lead one to conclude that women are inferior and unable to achieve equally with men. Feminist scholars were unwilling to conclude something was wrong with us. After all, if we were doing things professionally as well as (often better than!) the men we knew (while often doing most of the work at home), we could hardly conclude women as a group were inferior. If we believed we were made in the divine image, we had to figure out what went wrong, and it was clear something was wrong; something worked against women.

Women as Victims

The third strategy came with research by feminists on patriarchy—on systems of male dominance that oppress women. We discovered laws, religious ideas, social structures, public policies, and cultural attitudes that discriminated against women. Many great church theologians said degrading and demeaning things about women and did horrible things to them. Laws sanctioned the rape and battering of wives, and many Christian theologians, such as Calvin and Luther, agreed with the laws. The church often treated married women as nonpersons, as property. Women were blamed as temptresses for their own victimization. Church theologians—many of whom were celibate monks who may never have known any woman well—called women "misbegotten males" (Aquinas) or "the gateway of the devil" (Tertullian) and denied women ordination to ministry. As the magnitude of such systems became clear, a common response has been outrage and a state of consciousness we might call "the system is unfair and sexist."

This outrage has enormous energy in it for change. Feminists have reclaimed the outrage of the biblical prophets, who had a passion for justice. Beverly Harrison, who teaches Christian ethics at

Union Theological Seminary, proclaimed in an essay entitled "The Power of Anger in the Work of Love: Christian Ethics for Women and Other Strangers":

> A chief evidence of the grace of God—which always comes to us in, with, and through each other—is this power to struggle and to experience indignation. We should not make light of our power to rage against the dying of the light. It is the root of the power of love. So may it never be said of any of us feminist theologians that we merely stood by, ladylike, when that power of love was called for or that we sought refuge in an Otherworld when we were needed here and now, in the line of march....Like Jesus, we are called to a radical activity of love, to a way of being in the world that deepens relation,...[and] passes on the gift of life. (Harrison: 20, 18)

The energy of such anger has been used to break silences about the harm done to women and children and to make positive changes for women, for example, by starting hundreds of rape crisis hotlines and shelters for women and children who live with domestic violence. However, stereotypes about angry, man-hating women proliferated from these analyses of male dominance because anger is so unacceptable in women. After all, the socially acceptable (and lovable) woman was a chaste, pure, long-suffering, kind, patient saint— a perfect lady. Nonetheless, a great deal of feminist work was accomplished to make society and the church aware of the oppression of women, including exposing some of the most devastating aspects of male dominance, such as domestic violence, rape, incest, child molestation, and sexual harassment. Women have been expected around the world to feed others, to support them, and even to love those who oppress them. Millions of women's and children's lives and psyches have been saved by feminist work—the importance of which is hard to overestimate.

The anger of women against male dominance empowered thousands of women to tell the truth of the pain of their lives and to enable others to do the same. The creation of safe communities for women has sometimes involved strategies of separation from men and even of feminist separatism for some women, though few women use such separation as more than a temporary means for healing and sanity. Feminists developed hundreds of kinds of support systems and organizations to help women heal, to organize women for change, and to end male dominance. Feminists have large visions!— and prophetic outrage can be very empowering.

Some people outside this feminist work have found it hard to believe the extent of suffering involved, partly because discrimination and domestic crimes are often hidden. For example, a feminist theologian who gave a lecture at a conference on domestic violence was told by a male pastor that he was sure such things did not happen in his congregation because he had not heard of any cases. The theologian said to him, "I want you to do just one thing next Sunday in worship. Mention that you attended this conference and give the subject of it. You don't have to preach about it or do anything else. Just mention that you were here." He did so and called her two weeks later to tell her three women from his congregation had already talked to him about the violence that was happening to them—one was the wife of an elder.

There are limits with this third phase too, however. For one thing, being outraged much of the time can be exhausting and keep us in a reactive, uncentered state. We can become paranoid about anyone who belongs to a group perceived as powerful and be too quick to react and place blame. In addition, portraying women exclusively as victims of an oppressive system can be limiting to our ideas of women. While focusing on oppression may call attention to a serious problem, feminists are aware that women are more than the sum of the harm inflicted on us. After all, most women go about our lives and struggles without dwelling on unfairness and on oppression. In fact, it is far more empowering to know that women have survived, and sometimes even thrived, under highly adverse circumstances. Many women who have been violated and abused are able to nurture others and lead humane lives. For the sake of accuracy, women must also be seen as strong, courageous survivors.

Women-Centered

Feminists, on the whole, respect women, including ourselves, and that respect means we have to explore women's strengths and creativity. Feminist research shifted focus in the 1980s toward alternative values and strategies women have created in the worlds of female activity. As Beverly Harrison reminds us:

> Women have always exemplified the power of activity over passivity, of experimentation over routinization, of creativity and risk-taking over conventionality....*If* women throughout human history have behaved as cautiously and as conventionally as the 'good women' invented by [nineteenth-century] bourgeois spirituality, *if* women had acquiesced to the 'cult of true womanhood,' and *if* the social powerlessness of women that is the 'ideal' among the European and American 'leisure classes' had prevailed, the gift of human life would long since have faced extinction. (Harrison: 9)

From a perspective that affirms women's lives, wanting to be equal to men might look like a lack of ambition; for, if one examines the system that has hurt women and children, wanting equality within that system appears like a desire to join the ranks of those who inflict pain and create injustice. Feminists have often found ourselves in the paradoxical situation of fighting for equality within a system hard-put to include us, at the same time we also work to transform that system at its very roots. A woman uncomfortable with the hierarchy of authority that surrounds ordination may still work hard to be ordained and be called to a church. Once in a church, however, she may encourage more lay preaching and congregational participation in worship leadership as a way to minimize hierarchy and focus more on her role as facilitator, enabler, teacher, and counselor. In effect, she struggles to gain authority that enables her to share it with others, rather than to elevate herself higher. Out of such paradoxes, feminist research presented nonandrocentric (andros=male) values for measuring change that focused on the actual lives and contributions of the majority of American women. The state of consciousness that accompanies this strategy might be called "affirming women's lives and valuing what we offer for changing the world." Ruddick, above, has done this in philosophy with her work on maternal ethics.

This fourth phase has produced exciting and visionary research, as the passion behind anger about oppression has been combined with a deep respect for the gifts of women and a profound hope for change. How women do things and what women feel and think have much to teach the world about coping with many kinds of problems. Feminist research points to values centered on nurture, care, cooperation, egalitarian fairness, and other values associated with the roles and worlds assigned to women. Feminists who use a women-centered strategy highlight the impact of the neglect of women's ideas and female values on the larger society. Original research on women's psychological development, health care, spirituality, and organizations, to name just a few of the new areas of research, continues to appear. Feminist Christian scholars have worked to make the church and society more accountable to these woman-centered values while trying to avoid the gender stereotyping of sexism by showing how these values should be part of the whole society, not just women's work. New styles of leadership, ministry and preaching, new theological perspectives, new forms of biblical interpretation, new criteria for historical importance, new visions of hope for the future, and new language and images for God are contributions of this phase— and this book is a sampler of many of these, for example, in Jane McAvoy's essay on inclusive language.

One of the most important works to energize this Women-Centered Strategy was Carol Gilligan's book *In a Different Voice: Psychological Theory and Women's Development.* In that landmark study, Gilligan argued that Western psychological theories for determining maturation and ethical decision making were created by observation of the lives of men, who are pushed toward autonomy and independence as adults. These theories meant that women looked immature, less ethical, or inadequate. Why? Because women live more deeply bonded in relationships throughout our adult lives, usually without needing as much autonomy as men. To take account of women's difference, Gilligan created an alternative theory to measure women's maturity and ethical decision-making processes. She gave priority to how women maintain relationships of care. Gilligan said that, on the one hand, the male model lifts up the highest ethical stage as the ability to make choices based on abstract principles independent of particular circumstances, relationships, and contexts— the ideal use of reason. She argued, on the other hand, that women look for means, within a particular context, to find a strategy for causing the least amount of harm to all involved, what is now called an ethics of care. This more field-dependent or contextually based way of thinking, according to Gilligan, is as ethical as the other model, and might perhaps be more humane. She did not argue that all men use one way and all women the other. Rather, she insisted that her model existed in some women and that attention needed to be paid to its benefits for ethics. Kay Bessler Northcutt expands these insights into ideas of prayer in Section III.

Nel Noddings in *Women and Evil* has elaborated Gilligan's research into a study of how the Christian tradition has misunderstood evil and creates it by its ethical strategies that emphasize conflict and winning and losing. Noddings proposes a new ethical model based in the experiences of many women trying to heal, protect, and nurture other human beings. The essays by Sondra Stalcup, Kris Culp, and myself in Section II discuss aspects of theology when women's voices and perspectives become the lens through which we examine God, Christ, and the church.

Include Everyone

The success of this fourth phase points also to its limitations. Since many of the researchers have been middle-class white women, their pool of experiences and research subjects has often been limited to women similar to themselves. Women of color and other marginalized women, as well as feminists who also work in the civil rights and other liberation movements, have criticized feminist research as too narrowly focused on particular types of women—a criticism feminists had leveled at men's studies that pretended research on men was research on all humans. Because of this criticism, more attention has been paid in the last ten years to the types of women used in feminist generalizations about women. For example, the feminist focus on abortion rights, while important to many women of color, has tended to neglect the history of forced sterilization of women of color by the government and more overall issues of adequate health care for poor women. To focus on the right to limit birth options also tends to ignore the reality that not all cultures disvalue children as much as a consumer-oriented, business-driven society, which often discusses children's value in financial terms. We might think of the difference in ethical choices between asking how a woman can have a child she can't afford and asking how our friends and communities can support her so the child gets what she/he needs.

The state of consciousness behind this fifth strategy comes from an awareness of "the people who aren't there"—a return, in modified form, to the first state of consciousness described when women became aware of the absence of women. Now, however, we are more aware of all those who have been left out and the limits of our right to speak for any group of people outside our knowledge and experience.

As the focus of feminist research has shifted to women who have been marginalized in the male-dominant society and by mainstream feminism, interest in the diversity of women's lives has increased. Poor women, disabled women, lesbian women, women of color, and Two-Thirds-World women began to be included in the question of what women offer to our understanding of human beings. As doubly and triply marginalized women increasingly have raised criticisms, the limitations of white, middle-class feminism have become more and more obvious. The new, hopeful, visionary world of women-centered work did not always address the racism of white women, the classism of privileged women, the structure of labor in which some women exploit other women, the relation of First World affluence to the poverty of two thirds of the world's women, or the racially divided nature of the church and feminism itself.

Some African-American feminist theologians such as Jacqueline Grant, Delores Williams, and Kelly Brown Douglas, who call themselves womanist theologians, raised questions about the servant language used by feminists who argued that Jesus came as a servant and both men and women must be servants. Slave women and men were forced to serve white masters, and poor women of color have continued to be exploited cleaning the homes of affluent women. Hence, the concept of servant, which continues to require a hierarchical structure of one who is served by a servant, offers no liberating or helpful good news to African-American women, according to Grant and Williams. Womanist theologians turn to the language of Sojourner Truth and the Gospel of John in describing Jesus and God as friend or comforter. Womanists look to biblical women such as Hagar, who was outcast and survived, for mirrors of their own lives. Their good news is that we are not to serve each other, but to befriend and comfort each other, as Jesus is friend and comforter. In addition, womanist ethicists such as Katie Cannon have examined the survival skills and ethics of African-American women as resources for understanding how we can "make something out of nothing." In Section I, the theme of friendship is developed in a different direction by Marti Steussy who talks about women's relationship to the Bible as friend.

Through these criticisms on the limitations of women-centered research, we see how many other ordinary people are excluded by the larger, male-dominant society—including many men. We must ask frequently how many other views of the world have been silenced or even destroyed. Feminists have begun to see the need to include diverse points of view and diverse histories if we are to understand the fullness of human life and the gospel's relevance to that life, and if we are to understand the full cost of racism on women's lives. This inclusive perspective has been more characteristic of women of color, who have always had to find solidarity with their own diverse communities in the struggle against racism, sexism, *and* economic oppression.[3]

In some ways, this Everyone Included Strategy is similar to the Add Women and Stir Strategy. It might even be called Add Everyone and Stir. Groups marginalized by the dominant white culture's feminism are being included in woman-centered visions. This strategy has been criticized, however, for being implicitly exclusionary. The frameworks and questions of theology and research and definitions of oppression are already set by white feminist values and ideas into which those excluded are added. As yet, those excluded have not had an equal voice in determining the frameworks and questions, as is evident from this book in which only two authors, myself and Belva Brown Jordan, who wrote the Study Guide, are women of color. Jordan, in her Guide, invites each reader to bring her or his personal experience into each essay so that, while each work is limited to the perspective of its author, the reader might find ways to bring her or his life to bear on the ideas presented. By this process we

---

[3] See Henry Louis Gates' *Reading Black, Reading Feminist* for a discussion of this more inclusive view of African-American feminists.

hope to create conversations, rather than to expect agreement or adherence to finished products.

As different groups of women have begun to articulate their struggles and values, they have formed separate associations and studied women on their own terms, not necessarily on the terms of white, middle-class feminism. African-American women have started womanist theology, and Hispanic women are engaged in mujerista theology. Native American and Asian-American women have begun to write about our own cultural heritages. It is not that women of color have not been active all along, but marginalized women have only recently begun to be visible to white feminists. Men of color and other pro-feminist men have formed alliances with feminists, as has been the case throughout the entire history of feminist movements. White feminists have responded by reexamining the starting premises of feminism—its definitions of "woman," its analyses of male dominance, its understanding of community and the church, and the use of language. These reexaminations inform many of the essays in this book. We seem to be on the edge of a sixth strategy, as yet undetermined.

While these strategies loosely describe the development of feminist thinking over the last twenty-five years, they are neither fixed nor permanent. Research reflecting each strategy continues and many organizations work for both equality and for transformation, sometimes at the same time. Feminist theology is no exception. It reflects the many varied perspectives women bring to their work on Christian thought, the Bible, and the church. And women of color have entered the discussion. African-American women, Hispanic women, Native American women, and Asian-American women now have Ph.Ds in Christian theology, ethics, church history, social sciences and religion, and biblical studies, and more seminary-trained women of color have published scholarly work. The Christian Church (Disciples of Christ), as of 1994, has one African-American woman, one Asian-American woman, and one Hispanic woman with Ph.Ds.

Conclusion

While feminist theologians may conduct research using any or all of these strategies, once one has journeyed through the states of consciousness of each strategy, one does not move to another strategy unchanged. The Add Women and Stir Strategy looks different from the perspective of Women-Centered, or Everyone Included Strategies, such that a feminist asks new and different questions of what she finds. For example, in addition to proving that Julian of Norwich of the fifteenth century had theological ideas as innovative and sophisticated as the men of her day, a feminist historian would want to know now what distinctive perspective she represents as a woman who was unlike the men of her day. Why did she call Jesus "Mother" and God "Lover"? We would want to know what her life was as a woman and what social, economic, and cultural forces helped her become who she was. We would also want to know what social privileges allowed her to get an education, as well as what less-privileged women of her time might have been doing and thinking. An example of such research is Nadia Lahutsky's essay in Section III, in which she examines the medieval practive of women who fasted in relation to current relationships of women to food.

Few social movements in the latter half of the twentieth century have affected the church more than feminism. Women have changed dramatically and the Christian Church has felt the impact at the local, regional, and general manifestations of church life—from women in the pulpits of our churches to the women presidents of major units of our church structures. Feminist, womanist, and mujerista theologians offer Christians new angles for understanding God, faith, sin, redemption, worship, and theological language. Pro-feminist men have found conversation partners as they have struggled to articulate the negative impact of male dominance on men, a breaking open of privilege so that its ugly underside is exposed. We have all unlocked a fuller history of human lives in the church and given the church a better Christian story. Women biblical scholars have given us new eyes for reading the Bible and new ears to hear the stories. Feminists, womanists, and mujeristas in the Christian church call on the church to continue changing its institutions to be truer to the gospel message and to create a church for the future, a future in which everyone may be included. We continue to create new visions—to unset and reset the table so that it might welcome all of us equally.

This book is a glimpse of those changes and visions as they have impacted Christian thinking in the areas of biblical studies, theology, and understandings of Christian life. Each author discusses an aspect of feminist thinking that sheds new light on old texts, issues, and practices. This contribution of the Forrest-Moss Institute, an association of women scholars of the Christian Church (Disciples of Christ), is presented as part of the ongoing work of women in transforming the wider church and its theological insights. We hope you will join us at the table.

Works Consulted

Anderson, Bonnie S. and Judith P. Zinsser. 1988. *A History of Their Own: Women in Europe*. New York: Harper & Row.

Beauvoir, Simone de. 1952. *The Second Sex*. New York: Alfred A. Knopf.

Daly, Mary. 1968. *The Church and the Second Sex*. New York: Harper and Row

—. 1973. *Beyond God the Father: Toward a Philosophy of Women's Liberation*. Boston: Beacon Press.

Douglas, Kelly Brown. 1994. *The Black Christ*. Maryknoll, NY: Orbis Press.

Ehrenreich, Barbara and Dierdre English. 1973. *Complaints and Disorders: The Sexual Politics of Sickness*. Old Westbury, NY: The Feminist Press, Green Mountain Pamphlet #2.

Friedan, Betty. 1963. *The Feminine Mystique*. New York: Dell Publishing Co.

Gage, Matilda Joslyn. 1972. *Woman, Church and State*. 2nd ed. New York: Arno Press. Originally published in 1893.

Gates, Henry Louis, ed. 1990. *Reading Black, Reading Feminist: A Critical Anthology*. New York: Meridian.

Gilligan, Carol. 1983. *In a Different Voice: Psychological Theory and Women's Development*. Boston: Harvard University Press.

Harrison, Beverly. 1985. *Making the Connections: Essays in Feminist Social Ethics*, ed. by Carol Robb. Boston: Beacon Press.

Keller, Catherine. 1986. *From a Broken Web: Sexism, Separation, and Self*. Boston: Beacon Press.

Kimmel, Michael and Thomas E. Mosmiller, eds. 1992. *Against the Tide: Profeminist Men in the United States, 1776-1990, a Documentary History*. Boston: Beacon Press.

Lerner, Harriet. 1985. *The Dance of Anger*. New York: Harper and Row.

Mairs, Nancy. 1993. *Ordinary Time: Cycles in Marriage, Faith, and Renewal*. Boston: Beacon Press.

McIntosh, Peggy. 1983. "Interactive Phases of Curricular Re-Vision: A Feminist Perspective." Working Paper No. 124, available from the Wellesley College, Center for Research on Women, Wellesley, MA 02181.

Ringe, Sharon and Carol Newsome, eds. 1992. *The Women's Bible Commentary*. Philadelphia: Westminster Press.

Ruddick, Sara. 1989. *Maternal Thinking: Toward a Politics of Peace*. Boston: Beacon Press.

Ruether, Rosemary Radford and Rosemary Skinner Keller. 1981. *Women and Religion in America*. New York: Harper and Row.

Schüssler Fiorenza, Elisabeth, ed. 1993. *Searching the Scriptures: A Feminist Introduction*. Vol. I. New York: Crossroads Press.

—, ed. 1994. *Searching the Scriptures: A Feminist Ecumenical Commentary*. Vol. II. New York: Crossroads Press.

Williams, Delores. 1993. *Sisters in the Wilderness: The Challenge of Womanist God-Talk*. Maryknoll, NY: Orbis Press.

The Bible
Section I

Introduction

to Section I

Claudia V. Camp

O n the last day of class last semester, when students were invited to raise whatever issues still haunted them, one woman mentioned with much condescension, even sarcasm, a news report she'd encountered about *somebody* who was going to publish one of *those* (read: "stupid") Bible translations that attended closely to inclusive language. This translation would go so far as to put "Mother" in parentheses when the text referred to God as "Father." Now wasn't this just the most ridiculous extreme of political correctness?!

Packed into this plaintive question are many if not all the issues feminists have attended to in our work in biblical study and interpretation, an enterprise sometimes referred to as *feminist hermeneutics*. ("Hermeneutics" involves the process and theory of interpretation, including the awareness that *the perspective of the interpreter influences the results obtained*.) Let me see if I can isolate some of these issues so you can decide if you want to affirm the complaint or, as this student did after some discussion, acknowledge that there's more to the matter than meets the casual eye.

1. *Translation: the gender of people and the gender of God.* No language can be perfectly translated into another without some loss or alteration of meaning. All translation involves some degree of interpretation, including that of the Bible's ancient forms of Hebrew and Greek. Translators have to balance two competing values: first, that of faithfulness to the vocabulary, style, and word order of the original, to the degree they can recreate these; second, that of readability in modern English. Movement too far in the first direction risks woodenness and archaism that make understanding difficult; too far in the latter direction substitutes ease of reading for wrestling with the real differences in worldview that are often reflected in language.

How do these concerns relate to gender? Like modern English until very recently, biblical Hebrew and Greek tend to subsume the existence and presence of women under male-gendered vocabulary. There is, for example, a Hebrew word for "boy" and another for "girl." But if one wanted to talk about "children," one would use the plural for "boys," even if girls were also included. Similarly, when Paul writes to the early Christian churches, he often addresses himself to "brothers." We know, however, from many examples of active Christian women in the New Testament—including coworkers with Paul—that his letters were meant for women too. What, then, is the best translation of the Greek? Is it "brothers," the most exact literal English equivalent for the vocabulary item used by Paul? Or is it "brothers and sisters," representing the actual makeup of Paul's audience? Legitimate arguments could be made for either choice, but you can see that "brothers and sisters," while not a literal rendering, has a historical accuracy of its own that could otherwise be missed. The choice may depend on whether the reader feels comfortable with the "just like a man" perspective noted in the introduction or decides that situations that "include everyone" should have language that includes everyone.

OK for people, you might say, but what about changing the words for God? This issue is dealt with in detail in Section II of this volume, so I will address it only briefly here, as it relates to translation. In part, translators have a legitimate concern for rendering terminology for the divine as literally as possible in order to best represent the theological ideas of the Bible's authors. If the Bible consistently refers to God as "he" (which it does) there may be a disservice in pretending it says otherwise. However, most English-speaking readers are unaware that some of the Bible's most important terminology for God underwent changes in the course of history. Christian readers, especially, rarely know that the most significant name for God in the Hebrew Bible is a proper noun, YHWH. How it was pronounced in ancient times is uncertain (scholarly consensus has it as "Yahweh"), because Hebrew was written without vowels. At some point in Jewish history, however, the belief arose that the divine name was too holy for the human mouth to utter; thus, when an oral reader of the Bible encountered the name YHWH, the reader instead spoke aloud a circumlocution, substituting the Hebrew word for "the Lord" (*adonai*). When vowels were eventually put in the Hebrew manuscripts, the vowels for *adonai* were used with the consonants YHWH, creating a hybrid that Jewish readers immediately understand to mean "see YHWH, say *adonai*." Modern English translators have tended to respect the oral convention rather than the written. Thus, we usually find "the Lord" rather than "Yahweh" when we read. (The exception to this practice is the translation "Jehovah," which uses the consonants and vowels of the Hebrew hybrid, an odd practice in Jewish eyes!)

The point in all this is simply to say that modern Christians are unwittingly accustomed to using terminology for God that is the result of a change made for theological reasons; so accustomed, in fact, that the use of YHWH, *which is what the text actually says*, seems strange at best. There is a strong precedent, then, embedded in the Bible itself, for adapting God's name to meet changing theological perspectives. Why could this principle not apply to gendered terminology as well?

2. *What do feminist biblical scholars do?* Good translation and interpretation of the Bible depend upon understanding the social and historical contexts in which it was written, its use of literary forms and imagery, and its implicit and explicit ideological and theological motivations. On the one hand, feminists often share in these questions asked by all biblical scholars; we perform our task "just like men." But not *just* like men, because we bring some special perspectives as well.

Elizabeth Thomsen's essay in this section shows how some of the earliest feminist work, in *The Woman's Bible* of the last century, helped to "add women" to the roster of characters drawn from the Bible (phase two of feminist consciousness), and Nancy Pittman draws a picture of how this interest can show up in the lives of individual women. Whether women are portrayed as characters in biblical narratives or as objects of subordinating laws, researchers have been unable to ignore their frequent role as victims of a patriarchal society, generating the anger characteristic of phase three. Again, the essays by Thomsen and Pittman show how this feeling has motivated feminist authors of the past, as well as present-day Christian lay readers. Recent scholars have treated these issues in more complex ways. We have come to realize that while there are more female characters in the Bible than we're often taught, and that they are often victimized, there is still much missing if one focuses solely on what the Bible says about particular women.

For example, the Bible's portrayal of women is often oriented to exceptional women, for better or for worse: Eve the first sinner, Deborah the great judge, Mary the mother of Jesus. But what about the lives of ordinary, everyday women like you and me? What were their lives like? What occupied them from the time they arose in the morning until they went to bed at night? How much power or authority did they have that does not show up in the biblical accounts? Working as *social historians*, using the fruits of archeology, information from anthropological studies of similar societies, and sometimes the smallest of clues from the Bible itself, some feminist scholars have sought answers to questions like these (see, for example, the work of Carol Meyers and Elisabeth Schüssler Fiorenza).

But there is more missing as well, and that is the voice of the ancient women themselves. Because the Bible was largely written by men, and elite, scribally trained men at that, virtually all the female characters who do appear in the Bible have been filtered through the minds and words of those authors. (Note that the life and thoughts of the common *man* are also lost in this way!) For this reason, feminist biblical scholars often become *literary critics*, choosing to read the Bible as a piece of literature, rather than a report of history. We ask why a female character is portrayed in the way she is. What purpose does that characterization serve in conveying either the author's intended meaning or his implicit gender, class, or race biases?

For example, in the book of Proverbs, there are two poetically presented female characters, referred to as Woman Wisdom and the Strange Woman. The poems advise young men to seek the former and avoid the latter. Notice how female readers are excluded from the audience from the get-go. Of course, there may well be a desirable purpose served by these poems insofar as they encourage readers to seek a godly way and avoid the path of evil. But what does it do to or for women to be characterized as either completely good or completely evil? The parable of the ten maidens, as analyzed here by Thomsen, makes a similar point: on the one hand we may want to affirm, as that parable does, that something is required of those who seek to follow Christ. On the other hand, what happens to women when a story is told that pits one group of women against another? Indeed, what happens, Thomsen asks, to a church so divided? Asking questions like these is sometimes called *ideological criticism* because it seeks to uncover the deeper assumptions and biases—the systems of thought, or ideologies—that motivate both authors and interpreters and that are revealed in our approaches to female characters.

3. *What authority should the Bible have for women?* Feminists working as social historians, literary critics, and ideological critics have found that, more often than not, the Bible excludes women, victimizes them, or presents them as symbols of evil. We should note that this negative assessment does not always hold true. There are indeed some women portrayed as both authoritative and good and, in fact, even God is occasionally presented with female characteristics. Even in these cases, however, there is often a problem, for the Bible's "good" women tend to be those who contribute to upholding the patriarchal society. Given these facts, the question of the Bible's authority for feminist women becomes a serious question.

Feminists who have chosen to remain in the biblical faith traditions (and many have opted out!) have articulated a variety of ways of thinking about and relating to the Bible (see Marti Steussy's essay, "My Friend the Bible: Proposal for a Metaphor," in this volume, and the various essays in *Searching the Scriptures, Vol. 1,* edited by Fiorenza). One of the first academically trained women in the most recent wave of feminism, Phyllis Trible, has published two important books. As the essay by Steussy suggests, the first of these, *God and the Rhetoric of Sexuality,* adopted an "Add Women and Stir" approach, but did so with a depth that continues to influence many. Trible showed the thread of female imagery for God that runs through the Hebrew Bible (=Christian Old Testament) and also revealed the significance, for the life of faith, of other texts about women such as Ruth, Eve, and the lovers in the Song of Songs. Trible's second book took a more difficult turn. *Texts of Terror* deals with four stories in which women are brutally treated: Hagar, Jephthah's daughter, Tamar, and the Levite's concubine. To abandon the Bible, she suggests, is to abandon the memory of women who suffered like these.

I said above that, as feminist scholars do our research, there's a sense in which we do it "just like men." As we approach the question of the *authority* of the Bible, however, I think one could make the case that, to some degree, we always begin with a phase four, women-centered approach. Thus, although Trible's two books may use the strategies of phases two and three, her underlying presupposition is that it makes a difference when a woman reads the Bible with women's concerns and experiences in mind. This presupposition marks all feminist work on biblical authority. It is articulated even more forcefully in the work of another of the most well-known feminist biblical scholars, Elisabeth Schüssler Fiorenza.

Fiorenza has argued that *the authority of the Bible is found in the lives of biblical people* (*Bread Not Stone:* 140). To the extent that the Bible can provide liberation and wholeness to women, it is worthy of proclamation. But it must also be subjected to what she calls a "hermeneutics of suspicion," that is, an interpretive approach that begins by testing its capacity to provide such wholeness, and rejecting it to the extent it does not.

The essays in this section all in some measure take up the question of biblical authority. "My Friend the Bible," by Marti Steussy, does so most explicitly. She develops how Brock's five strategies appear in feminist interpretation and how they interact. Most important in terms of the question of authority, she argues that women's decisions about which texts to use for our life of faith, and how to evaluate them, depend on women's experience that "balances biblical authority against our own God-guided discernment." Steussy then proposes a new way of thinking about the believer's relationship with the Bible, using the metaphor of friendship to reframe our understanding of the nature of biblical truth.

You may find Steussy's perspective quite challenging. She does, after all, ask that we think of truth in *relational* terms (notice I did not say *relativistic*—can you discern the difference?) rather than absolute terms. Moreover, by describing the Bible as a friend, she puts it to a large degree on our level, something that's often avoided with the word of God. While these ideas may feel threatening in the abstract, Nancy Pittman's essay provides stories of concrete experiences of women's encounters with the Bible. Maybe you'll find yourself there, or someone you know. At the very least, I suspect you'll find it hard to discount the integrity of these encounters, even though they demonstrate the very points Steussy has made about the importance of the reader's experience—and in particular women's experience—both in the interpretation of biblical texts and conclusions about their authority. Elizabeth Thomsen sums things up when she says "as in a conversation, the authority of biblical texts is born in the dynamic meeting between the hearts, minds, souls, and situations represented in the texts, and the minds hearts, souls, and situations of readers" and when she concludes, regarding the meaning of the parable of the ten maidens, that "the author or editor of Matthew has thrown the ultimate questions of judgment and mercy back on us! *We* decide whether and how this story illustrates the 'kingdom of heaven.'"

4. *So aren't there any standards for anything anymore?* My student who bewailed the "excesses" of inclusive language gave voice to, among other things, her deep discomfort with the implication that one could not depend on the Bible to say the same thing consistently, no matter who reads it or what their circumstances. As I have noted, all the essays in this section hold up precisely that concern for open discussion and conclude that not only might it be a *valuable* thing that the Bible does not say exactly the same thing to everybody

in every situation, but that this is just the way it is and we had better deal with the fact!

Now, I have other students who revel in the implications of relativism in this statement: "No problem, you interpret it your way, I'll interpret it mine, and we'll each go our merry way." But is this really what Jewish and Christian feminists want to say? I don't think so. You no doubt observed a moment ago that I made a distinction between "relativism" and "relationality." Like relativism, a relational approach to interpretation does value flexibility and adaptability to circumstances. Unlike relativism, relationality by definition *cannot* simply say "to each her own." My interpretive efforts must always be done in service to and respect for others. But which others? Isn't it the case that an interpretation that serves and respects one person or group will injure another? Yes, this can easily be the case, and it's important to recognize that there is no perfect solution to this dilemma.

Feminist biblical scholars respond to the dilemma by adhering to the flexible-but-not-relativistic standard of the liberation and wholeness of women. Probably the first question that pops into your head when I say this is, "But what about men?" In contrast to media conjurings of "man-hating libbers," it is important to recognize that there are few feminists who cannot distinguish between the *oppression caused by the patriarchal system* and the intentions of individual men. This awareness has always existed in feminist thought. Thomsen, for example, notes the statement by Elizabeth Cady Stanton, the nineteenth-century editor of *The Woman's Bible*, that "the degradation of women degrades men also." Feminists also feel the need to say, however, that historically it has been *women* who have been degraded. One must begin, from the standpoint of feminist values, at the point of pain.

Perhaps less obvious to the beginning student of feminism is the fact that the meaning of "the liberation and wholeness of women" is not as self-evident as it may seem. Indeed, as the introductory essay by Rita Nakashima Brock makes clear, it is only recently that many feminists—heretofore mostly white, well-educated, middle economic bracket women—have noticed their own lack of inclusivity. Women of color—both in North America and in the Two-Thirds World—have had to forcibly remind white feminists that the concept of "women's experience" hides a multitude of experiences. While Stanton might have felt herself "inclusive" in her own time—she did after all, seek contributions to her *Woman's Bible* from women of varied views from several different countries—her purview did not extend beyond the bounds of the United States and Western Europe. Her acceptance of white supremacy, moreover, is a sad reminder of the limitation of assuming that "women's experience" is a unified notion. This limitation continues to afflict us if we fail to set Stanton alongside African-American feminist biblical interpreters of the nineteenth century, such as Jarena Lee, Sojourner Truth, and Anna Julia Cooper, not to mention, as Steussy does, a recent African-American scholar such as Renita Weems or, one might add, a Central American such as Elsa Tamez. The essays in this section are, however, all written by white feminists. We hope that some, if not all, our observations will speak more widely—conversation between different groups is not, after all, impossible! Nonetheless, we encourage our readers to seek out other voices as well.[1]

In sum, as the essays by Steussy and Pittman make clear, each in its own way, the woman-centered phase four perspective, already embodying the unrelativistic assertion of relational value, must finally open onto phase five's "include everyone." Not just men, but also women; and not just women in general, but women in our many particulars. Yes, Virginia, there *are* standards, even for feminist biblical interpretation.

---

[1]The recent collection of essays in *Searching the Scriptures, Vol. 1* is an excellent introduction to many such voices. See also the bibliographies both there and in this volume.

Works Consulted

(The lists of works consulted that follow the essays of Steussy and Thomsen contain many important references. I cite here a few others that are not in those lists.)

Felder, Cain Hope. 1991. *Stony the Road We Trod: African-American Biblical Interpretation*. Minneapolis: Fortress. See especially the essays by Renita Weems, John Waters, and Clarice J. Martin.

Pobee, John S., and Bärbel von Wartenberg-Potter. 1987. *New Eyes for Reading: Biblical and Theological Reflections by Women from the Third World*. Oak Park, IL: Meyer-Stone.

Sanders, Cheryl J. 1995. "Black Women in Biblical Perspective." *Living the Intersection: Womanism and Afrocentrism in Theology*, ed. by Cheryl J. Sanders. Minneapolis: Fortress.

Schüssler Fiorenza, Elisabeth, ed. 1993. *Searching the Scriptures. Vol. 1: A Feminist Introduction*. New York: Crossroad.

van Wijk-Bos, Johanna W. H. 1991. *Reformed and Feminist: A Challenge to the Church*. Louisville: Westminster/John Knox.

2

My Friend the Bible

Proposal for a Metaphor

Marti J. Steussy

The Issue

B iblical authority is a hot and often painful issue in American churches, partly because it lies at the firing line between liberal and conservative camps. ("Liberal" and "conservative" are oversimplified labels, but I suspect you know what I'm talking about.) Whether the topic is abortion or AIDS, many a supposed dialogue degenerates into competing claims that "we are more biblical than thou." Such assertions persuade only the already-convinced.

The biblical authority issue troubles feminist circles as well. A Christian feminist who upholds the Bible's authority finds herself under attack from two sides. A vocal group of religious traditionalists tells her that as a Christian she must give up feminism. An equally vocal group of feminists tells her that as a feminist she must deny the Bible's authority. These opposing groups do agree on one issue: both believe that the Bible demands subordination of women.

One can see why they come to this conclusion. Passages such as Numbers 30:5–8 (which allows fathers and husbands to annul women's vows) and 1 Timothy 2:11–12 (which mandates silence for women) stand in stark contradiction to the agendas of most modern women's movements. But many feminists, including myself, remain committed to both biblical faith and gender justice. In fact, some of us believe that our biblical faith requires gender justice. What do we say about biblical authority?

Some Christian Feminist Approaches to the Bible

In the introductory essay of this book, Rita Nakashima Brock describes five strategies women use to understand their place in the church and the world. Women use these same strategies to approach scripture. This yields a variety of ways to think about biblical authority. Modern as these understandings may seem, all grow from ancient Christian roots.

1. *Just Like a Man/Overarching Theme.* Historically, most women haven't felt the need for a special approach to the Bible. Catholic women have taken names such as Sister John Mark, and Protestant women have modeled their faith on Abraham's, because they assumed a woman's faith can and should be "Just Like a Man's."

Today's feminists, having wrestled mightily with prejudice and exclusion from the church, tend to be more keenly aware of the imbalance in biblical treatment of men and women. Many ardent feminists nonetheless continue to believe that women's and men's faith houses should be built on the same biblical rock, whether it be the prophetic demand for justice, the vision of God's realm, or the "New Testament ethic" of love. (The "New Testament" language unfortunately suggests a contrast with the Old Testament and Judaism. Passages such as Leviticus 19:18, 34 and Micah 6:8 should have taught us that the "love ethic" is not a New Testament invention.) These approaches give authority to a central, overarching biblical theme. This provides a basis for critiquing practices, interpretations, and even other biblical passages that go against that standard. Christians have used this kind of strategy for many centuries: Luther's emphasis on salvation by grace is an example.

2. *Add Women and Stir/Canon Within the Canon.* Although many women have been content to model their faith on biblical men, others have wanted to find out about the Bible's women. Guided by books such as Edith Deen's *All of the Women of the Bible*, generations of CWF circles have discovered sisters like the Israelite prophets Deborah (Judges 4—5) and Huldah (Kings 22:14–20 = 2 Chronicles 34:22–28). Women play a key role in the Easter story. Paul sends greetings to Junia (Romans 16:7) as an apostle of more seniority than Paul himself.

In addition to these stories about specific women, the Bible contains some fascinating theological statements about women's status.

Genesis 1:27 stresses that male *and female* are created in the image of God. Galatians 3:28 proclaims, "there is no longer male and female; for all of you are one in Christ Jesus." Such statements argue powerfully against sexual discrimination.

Many Christian feminists use these biblical examples and teachings about women as a "canon within the canon." (I will reserve this term specifically for emphasis on texts *about women*, although in a general way the phrase "canon within the canon" could also describe the overarching theme strategy.) The canon within the canon approach does not challenge basic church structures, but rather asks for women's access to them. It asks the church to "add women and stir." (By contrast, the women-centered approaches will stress alternative roles and values.) Canon-within-the-canon feminists do not deny that the Bible says negative things about women, but they subordinate these to the pro-equality teachings. Phyllis Trible takes such an approach in her influential book, *God and the Rhetoric of Sexuality*, where Genesis 1:27 becomes the "hermeneutical key" to a series of other Hebrew Bible texts.

3. Women as Victims/Remembrance. With such positive biblical precedent, why aren't women more visible in the church? One reason is that churches have silenced or distorted stories and teachings that are favorable to women. For instance, the RSV and NIV follow medieval tradition in designating the second apostle of Romans 16:7 as a man, Junias (Lampe: 1127). (The King James Bible and NRSV, like earlier Greek manuscripts, give a woman's name, Junia.) Trible's study of the Eden story (Genesis 2—3) shows that the bulk of its supposedly anti-woman teachings have been imported by interpreters (Trible, 1978: 72–143). Historian Elaine Pagels, in *Adam, Eve, and the Serpent*, tracks this interpretive history in much greater detail, tracing the religious and social needs served by different interpretations in different periods.

Some of my own students have been told that Sarah's silence during the sacrifice of Isaac (Genesis 22) proves that women should obey their husbands even when husbands threaten children's lives. The story itself does not say whether Sarah knows about Abraham's action, but the news that she dies in a different city (Kiriath-arba, Genesis 23:2) than Abraham lives in (Beersheba, 22:19) suggests that she did not care to stay with a child-sacrificing husband.

Tradition has made the Bible sound more sexist than it is, but this is not the end of the problem. The Bible has its own patriarchal horrors—rules and instructions that treat women as men's property, stories in which women suffer terribly with no protest from the narrator. These images of "Women as Victims" have, we know, led some feminists to abandon the Bible altogether. Others, just as aware of biblical misogyny, refuse to set the stories aside. Trible uses this "remembrance" strategy in her second book, *Texts of Terror*. "Such an approach...interprets stories of outrage on behalf of their female victims in order to recover a neglected history, to remember a past that the present embodies, and to pray that these terrors shall not come to pass again" (Trible, 1984: 3). To 2 Timothy's statement that "all scripture is inspired by God and is useful for teaching, for reproof, for correction, and for training in righteousness" (3:16), remembrance theology responds that scripture instructs through bad examples as well as good ones. This in itself is not controversial—the murder of Uriah (2 Samuel 11) and Peter's denial of Jesus (Mark 14:66–72 and parallels) are widely recognized as "bad examples." But how do we decide which other stories are bad examples?

We have already named some ways. One may judge stories and teachings against a central biblical principle such as justice or love ("overarching theme" approach). One may critique them on the basis of scriptures that speak more positively of women ("canon within the canon"). Opponents argue that these strategies involve "picking and choosing" or "human interpretation" rather than acceptance of God's entire Word. Feminists reply that giving 1 Timothy 2:11 ("let a woman learn in silence with full submission") priority over Galatians 3:28 ("no longer male and female, for all of you are one") is equally a case of "picking and choosing." They also point out that *no one* embraces the whole Bible without interpretation. We interpret *any* words when we read or hear them—there is no such thing as uninterpreted language. The Bible's diversity particularly demands interpretation and prioritizing—otherwise faith becomes an incoherent muddle.

4. *Women-centered strategies.* Another ground for distinguishing between inspired teaching and bad example is women's experience. No woman who has been raped can comfortably accept the Levite's treatment of his concubine (Judges 19). A woman whose spouse treats her demonically may rightly deny that God intends her to be "subject, in everything" (Ephesians 5:24) to that husband. Experiential critique may recognize divine inspiration in scripture, but it also sees human influences—including some very self-interested ones—in the text. These self-serving viewpoints are—not surprisingly—more evident to people they harm than to people who benefit from them. Theologically, this position uses respect for every person as a child of God, and the spirit-given ability to discern truth in an ongoing history (John 14:16–17, 15:26), to check and balance the authority of scripture and/or its traditional interpretations. In its feminist form, which appeals especially to women's experience, we may call this approach "Women-Centered."

While much women-centered study looks at the Bible through the experience of contemporary women, feminist scholars have also worked to recover the experience and values of biblical women. Carol Meyers, in *Discovering Eve*, uses archeology, anthropology, and the Bible itself to probe the lives of ancient Israelite women. She highlights the Eden story's concern with food (the first thing God talks about), farming, and the need for farm women to bear children as well as work in the fields. Her work reveals a whole set of family-centered values that traditional exegesis (focused on sin and mortality) largely ignores.

Elisabeth Schüssler Fiorenza's book, *In Memory of Her*, provides another example of women-centered historical research. Her study of the New Testament reveals that early Christian practice was more egalitarian than the New Testament writers' own values—for instance, Paul's greeting to Junia shows acceptance of women apostles despite Paul's uneasiness about women's place. Schüssler Fiorenza suggests that the New Testament church's "walk" provides better values for us than its "talk."

Women-centered scholars also call attention to the oft-neglected "feminine side" of God in the Bible—God as mother, God as midwife, God as hostess, and so forth. Virginia Ramey Mollenkott explores such images in her popular book *The Divine Feminine*. The figure of divine wisdom, Sophia, particularly attracts women. For more about Sophia in the Bible, see *Wisdom's Feast* by Cady, Ronan, and Taussig.

5. *Include Everyone.* Women are not the only people to discover that their experience brings out new meanings in scripture. African Americans, Caribbean farmers, Asian factory workers, and many other groups are reading the Bible in new ways. Dialogue with them has shown well-educated white feminists how self-serving our own theology can be. If all readings succumb to self-interest, you might ask, is there any hope of finding truth? Yes—by working together to discover and correct blind spots. The more kinds of people we involve, the better we hear God's voice. Brock calls this the "Include Everyone" strategy, and it opens up new vistas in biblical faith. *Just a Sister Away*, a book of Bible meditations and discussion questions by African-American scholar Renita Weems, shows how fruitful—and accessible—this approach can be.

6. *Summary Observations.* In general, when Christian feminists speak of the Bible as "inspired," they mean it has shown itself to be *adequate* for salvation—capable of bringing us into genuine faith and relationship with God. They do not see it as *inerrant* (free of all mistakes and human axe-grinding). This is not a new idea. Even 2 Timothy 3:14–17 associates inspiration with "profitableness" or "usefulness" rather than flawlessness.

The "overarching principle" and "canon within a canon" strategies have an additional common ground with tradition in that they treat the Bible as a source of teachings (by rule, principle, and/or example) for the faithful person to accept and act upon. "Remembrance theology" uses the Bible in a different way. It respects the Bible's *bad* examples by continuing to interact with them rather than refusing to talk about them. It grants the Bible authority as our source of stories, symbols, and images, but claims a great deal of freedom in its use of these—sometimes using a story in a sense opposite to that which the writer may have intended. To the extent that women's experience decides which stories are "bad," this approach also balances biblical authority against our own God-guided discernment. The "include everyone" strategy introduces another balance by checking our own perceptions against other points of view.

These strategies are not mutually exclusive. One may take Genesis 1:27 as an authoritative statement on equality of the sexes (canon-within-the-canon) while also arguing that prophetic demands for justice rule out oppression of women (overarching theme). One could then hold up Hagar's story (Genesis 16, 21) as a warning of how easily patriarchal systems can set women against one another (remembrance), having been led to this insight by an African-American woman's reflection on her experience (woman-centered, everyone-must-be-included). Christian feminism offers a range of ways for thinking about biblical authority, rather than a single answer.

Truth and Authority

Quite a lot of people functionally adopt some combination of the interpretive strategies I've described, but aren't comfortable calling it "interpretation" or openly discussing (as feminists tend to do) the standards they apply to get where they are. Much of this discomfort comes from the fact that we've been taught to think about "truth" and "authority" in very concrete and limited ways.

Mention biblical truth, and most people think of a truth such as the law of gravity. (This connects historically to people's fascination with Newtonian science and their desire to find a similar level of exactitude in religion.) Gravity exists independent of human beings.

It works the same way in all times and places. It affects prime ministers as it affects beggars. We can express it in a brief mathematical formula that does not alter when translated into a different language. Gravity is a given, with which we cope in one way or another. Its sway is non-negotiable. Gravity will have its due, science fiction fantasies notwithstanding.

Mention biblical authority, and most people think of an absolute monarch proclaiming edicts. Disobedience to such laws challenges the monarch's power, tweaks the lawgiver's nose. Only a fool would do this to God!

These are the ways we usually think about biblical truth and authority. Yet biblical truth is not the unconditional truth of natural law, but a truth sensitive to the everchanging circumstances of human life. (Note how the proclamations of condemnation and punishment in Jeremiah and Ezekiel change to consolation and comfort when Judah falls.) On the authority side, how do we square our image of the despotic lawgiver with a faith that proclaims God crucified, and whose chief apostle says, "all things are lawful" (1 Corinthians 6:12)? (Paul quotes his opponents here—but he does not deny their statement, only nuances it with the criterion of helpfulness.) In the next section of this essay I will propose a metaphor that offers some different and perhaps more helpful(!) ways to think about biblical truth and authority. I developed this metaphor in response to a question from seminary trustees about my classes—not a specifically feminist context—but it reflects a consciousness informed by both feminism and biblical scholarship.

My Friend the Bible

Picture the Bible as a wise and cherished friend. I imagine this friend as a woman—because I am a woman, because in our society this sort of friendship is more common among women than men, but also because an ancient tradition describes scripture as a lovely woman who gives life to humankind (Baruch 3:36—4:1—this appears in the "Apocrypha" section of Protestant Bibles). Let me draw out some implications of this image.

1. *Friendship takes time.* We may recognize a kindred spirit at first acquaintance, but deep life-sustaining friendship takes time to develop. (Clock pressure is one reason men seldom create and maintain intimate friendships—career women frequently suffer the same difficulty.) Just so (as churches have long known!), time spent with the Bible over many years makes it much easier to lean on her in times of crisis. One of the most vivid testimonies to this comes from hostages and political prisoners who sustain themselves through torture and deprivation with psalms memorized long ago in church school. Perhaps you yourself have opened a Bible and dropped your finger onto the page with your eyes closed, to see what wisdom God offered in a time of trouble. Many have found help in such a manner. But how much richer to read the book with your eyes open, exploring new ideas and learning where to find words that speak to your condition!

2. *We need to understand where the Bible comes from.* It takes time to make friends with the Bible in part because she comes from a very different culture. She grew up far away and long ago, and sometimes makes assumptions very different from our own. When she was a girl, there was no Medicare or Social Security—elderly people were cared for by their children. This left childless widows in a dangerous position. The solution was for the widow to have a child by her dead husband's brother; that child then inherited the property and took care of the mother (Deuteronomy 25:5–10). It seems obvious to the Bible that this should be so; she bubbles with indignation when Judah refuses to set up his twice-widowed daughter-in-law, Tamar, with his remaining son, Shelah (Genesis 38). Tamar solves the problem by dressing as a prostitute and soliciting Judah himself to get her pregnant. The Bible greatly admires Tamar and cites her as a founder of the faith (Ruth 4:12, Matthew 1:3). Inquiring into the background (in the Bible itself or with the aid of Bible dictionaries and commentaries) helps me appreciate Tamar's courage and the Bible's approval of her. In this way, taking my distance from the Bible seriously actually brings me closer to her. But it also prompts me to set aside certain pieces of the Bible's well-meant advice. I do not recommend Tamar's strategy—or even Deuteronomy's—for widows today.

3. *The Bible has seen a lot.* We've all known people who were very nice, but just too inexperienced to understand or advise us about life's difficulties. No such problem with the Bible! She's been around several millennia longer than you or I, and she's been a lot of places. She has sat with kings in their palace councils and camped with runaway slaves in the desert. She knows the history of entire nations, but she has also followed the loves and jealousies of individual households. She ponders the injustices of a world where people don't get what they deserve (Job, Ecclesiastes) and collects advice to help them make their way (Proverbs). Sometimes folks who've been introduced to her on only one occasion, such as when she reports a law about male homosexuality in Leviticus 18:22, mistake that for the extent of her experience. She sounds quite different as she quotes David's lament over Jonathan (2 Samuel 1:26).

4. *The Bible cares.* The law of gravity has been a lot of places too. But unlike the law of gravity, our friend the Bible cares deeply about what she has seen. Cold rage—even vengefulness—fills her when she contemplates the misery wrought by wealthy arrogance (Amos 2:6–8, Isaiah 5:8). Sometimes she turns on oppressors with biting sarcasm (Amos 4:4–5, Isaiah 5:22–23). Other times she finds their pretensions simply laughable (Numbers 22, where Balaam's donkey sees what the supposed prophet cannot). Yet fundamentally she loves us (Proverbs 8:31), and she weeps alongside us over the devastations of war (Lamentations). For all the suffering she's seen, she still laughs with delight to see lovers flirting in a garden (Song of Solomon), and dreams of a day when all wounds will be healed (Revelation 21:1–4, 22:1–2).

Knowing the Bible's passionate nature, we must be sensitive to her moods and tones of voice. Does she mean it, or is it sarcasm, when she tells Israel to come to Gilgal and sin (Amos 4:4)? Does she approve of Jephthah's human sacrifice (Judges 11:29–30), or is this one more tragic example of a man doing what is right in his own eyes? Is human nature "only evil continually" (Genesis 6:5, 8:21), or does God also see good (Genesis 6:8–9)? The Bible's truths are always tactical, always related to situations. We must be careful to hear them as they are meant.

5. *Our friend is flexible.* This leads us to a final point: the Bible (again unlike the law of gravity) does not say the same thing to all persons and in all places. She usually gives down-and-outers the benefit of the doubt (Deuteronomy 10:17–19)—although, like most of us, she has been known to play favorites (Deuteronomy 15:1–3). When it comes to the privileged she tends to hew a harder line (Luke 12:48, Romans 15:1). Nor does she always enforce edicts. Certainly she disapproves of young widows who crawl under the covers with drunken men. Yet in Ruth's case (3:7–9) she understands that desperate circumstances require desperate action. Jesus quotes her in a similar vein in Mark 2:25–26.

Sometimes, the Bible wavers because a question just doesn't have an easy answer. Is faith conducive to good family life? No, she says— you've got to put God's realm above everything else, and the homefolk aren't going to like it (Matthew 10:35–36). Yet surely Christians should be at least as decent in carrying out their duties as pagans are (1 Timothy 5:8). Do the sins of ancestors land on their descendants? Yes (Exodus 20:5 and elsewhere), in everything from fetal alcohol syndrome and toxic waste to ruined economies. Yet surely God will deal with each as he or she deserves (Ezekiel 18:1–4). So why do righteous people perish, and the wicked prosper (Ecclesiastes 7:15)? The mystery lingers.

The Bible's adaptability means you don't really have a full grasp of her talents until you've seen her in a wide variety of situations. She shows different gifts at a day care center or disaster site than at a board meeting. People who've known her in only one setting sometimes underestimate her capabilities. Her adaptability also requires us to ask when she is speaking to us, and when to our neighbor. Much as we enjoy her words of comfort (Luke 6:20–23), we may need her words of warning as well (Luke 6:24–26).

Reflections

Talking about cultural assumptions, passion, and flexibility in the Bible upsets many people, for it feels like the edge of a slippery slope. How can we depend on the Bible, if it's not consistent? I answer that the Bible *is* consistent, but not mechanically, mathematically consistent. The Bible is consistent the way a human personality is consistent. A person is shaped by her experience, has different moods, and waffles on certain issues, yet if we know her well, we can usually anticipate her reactions. Once in a while, of course, she will surprise us—it's the surprises that keep friendship growing. In the same way the Bible, for all her variety, shows generally predictable patterns. She also surprises us once in a while—perhaps even in a verse we have studied many times before. Could we expect less from the word of a living God?

The Bible's truth grows out of her long experience with human relationships, good and bad, with one another, other creatures, and God. Her authority rests not in legal sanctions (especially since "all things are lawful") but in her wisdom. Generations testify that her advice is well worth seeking ("wonderful words of life," says Philip Bliss's hymn), and we are fools if we fail to consult her. Yet we can and should weigh her words carefully. They may be grounded in a quirk of upbringing (remember Tamar), directed toward a different kind of situation (instructions for Temple sacrifice), or even tongue-in-cheek (2 Corinthians 12:13). Therefore we must not act like slaves, but stand fast in our freedom (Romans 8:15, Galatians 5:1) and discern how God needs to be at work in us (Philippians 2:12–13). Our friend the Bible expects no less of us. She is not a monarch to behead us for making our own decisions.

Is it blasphemous to regard God's Word so familiarly? I think not. The idea of "friend" has a long and significant faith history, far beyond the texts which speak of Lady Wisdom/Torah and her desire to be our friend. Moses, the human partner in the Torah-giving process, spoke to God "as a man speaks to his friend" (Exodus 33:11). We should note that this friendship included a number of arguments, some of which Moses won! As Christians we also are called into friendship with God (John 15:12–17). (For more on God as friend, see McFague, 1982: 177-192). Let us now accept the biblical Word, like the incarnate Word, as Friend.

Works Consulted

Cady, Susan, Marian Ronan, and Hal Taussig. 1989. *Wisdom's Feast: Sophia in Study and Celebration*. San Francisco: Harper & Row.

Deen, Edith. 1955. *All of the Women of the Bible*. New York: Harper.

Lampe, Peter. 1992. "Junias," in *Anchor Bible Dictionary*, III: 1127. New York: Doubleday.

McFague, Sallie. 1982. *Metaphorical Theology: Models of God in Religious Language*. Philadelphia: Fortress Press.

Meyers, Carol. 1988. *Discovering Eve: Ancient Israelite Women in Context*. Oxford: Oxford University Press.

Mollenkott, Virginia Ramey. 1984. *Divine Feminine: The Biblical Imagery of God as Female*. New York: Crossroads.

Pagels, Elaine. 1988. *Adam, Eve, and the Serpent*. New York: Random House.

Schüssler Fiorenza, Elisabeth. 1984. *In Memory of Her: A Feminist Theological Reconstruction of Christian Origins*. New York: Crossroads.

Trible, Phyllis. 1978. *God and the Rhetoric of Sexuality*. Overtures to Biblical Theology. Philadelphia: Fortress Press.

—.1984. *Texts of Terror*. Overtures to Biblical Theology. Philadelphia: Fortress Press.

Weems, Renita. 1988. *Just a Sister Away*. San Diego: LuraMedia.

3

Women Studying the Bible

Footsteps on the Road from Past to Present

Elizabeth Lee Thomsen

Pilgrim

This is a road
   One walks alone;
Narrow the track
   And overgrown.

Dark is the way
   And hard to find,
When the last village
   Drops behind.

Never a footfall
   Light to show
Fellow traveller—
   Yet I know

Someone before
   Has trudged his load
In the same footsteps—
   This is a road.
   —Anne Morrow Lindbergh

Miracle

The bush burns
A spark flies
Fireworks
    burst into the skies
    of darkness
Lighting pilgrim paths
    in the wilderness;
Perfecting the beauty
    of hope.
Mere spark
Now star
    which even the "wise"
    must follow.
        —*Elizabeth Lee Thomsen*

Introduction

More than one hundred years ago Frances Willard, a proponent of women's rights, realized that women's reading of the Bible was important to any adequate understanding of "truth." She claimed that, "We need women commentators to bring out the women's side of the book; we need the stereoscopic view of truth in general, which can only be had when woman's eye and man's together discern the perspective of the Bible's full-orbed revelation."[1]

The question upon which this chapter is based is the following: Given the five stages of feminist consciousness described earlier, can the Bible make a claim to authority for women? If so, how? The experience and circumstances of my life have led me to answer the first part of the question with a resounding "yes." This essay will spell out a little about that affirmation, with reference to history. The crux, however, lies in the "how?" The second half of this chapter will attempt to show some answer to that part of the question by dealing with a particular New Testament text.

If, recently, you have been to a bookstore and perused the "Women and Religion" section, you may think that Willard's claim, made in 1888, has been realized. There are seemingly innumerable books and articles these days written by women who are earnestly grappling with their quest for what is authoritative about the Bible.[2]

---

[1] Frances E. Willard, *Woman in the Pulpit* (Boston: D. Lothrup C., 1888), 21.

Still, we deceive ourselves if we think that this plethora of publications means woman's eye along with man's now serves to provide us with a "stereoscopic" view of the Bible.

One simple glance at rough statistics involved in two of the "learned journals" prominent in biblical studies in America proves the point. Over the last ten years the *Journal of Biblical Literature* has printed hundreds of articles—articles which are used in classrooms and assigned as reading to persons preparing for the ministry. The authors of those articles are 90 percent men; 10 percent women. The experimental journal *Semeia* has a better track record over the last decade, with about 24 percent of its authors being women. Still, the difference between the contributions of men and women is staggering, and points up the fact that, if we fail to name and claim our history in the realm of biblical scholarship, we keep reinventing the wheel, and deny our integrity.

This chapter aims to do two things: 1) keep alive and in our vision the history of *The Woman's Bible*, a revolutionary two-volume commentary on the Bible resulting from the collaborative efforts of a group of women, whose centennial is being celebrated in 1995; and 2) to present a "sample" study of a biblical text from a woman's point of view. It is hoped that, together, these things will facilitate the very stereoscopic vision that Willard so rightly demanded. For the purposes of this chapter, "feminist" will be a defining word for all, women and men, who agree with Willard's claim regarding truth. The agenda of feminist biblical interpretation then, is not to deny the vision and authority of men, but to bring up and explore women's "view" of biblical message and truth.

While we may mistakenly be led to believe that "feminist interpretation of the Bible" is a newfangled concept, it is imperative to keep in mind that Willard's comment regarding the need for a stereoscopic view of truth was typical of opinions held by many women in her own day, it remains typical of the concerns that contemporary biblical scholars bring to their work, and it is also a link in a very long history of women's queries about God's authority regarding Word. In Numbers 12:2 Miriam, along with her brother Aaron, frustrated with the strategy that Moses is using to bring the people out of Egypt, asks, "Has the LORD spoken only through Moses?" The theological, interpretive, and ethical implications of this question con-

---

[2] See, for example, Christina Buchmann and Celina Spiegel, eds., *Out of the Garden: Women Writers on the Bible* (New York: Fawcett Columbine, 1994); Elisabeth Schüssler Fiorenza, ed., *Searching the Scriptures: A Feminist Commentary* (New York: Crossroad, 1994); and Carol A. Newsom and Sharon H. Ringe, eds., *The Women's Bible Commentary* (London: SPCK, 1992).

tinue to reverberate. And it is worthy of note that although Miriam was, for her insubordination, struck with leprosy, the *whole nation* waited for her cure before moving on.

For women, this fact points directly back to concern with biblical interpretation. As women, and as scholars, we are particularly aware that there is more to interpretation than just opening the container (a text; the Bible) and naming a single "meaning" found in it. As will be shown, the authors of *The Woman's Bible* recognized in the last century that interpretation involves the psychology, history, economic status, gender, and so on of each interpreter and interpretive community throughout the long history of the religious text we call the Bible. Responsible biblical interpretation proclaims that "the hopes and fears of all the years" meet in the interpretive endeavor. The term *interpretation* gives tribute to the fact that through the ages people have earnestly read the Bible in different ways and that all their interpretations are part of our legacy surrounding this pivotal book. As in a conversation, the authority of biblical texts is born in the dynamic meeting between the minds, hearts, souls, and situations represented in the texts, and the minds, hearts, souls, and situations of readers.

The Woman's Bible

Let us now take a look at the nineteenth-century women who produced *The Woman's Bible*. It may come as a surprise that several stages of feminist identity described by Rita Brock at the beginning of this volume are precisely and accurately descriptive of this work done exactly one hundred years ago. Elizabeth Cady Stanton, whose work in the arena of suffrage has been touted much more than her religious views, was the driving force behind the document. Stanton's life itself poignantly illustrates motion in and through Brock's five stages.

Elizabeth Cady Stanton was born into material privilege. Her father was a prominent lawyer in New York, and as a young girl she was allowed, even challenged, to keep up with the boys at everything from scholarship to sports. She was given material from her father's extensive library so that she could keep up her end of the conversation at dinner discussions with his law clerks. Once she reached puberty, however, Elizabeth found, to her mortification, that the very excellence which had once been the source of his pride was now grounds for her father's anger. Although he allowed her to attend a boarding school to "finish" her cultural skills, Judge Cady responded when Elizabeth won the Greek Prize by bemoaning the fact that she was not a son. He never could be persuaded to let her pursue the college education she so vehemently desired.

When Elizabeth met and married reformer Henry Stanton, her world expanded into realms of social reform. Abolition and temperance were two of the reform movements she entered with great fervor. Attending an international abolition conference in London on her honeymoon, Elizabeth was chagrined and angered to find that women delegates were seated behind a curtain, and not allowed to speak to the assembly. There in London she made a network with other outraged women from Europe and the United States, and ever after she worked tirelessly to improve the lot of women.

You may be wondering how this information connects with religion and biblical interpretation. The connection is absolutely foundational. Elizabeth's experience in the Old Scotch Presbyterian Church during her childhood, and her experience of revival religion while at boarding school, set in motion a train of thought with which she grappled throughout her long lifetime. Stanton held the Bible (and its use by patriarchal religious institutions) directly responsible for a great deal of the evil perpetrated upon women, and she assured her women readers that, "Whatever your views may be as to the importance of [*The Woman's Bible*], your political and social degradation are but an outgrowth of your status in the Bible." Hence, enlightened interpretation or "revision" of the Bible took on phenomenal importance.

In writing *The Woman's Bible*, Stanton and her committee set themselves the challenge of reading the Bible self-consciously *as women*. They wanted to discover for themselves how Judeo-Christian scriptures functioned to liberate or oppress their sex. Their project exhibits great seriousness of purpose, and also shows a feisty and energetic spirit regarding biblical interpretation.

The rationale for *The Woman's Bible* was blatantly political, and shows all the signs of Brock's third state of feminist consciousness. These women were enraged, and made no bones about it. On the other hand, they were not irrational man-haters, intent on making war on all males. Indeed there were men among the reformers who actively supported the cause of women's rights, and Stanton was in constant correspondence with ministers and scholars.

When women in nineteenth-century America began to wrestle with the forces that held them in subjection, many of them were stymied by the weight of tradition which held that the Bible was literally the Word of God. Stanton, aided by new academic research, saw *The Woman's Bible* as a forum to help women formulate and value their own opinions about scripture. They showed characteristics of stages two and three in the feminist consciousness model assumed for this book.

Volume One of *The Woman's Bible* was published in 1895, Volume Two in 1898. Stanton elicited and edited the collection of essays. Her "Revising Committee" was comprised of twenty women from the USA; five from "foreign" countries: England, Finland, Austria, Scotland, and France. Part I dealt with material in the Pentateuch (the first five books of the Hebrew Bible/Old Testament). Part II covered material from Joshua in the Hebrew Scriptures to Revelation in the New Testament. It also included an Appendix consisting of letters and comments voicing positive and negative opinions of *The Woman's Bible* project. The document also included the resolution passed by the National American Woman Suffrage Association which repudiated the book, because a slim majority felt that politics should be addressed before religion, and that the women's movement should keep its energy focused upon one issue at a time.

The process of researching and writing the commentaries was aided by an academic approach to the Bible that demanded it be studied as any other piece of literature, not as a special case exempt from critical methodologies such as historical, sociological, and literary theories. Although not formally schooled in the techniques of this so-called "Higher Criticism," the women of the Revising Committee often made comparisons and observations very much in line with these methods being used by the reputable scholars of the day.

Although Stanton had had a long-standing and passionate interest in the project of a feminist commentary, the rearing of her seven children, along with her political activity, delayed the project. In 1886, she had the opportunity to begin to take action on what she conceived as a corrective to the low estate women held with regard to religion. The time was especially ripe, according to Stanton, because as women were being admitted to institutions of higher learning in increasing numbers, they were studying theology and asking to be admitted to the power structures of religious organizations.

In an almost eerie realization of stage one consciousness of feminist reality, Stanton claimed, "We found that the work would not be so great as we imagined, as all the facts and teachings in regard to women occupied less than one-tenth of the whole Scriptures" (Stanton, 1898: 391). Clearly, the absence of women had been duly noted!

With regard to methodology, according to Stanton's description, "We purchased some cheap Bibles, cut out the texts, pasted them at the head of the page, and, underneath, wrote our commentaries as clearly and concisely as possible. We did not intend to have sermons or essays, but brief comments, to keep 'The Woman's Bible' as small as possible" (391). Indeed, Stanton and her Revising Committee were concerned not only to make their document small; they were determined that it be inexpensive, so that women in general could have access to it. They insisted that it be printed in paperback, to cut costs.

However, it soon became apparent that the task of the Revising Committee would not be very simple after all. Stanton, her daughter Harriot Stanton Blatch, and Miss Frances Lord applied themselves to the task with enthusiasm. But others who had been invited to join the project demurred, for a variety of reasons. Those scholars who had the requisite knowledge of languages did not wish to associate themselves with such a radical undertaking for fear of losing their jobs. Other women thought that the Bible had "no special authority with them," and thus did not deserve the effort of special study. Others accepted as correct the view that scripture mandated second-class citizenship for females, and still another group said that the male revising committees had made such a mess of things that it would be a horrible mistake if women addressed themselves to the task of revision. Still, Stanton, now some eighty years old, pressed forward with *The Woman's Bible*.

Perhaps the most urgent conviction behind her dogged determination to see the project to completion was her belief, which grew even stronger as she grew older, that one of the primary roadblocks to the liberation of women was the fact that women believed their primary duty to be that of self-sacrifice, rather than self-development. It was obvious to her how much the church, through its interpretation of scripture, had inflicted this "virtue" of self-sacrifice upon women, and had nurtured it with an amazing vengeance. Commenting on the Matthean parable of the wise and foolish virgins, she declares that,

> Woman's devotion to the comfort, the education, the success of men in general, and to their plans and projects, is in a great measure due to her self-abnegation and self-sacrifice having been so long and so sweetly lauded by poets, philosophers and priests as the acme of human goodness and glory.

Furthermore, she contended that,

> It is not commendable for women to get up fairs and donation parties for churches in which the gifted of their sex may neither pray, preach, share in the offices and honors, nor have voice in the business affairs, creeds and discipline, and from whose altars come forth Biblical interpretations in favor of woman's subjection. (*The Woman's Bible*, II: 125)

The result of the labor that Stanton and her committee expended in coming to grips with scripture was neither a summary rejection of the Bible nor a wholehearted acceptance of it. Stanton claimed that, "The Bible cannot be accepted or rejected as a whole, its teachings are varied and its lessons differ widely from each other" (*TWB*, I: 13).

According to the preface to Part I written by Stanton, the goal of *The Woman's Bible* was "to revise only those texts and chapters directly referring to women, and those also in which women are made prominent by exclusion" (*TWB*, I: 13). Although Stanton terms the committee for this project a "Revising Committee," and speaks of the task of "revising," she also uses the word "commentaries" to describe the contents of *The Woman's Bible* (*TWB* I: 10). Although the terms "revision" and "commentaries" may seem to indicate very different things, Stanton's usage of them makes apparent just how intertwined the two are. The juxtaposition of these terms and tasks presents the interpretive process in a nutshell, and the configuration makes obvious vital questions faced by both Stanton and her committee *and* by contemporary feminist biblical interpreters. What exactly is to be revised? The text of scripture itself? Our understanding of scripture? Our understanding of ourselves in light of the Bible? Or, is our task only to "comment"?

The Woman's Bible was, in many respects, a watershed document. As the exegetical passage later in this chapter will show, many trajectories of interpretation identifiable in that document continue to guide contemporary work in the biblical field. Following are just a few strengths of *The Woman's Bible* that are discernible in our work today.

First, several commentators point out that women in the Bible often exhibit tremendous strength of character. The Revising Committee did a great service in bringing this strength to light, and in suggesting how it could serve as inspiration and encouragement for contemporary women. Characters such as Vashti, who in the book of Esther refused to parade her womanly charms before her husband's drunken friends, received "good press" in *The Woman's Bible*, and set the stage for appreciation of biblical women as role models as spokespersons for their sex.

Second, Stanton, more than the other commentators, seemed to underscore the paradoxical tension between the view of the Bible as historical record and the view of it as a literary creation. She seemed to understand that this tension could be creative, rather than negative. Sometimes she referred to biblical authors as "sacred fabulists," at other times as "sacred historians." I believe that she was recognizing the mythopoetic nature of biblical language and was, in a sense, setting forth an important agenda item for feminist hermeneutics.

Third, the members of the Revising Committee were very bold in their opinions. They named and openly objected to the misogynist judgments and practices reflected in biblical texts, and vigorously stated their doubt that God could have been the source of many laws found there. Of the statutes concerning the validity of vows found in Numbers 30, where the "sacred" vows of women are declared to be invalid (such vows were subject to the approval of fathers and/or husbands), Phebe A. Hanaford says, "Could the Infinite Father and Mother have given them to Moses? I think not" (*TWB*, II: 57).

Fourth, many essays contained in *The Woman's Bible* show a great latitude in interpretation. For the Revising Committee, plurality and ambiguity seem to have been positive facts of life regarding interpretation. The members of the Committee disagreed with one another, and encouraged the hearing of many voices. Some thought that, properly read, biblical texts were liberating for women. Others thought the same texts stultifying. The creation story, for example, was the source of liberating equality for some, who claimed that man and woman alike were created in the image of God. For others, the secondary creation of woman represented a curse.

Fifth, although the feminist politics and philosophy of Stanton and the Revising Committee were often clearly iconoclastic with regard to the content and intent of scripture, inclusion was also an important facet of their work. *The Woman's Bible* was certainly iconoclastic in that it tore down false idols of biblical interpretation which, through the centuries, had done such harm to women. On the other hand, there was an important aspect of the document that involved "including women into" the Bible and its interpretation. Furthermore, the essays of *The Woman's Bible* often express the conviction that the progress or regress of either of the sexes is inextricably tied together. As Stanton says, "No magnet is so powerful as that which draws men and women to each other. Hence they rise or fall together. This is one lesson which the Bible illustrates over and over—the degradation of women degrades man also." In a way, this spectrum of inclusion and iconoclasm—both finding a place in the biblical tradition and resisting it—is an illustration of the spiraling dance that feminist biblical interpreters must do to the "music" of the stages outlined by Brock.

The Woman's Bible has tremendous scope and an enlivening, empowering conversational format that easily accommodates sublime anger and tenderness, stupefying shock, and soul-shaking humor. For example, Stanton shocked scholars by calling for the "elimination of some of the coarser" biblical texts. On a humorous note, she paints a poignant picture of Balaam's ass as the unsung heroine of

Numbers 22. In their bold "attacks" upon the Bible and traditional interpretations, the Revising Committee showed great faith that the Bible could hold its own with respect to critical treatment. They took a great leap of faith in assuming that, given adequate scrutiny, the Bible could yield truth, whether or not that truth be comfortable.

Re-vision: The Parable of the Ten Maidens

In order to illustrate some principles of feminist exegesis that have been discussed in this chapter, we will now give brief attention to one specific text, the parable of the ten maidens found in Matthew 25:1–13. Parables are short, self-contained literary units most often characterized by an everyday or commonplace setting combined with some element of shock or surprise. A parable is a type of metaphor in which two things, seemingly quite different, are described in terms of each other. Literary critics have pointed out that in considering this type of extended metaphor we must be careful to realize that the figure of speech points us toward both how the things thrown together are alike and how they differ.

From a feminist standpoint, much of the significance of metaphor lies in the fact that metaphorical language is a language of *relationship*. Things usually considered distinctly different are seen and understood in a new light. According to feminist theorists, the epistemological development of females—how women come to know what we know—is oriented around "connected knowing."[3] That is to say that our "knowledge" evolves primarily from relationships between persons and things. I shall try to show how this woman's way of knowing relates to the use of parables.

At this point read the parable of the ten maidens in Matthew 25:1–13. As you read, try to identify for yourself what elements of the parable make it challenging and dynamic for you. What parts make it problematic?

It is difficult to designate a protagonist for this parable. After an opening formula, the characters are introduced rapidly in the first sentence. The focus falls first upon the ten maidens; these are immediately divided into two groups, and labeled "foolish" and "wise." These adjectives are affixed prior to the narrative explanation that tells the audience the reason for the descriptions. The delay, in narrative time, of the coming of the bridegroom is reinforced by the struc-

---

[3] Cogent discussion of feminine epistemology is addressed by such authors as Mary Field Belenky, Blythe McVicker Clinchy, Nancy Rule Goldenberger, and Jill Mattuck Rule, editors of *Woman's Ways of Knowing: The Development of Self, Voice and Mind* (New York: Basic Books, Inc., 1986).

ture of the passage. Readers or hearers of the story (like the maidens) must wait—wait until halfway through the story—for the actual appearance of the bridegroom. The descriptive sentences in the initial section of the parable are short and matter-of-fact: "'Then the kingdom of heaven will be like this. Ten bridesmaids took their lamps and went to meet the bridegroom. Five of them were foolish, and five were wise.'" Action begins with the direct speech of verse 6: "'Look! Here is the bridegroom! Come out to meet him.'" From this point on, the dramatic urgency of the story is made evident in the string of imperative verbs (behold, come out, go buy, open) that propel the plot forward.

Much of the dramatic impact of the parable arises from juxtaposition of opposites, producing shock effect. At the beginning of the parable, our attention is directed to the "kingdom of heaven." The audience is prepared for good news. And yet at the end of the story a happy, inclusive celebration is in progress on one side of the door; on the other a group of excluded members of the community remains, denied not only entry, but also recognition, identity. In the story world of this parable the themes of invitation and judgment, pleasure and pain appear, as does the theme of participation—radically actualized or forcefully denied.

Here we must consider the claim of Phyllis Trible, a twentieth-century feminist exegete, that, with biblical literature, context alters text; that the meaning of a particular story is to some extent determined by its place in the larger literary setting. The parable of the ten maidens (or, according to some translations, the "wise and foolish virgins") appears only in the Gospel of Matthew, although it does have thematic links such as light/dark, readiness, wisdom, etc., with the narratives of the other Gospels. The parable comes toward the end of what is often labeled one of five major sermons or discourses in Matthew's Gospel. Its narrative setting is the Mount of Olives, the speaker is Jesus, and the audience is made up of the disciples. According to preceding verses, it follows a scathing attack by Jesus upon the scribes and Pharisees. It is placed within a group of parables most often characterized as "eschatological," which is to say that the parables and narrative sections of this part of the Gospel describe "signs of the end"; they pave the way for the account of the Passion which will follow shortly. This passage is the first in a series of parables and teachings that make up chapter 25 of the Gospel of Matthew. This first parable deals with women. The next unit (verses 14–30) deals with men—a wealthy man who entrusts his male servants with his property while he takes a journey. The servants make very different uses of the property entrusted to them, resulting in the satisfaction or the ire of the master.

The teaching (verses 31–46) that ends the chapter and may be seen as its culmination, concerns the judgment the Son of Man will make when he comes in all his glory and occupies his throne. As in the previous two passages, one theme which characterizes the section is that of judgment. Verse 32 announces that at the momentous time envisioned, all the nations will be gathered before the throne and will be separated, as sheep are from goats, with the sheep, or obedient nations, assigned to the Son's right hand.

Here, however, the dramatic tension rises to an exquisite level, because the criterion given for the assignment to "sheep" or "goat" categories is the showing of mercy! Those who have fed, clothed, visited, and welcomed "the one of the least of these who are members of my family" (NRSV) unknowingly, are said to have ministered to the Son of Man, God's earthly manifestation. So the very context of the parable of the ten maidens argues against a simplistic interpretation of the text. The kingdom of heaven is not characterized by judgment instead of mercy. Rather, that "kingdom" is seen to involve a dynamic juxtaposition of the two.

Stanton considered the basic theme of Matthew 25 to be "the duty of self-development." In her commentary upon the parable of the wise and foolish virgins she notes the context of the story, and refers to Adam Clarke's[4] interpretation of the text. Clarke, along with many exegetes before and after him, interprets the parable allegorically, making the bridegroom represent Christ, the foolish virgins represent sinners whose hearts were not properly prepared for the kingdom of God, and the wise young women represent "the saints" who were spiritually ready for the age to come.

Stanton, however, makes a bold hermeneutical shift in her reading of the text. She interprets the wise and foolish young women in terms of themselves. She sees the development or stewardship of God-given abilities to be the crux of the parable's meaning. For her the foolish girls have been obedient to the "duty" of self-sacrifice. They have failed to make themselves self-reliant, capable citizens. Stanton vividly illustrates this failure:

> In their ignorance, women sacrifice themselves to educate the men of their households, and to make of themselves ladders by which their husbands, brothers and sons climb up into the kingdom of knowledge, while they themselves are shut out from all intellectual companionship, even with those they love best; such are indeed like the foolish virgins. (*TWB*, II: 125)

---

[4] Adam Clarke was a prolific, well-respected clergyman and scholar of his day. His work is often quoted in *The Woman's Bible*.

Stanton certainly does not stop with what we might term "blaming the victim." She makes perfectly clear her opinion that the type of person represented by the foolish maidens has been shaped by structures of society. According to Stanton, what we must learn from the parable is this:

> The wise virgins are they who keep their lamps trimmed, who burn oil in their vessels for their own use, who have improved every advantage for their education, secured a healthy, happy complete development, and entered all the profitable avenues of labor, for self-support, so that when the opportunities and the responsibilities of life come, they may be fully fitted to enjoy the one and ably to discharge the other. (*TWB* II: 126)

As contemporary feminist biblical scholarship shows, the radical imperative of Stanton's interpretation is as compelling and as necessary today as when she wrote it.

Much scholarly work on the parables discusses this passage in terms of a single, or at least predominant "point" that derives from the plot of the story. The foolish maidens are shut out of the feast, therefore this "fact" forms the basis of assumptions about *the* meaning of the parable. In putting their discussion on this foundation, scholars seemingly assume that the plot offers a solution or resolution from which moral, ethical, or religious lessons may be extracted. And surely the themes of preparedness, responsibility, watchfulness, and the realized possibility of being shut out do offer lessons related to the nature and the will of God. But according to the feminist interpretive principles we have explored, these assumptions are inadequate in that they stop too soon. To stop short is to sidestep the power of multiple meaning not only in this one parable, but also in the Gospel of Matthew, the New Testament, and scripture as a whole.

As the parable ends, relationships, lines of communication, stand ruptured. How can the bridegroom and the in-group of guests be seen as "successful" when the community is shattered? Surely they are "tragic" figures as much as the ones outside the door, in that they participate in the fragmentation of community. In the case of this story, we must, I believe, force ourselves to keep giving attention to the radically different situations on the two sides of the closed door, and to keep asking how this configuration can be seen as "like" and "not like" the kingdom of God. We must, like Phyllis Trible, approach this as a "text of terror," that is, we must identify with the horror represented rather than too easily identifying with the "good girls" within the house. We must also subject it to what Elisabeth Schüssler Fiorenza identifies as a "hermeneutics of suspicion," calling attention to the way that women are divided from each other by patriarchal institutions. In other words, we must remain open to the possibility that the "not like" dimension of the parable may indeed outweigh the "is like" dimension. We must push beyond the "givens" of the plot to raise questions about what essential issues are at stake.

If the parable as extended metaphor is kept open or tensive, there is much greater opportunity to interpret it in terms of communal, as well as individual salvation. It may be the emphasis that I, as a woman, put on relational issues that leads me to say that any adequate interpretation of this parable would have to address the shattered community depicted. And, as Stanton's commentary suggests, social systems as well as individual behaviors would have to be considered as part of the picture. In short, adequate interpretation needs to include both "the personal," the question of individuals' preoccupation with their readiness for the eschaton, the moment of God's final judgment, and "the political," the question of what models for social structures are mandated by the "Good News."

I am suggesting that an adequate feminist reading of this text raises questions, rather than necessarily providing answers. Questions such as: How is the "kingdom of heaven" like the situation described in the parable? Is the "kingdom" the happy celebration going on behind closed doors, or is it the vision of a larger picture? Does the "kingdom" necessarily involve the shattering of community: division and strife? Does it involve a believer's internalized battle? Why a "kingdom" as a symbol for salvation? Does the door slammed in the maidens' faces mean the end of an era? Must existing systems be shut down and out in order for salvation to occur? Finally, if the bridegroom represents Jesus, is this the sort of savior we, as individuals and communities, are willing to wait upon, follow, serve?

In the case of the parable of the ten maidens we may discover that by means of narrative strategy the author or editor of Matthew has thrown the ultimate questions of judgment and mercy back on us! *We* decide whether and how this story illustrates the "kingdom of heaven."

Works Consulted

Bach, Alice, ed. 1990. *The Pleasure of Her Text: Feminist Readings of Biblical and Historical Texts*. Philadelphia: Trinity Press International.

Bass, Dorothy C. 1982. "Women's Studies and Biblical Studies: An Historical Perspective." *JSOT* 22: 6-12.

Collins, Adela Yarbro, ed. 1985. *Feminist Perspectives on Biblical Scholarship*. Baltimore: Scholars Press.

Faludi, Susan. 1991. *Backlash: The Undeclared War Against American Women.* New York: Crown Publishers, Inc.

Fischer, Clare B., Betsy Brenneman, and Anne McGrew Bennett, eds. 1975. *Women in a Strange Land: Search for a New Image.* Philadelphia: Fortress Press.

McKenzie, Stevan L., and Stephen R. Haynes. 1993. *To Each Its Own Meaning: An Introduction to Biblical Criticisms and Their Applications.* Louisville, Kentucky: Westminster. John Knox Press.

Newsome, Carole A. and Sharon H. Ringe, eds. 1992. *The Women's Bible Commentary.* Louisville: Westminster/John Knox Press.

Ruether, Rosemary Radford. 1982. "Feminism and Patriarchal Religion: Principles of Ideological Critique of the Bible." *JSOT* 22: 54-66.

—. 1983. *Sexism and God Talk: Toward a Feminist Theology.* Boston: Beacon Press.

—. 1989. *To Change the World: Christology and Cultural Criticism.* New York: Crossroad.

Ruether, Rosemary Radford, and Rosemary Skinner Keller, gen. eds. 1982. *Women and Religion in America. Volume One: The Nineteenth Century, A Documentary History.* San Francisco: Harper and Row.

Russell, Letty M., ed. 1985. *Feminist Interpretation of the Bible.* Philadelphia: Westminster Press.

Schneiders, Sandra M. 1978. "Faith, Hermeneutics and the Literal Sense of Scripture." *Theological Studies* 39.

Schüssler Fiorenza, Elisabeth. 1977. "Feminist Theology as a Critical Theology of Liberation." In *Woman: New Dimensions,* ed. by Walter Burghardt. New York: Paulist Press. 19-50.

—. 1979a. "'For the Sake of Our Salvation...': Biblical Interpretation as Theological Task." In *Sin, Salvation and the Spirit,* ed. by Daniel Durkin. Collegeville, Minnesota: The Liturgical Press.

—. 1979b. "Word, Spirit and Power: Women in Early Christian Communities." In *Women of Spirit,* ed. by Rosemary Radford Ruether and Eleanor McLaughlin. New York: Simon and Schuster. 29-70.

—. 1983. *In Memory of Her: A Feminist Theological Reconstruction of Christian Origins.* New York: Crossroad Press.

—. 1984. *Bread Not Stone: The Challenge of Feminist Biblical Interpretation.* Boston: Beacon Press.

—. 1986. "Theological Criteria and Historical Reconstruction: Martha and Mary, Luke 10:38–42." *Protocol of the 53rd Colloquy of the Center for Hermeneutical Studies.* Berkeley, California: CHS.

—. 1988. "The Ethics of Biblical Interpretation: Decentering Biblical Scholarship." *JBL* 107/1: 3-17.

—. 1992. *But She Said: Feminist Practices of Biblical Interpretation.* Boston: Beacon Press.

Setel, T. Drorah. 1985. "Feminist Insights and the Question of Method." In *Feminist Perspectives on Biblical Scholarship,* ed. by Adela Yarbro Collins. Baltimore: Scholars Press. 35-42.

—. 1986. "Feminist Reflections on Separation and Unity in Jewish Theology." *JFSR* 2/1: 113-118.

Soelle, Dorothee. 1977. *Revolutionary Patience.* New York: Orbis Books.

—. 1982. *Beyond Mere Obedience*. New York: The Pilgrim Press.

Stanton, Elizabeth Cady, ed. [1895/1898.] *The Woman's Bible*. Reprint edition: Seattle: Coalition Task Force on Women and Religion, 1974.

—. 1898. *Eighty Years and More: Reminiscences 1815-1897*. New York: T. Fischer Unwin. Reprinted: New York: Schocken Books. 1971.

Tolbert, Mary Ann. 1979. *Perspectives on the Parables: An Approach to Multiple Interpretations*. Philadelphia: Fortress Press.

—, ed. 1983. *Semeia 28: The Bible and Feminist Hermeneutics*. SBL.

—. 1990. "Protestant Feminists and the Bible: On the Horns of a Dilemma." In *The Pleasure of Her Text: Feminist Readings of Biblical and Historical Texts*, ed. by Alice Bach. Philadelphia: Trinity Press International.

Trible, Phyllis. 1978. *God and the Rhetoric of Sexuality*. Philadelphia: Fortress Press.

—. 1982. "The Effects of Women's Studies on Biblical Studies: An Introduction." *JSOT* 22: 3-5.

—. 1983. "Depatriarchalizing in Biblical Interpretation." *JAAR* 41 (March): 30.

—. 1984. *Texts of Terror: Literary Feminist Readings of Biblical Narratives*. Philadelphia: Fortress Press.

—. 1985. "Jottings on the Journey." In *Feminist Interpretation of the Bible*, ed. by Letty M. Russell. Philadelphia: Westminster Press.

Willard, Frances E. 1888. *Woman in the Pulpit*. Boston: D. Lothrop Co.

4

Women Reading
Women in the Bible

Nancy Claire Pittman

W hen I was a young girl, I was quite interested, naturally enough, in "women's things." My interest was not just confined to Barbie dolls and Miss America pageants—though they were often presented as the appropriate feminine concerns for little girls—for I knew intuitively that "women's things" were not really defined by clothes and physical measurements. Rather, I was interested in the history of women, in their lives and stories, in the issues and questions that concerned them. As an avid reader, my weekly trips to the city library uncovered such wonders as the biographies of famous women, the novels of Louisa May Alcott, and the stories of Laura Ingalls Wilder. I enjoyed Greco-Roman mythology, because in it women appeared frequently and played major roles, and futuristic fantasies in which women governed societies with wisdom and grace. I discovered that the library, if one looked hard enough, could be a treasure-trove of information about women as they have been, as they are, as they might be. At the time, my reading was guided by no agenda, political or otherwise, except my ravenous interest in "women's things."

My attempts to satisfy my curiosity about women in Christianity, especially women in the Bible, however, were not so successful. In Sunday school, when I asked questions about the women in the biblical texts that we were studying, I was greeted with either blank stares or with long and confusing explanations, both responses invariably signaling that I had missed the point of the text, again. Secretly, however, I thought that surely something could be known about biblical women. So I turned to Edith Deen's *All the Women of the Bible* and fanciful historical reconstructions by Gladys Malvern or Taylor Caldwell. Not until I was an adult in seminary did I learn to read the Bible itself to find the stories and claims made about women within its pages. Reading the Bible out of an interest in "women's things" was becoming at last a legitimate enterprise in the church and in the academic community.

Reading about "women's things" in the Bible is not a very easy thing to do. On the one hand, very few women appear in its pages and very little information is offered about their personalities, their motivations, their lifestyles, their concerns. Often they are simply props in the stories of men. For example, the author of 2 Samuel never tells us much about Bathsheba other than that she had one husband and she attracted another when she took a bath in view of his rooftop. We find out a great deal about how David felt about her and what he had done with her, but we never hear about how she felt. In fact, the only hint we ever get about her emotional state in the whole episode comes when her child dies. Second Samuel 12:24 reads, "Then David consoled his wife"; she must have been upset enough to need consolation! Primarily, Bathsheba provides an occasion for David's sin; in other words, she is a prop. On the other hand, many texts in which women do appear are some of the most difficult texts in the Bible to understand. The story of Jephthah and his unnamed daughter in Judges 11 is terrifying. Try as they might, its interpreters have yet to offer a reading of the story that stills my fears about one man's promises and his understanding of a God who would demand that such promises be kept.

Nevertheless, in spite of these difficulties, women have been reading the Bible for centuries to find out what it has to say about themselves. In this essay I am going to tell the stories of five modern women who read the Bible out of their own questions and concerns as women. These five hypothetical women loosely correspond with Rita Nakashima Brock's five "states of consciousness" described in the introduction to this book. In fact, it might be said that these five women are embodiments of those states—a way of giving flesh and blood to the conceptual models Brock offers.[1]

---

[1] Brock and I envision the first two states, originally described by Peggy Macintosh, in a slightly different way. My first state, "The Woman Who Wasn't There," serves as an illustration of a starting point in the development of a feminist consciousness; my second state, "Just Like a Man (Only Different)," is an amalgam of Brock's first two states, "Just Like a Man" and "Add Women and Stir."

As you read their stories, picture in your mind's eye five women, all of whom are in different places, at different ages, with different needs and cares. For clarity's sake, I have given them names: Margaret, Anita, Rebecca, Yolanda, and Ming-li. Each brings to the various texts she reads certain assumptions and questions about what it means to be a woman in her own circumstances. What these women find as they read are parallels between their lives and the portrayals of the biblical women they read about, a rather common occurrence for all people in reading the Bible. At the same time, as they open themselves more vulnerably to the text, their understandings of themselves and of women in the Bible are challenged. Perhaps, as they reflect about themselves and about the biblical women about which they read, they grow.

Before I tell their stories, I want to clarify two essential points. The Bible, of course, was not produced by persons who can be identified with any of these states of consciousness or strategies, as Brock sometimes calls them. Thus, the individual texts read by these women are not demonstrations of the strategies themselves, although, to be sure, the texts have features that enable their readers to make comparisons between their own lives and the lives of various women in the Bible. Rather, it is the ways in which these stories are read that serve as the demonstrations of these divergent states of feminist consciousness. Reading is itself an interactive process between reader and text in which the text offers certain stories, claims, and comments to the reader, and the reader, in turn, brings her own experience, gifts, culture, perspectives. What comes out of this interaction is a reading, an interpretation, a way of understanding the biblical text—and a way of being understood by the text, which is, after all, part of our scriptures, our sacred writings. The significant point, then, is not simply what a biblical text says about women—although we must surely pay attention to any claims it does or does not appear to make—but what happens when text and reader are brought together.

Second, all of us—female, male, twentieth century, first century, child, adult—bring something to the Bible when we pick up and read it. All of us bring our own states of consciousness, feminist or otherwise, and our own interpretive strategies. There is simply no such thing as an un-interpreted reading of the Bible. Furthermore, what we bring to the text before we read greatly influences the outcome of our reading. The very way we ask the questions of the Bible shapes the answers we receive. Thus, the particularities of the lives of these hypothetical women may indeed pull things out of the text that you or I did not see at first. The particularities of your life will do the same. The real issue, then, is not whether these women are imposing something on the text; of course they are—they are imposing themselves. The issue is how they impose themselves and how honest they are about their impositions.

"The Woman Who Wasn't There"
Matthew 1 and 2

All her life, Margaret had tried to be perfect. She was not perfect, that fact she knew well, but she wanted to be perfect and the desire for perfection drove her through the tasks and cares of her life. If she tried to put her concept of perfection into words, which she did not try very often, it would be comprised of a list of "do's" and "don'ts." "Do be polite; do your homework or, now that you're out of school, do your housework, your volunteer work, your church work; do take care of your family; do attend PTA meetings; do go to church, and get your family to church, every Sunday morning." And, "don't call attention to yourself; don't wear white shoes after Labor Day; don't say anything if you can't say anything nice; don't rock the boat." At the end of the day, Margaret felt like she had at least approximated perfection if she could say to herself, "I got everything done, smoothly and efficiently, without any fuss." In fact, if she did things in such a way that no one around her seemed to notice what she had done, she thought herself even more content. On the surface of her life, it was all right with her if her family and friends took her for granted; at least they weren't finding fault with her or picking at her.

When she had been a child, Margaret had defined perfection a little differently. At that time, her ideal of perfection had been mostly tied up with how well she did in school. She had studied hard and excelled in subjects such as history and English literature. She loved reading about the great culture-making events of the world and of the men who made those events happen. She looked for women in the history of Western civilization and finally concluded that if they appeared at all, they surfaced as wives and mothers of great men, Queen Elizabeth I of England being one of the great exceptions. Margaret had done so well in high school that she and Jason Daly competed all the way to graduation for the head of the class. In the end, she was named salutatorian; Jason was valedictorian. At first she felt terribly disappointed, until one of her teachers pointed out that it was better for Jason to have been so named because it would help his career along. So Margaret, second banana, went to college, earned a bachelor's degree in education, and married a nice boy. If perfection could not be attained through her own intellectual gifts, it might be reached by becoming the perfect wife and mother—the perfect woman, or so Margaret thought. And no one bothered to disabuse her of that notion.

Now, when Margaret was quite honest with herself—a state of mind she usually tried to avoid—she wished she had done just a little more and seemed just a little less invisible. Sometimes, she seemed so unobtrusive that she even lost sight of herself in the network of relationships around her. It was during one of these rare periods of introspection that the Christmas holidays arrived, and with them the concomitant scripture readings of the story of Jesus' birth.

One evening, in preparation for a children's Sunday school class that she was teaching, she turned to the Gospel of Matthew to get some help in describing Mary to the children. The first thing Margaret noticed was the long list of "begats" that lead up to the birth of Jesus. Fathers played a pretty prominent role, she observed, and forty-one were named. Only five mothers were mentioned, and only four of those had names; the mother of Solomon was identified only as the wife of Uzziah. Margaret knew from all those years in Sunday school, however, that the mother of Solomon was called Bathsheba, so she supplied the name herself.

Having worked through these first seventeen verses, Margaret proceeded with the question, What can we find out about Mary from Matthew? Matthew 1:18 states, "Now the birth of Jesus the Messiah took place in this way. When his mother Mary had been engaged to Joseph, but before they lived together, she was found to be with child from the Holy Spirit." Being an English major, Margaret was immediately aware of the passive voice of the verbs, "had been engaged," "was found." "Who had engaged her to Joseph? Who had found her pregnant?" she wondered.[2] The text does not say, but the story continues.

Joseph evidently knew she was pregnant because he "planned to dismiss her quietly." However, just as he had decided to do this, he had a dream in which an angel appeared to him and told him that because her child was from the Holy Spirit he should keep Mary as his wife. The angel also told him what to name the baby, and how the baby would "save the people from their sins" (Matthew 1:21). So Joseph did what the angel said. Not a word in this part of the story is said about what Mary knew or what she thought or what she did about the things happening to her. Her character, motives, and responses remain unknown. Joseph, together with the angel, are the only real actors. In her imagination, Margaret saw Mary simply stand-

---

[2] In common English usage today, we often use the passive voice of the verb *engage*, as in "I was engaged to Jimmy," a usage that assumes the speaker's own wishes and actions in getting engaged to Jimmy. The Greek word in Matthew. 1:18, *mnésteutheisés*, is a passive that indicates that Mary is the object of someone else's intention and action.

ing at center stage, getting greater and greater with child, while the action took place around her and outside her.

At the right time, Mary gives birth to a son and Joseph names the baby Jesus, as he had been directed by the angel. The scene then shifts from Joseph and Mary to the intrigue of King Herod's court and the coming of the wise men. Mary next appears in the story when the wise men, following the star, enter the house and see "the child with Mary his mother." What follows from there Margaret could recite in her sleep after years and years of Christmas pageants. The wise men leave their gifts for the baby and, having been warned in a dream, depart for home in a different way. Joseph has another dream visitation from an angel who tells him that "the child and his mother" are in danger and that he should flee with them to Egypt. Immediately after the family leaves, all the male babies in the area are slaughtered in an effort by Herod to get rid of the threat to his power. When Herod dies, Joseph has yet a third dream in which an angel calls him to take "the child and his mother" back to Israel. Joseph eventually settles the family in Nazareth.

In all of Matthew 2, Mary is mentioned by name only once. The pattern begun in chapter 1, in which others (i.e., men) do the thinking, dreaming, deciding, and acting, continues in chapter 2. Mary is hardly anything more than a set-piece to be moved about the stage at will by others. And it occurs to Margaret that this story has very little to do with Mary at all! It is a story about Joseph and angels and Herod and wise men and a baby boy. Mary is just the receptacle, the vessel, for the Holy Child. She seems as invisible in her life as Margaret seems in her own.

Margaret closed her Bible, leaned her head back against the wall over her sofa, and thought about this parallel between her life and the life of Mary, as depicted by Matthew. Just like Margaret, Mary was a necessary, yet practically invisible, actor in the story of her own life. Being a mother was indeed important, but did a woman have to be so unassuming and so unapparent to be good? "When was it," wondered Margaret, "that I put together the equation, perfection = unruffled, unruffling invisibility? Why, like Mary, am I just a prop on the stage of my own life and not a major character? Surely, surely something more can be said about Mary and surely something more can be said about me. But what?"

"Just Like a Man (Only Different)"

Exodus 15:20–21; Numbers 12; 20:1; 26:59

When Anita was a little girl, her father loved to tell people, "Anita, not like her sisters, has a real head for business!" He was right, too;

even when she had been small, Anita loved piling numbers on top of numbers to get more and bigger numbers. The first toy she really loved was a calculator that could do things with numbers faster and better than she could imagine. She was also very enterprising. As soon as she had learned that numbers could stand for something real, like money, she began coercing her sisters into all kinds of money-making schemes, from lemonade stands when they were children, to door-to-door cosmetic sales when they got older. Her father was very encouraging all the way, just bursting with pride over the money they made each week. He would also remind her constantly of the successes of other women. "Listen to this," he would read to her from the newspaper, "Mary Kay has set another record in cosmetic sales!" Or, "Sherry Lansing is now the head of her own movie studio!" Or, "First National just promoted a woman to senior vice-president!" "Honey," he would say from behind his paper, "if they can do it, you can do it!"

Anita believed him. She went to college, excelled as an accounting major, and got a job in a major accounting firm. For five years, she climbed the corporate ladder, working such long hours that she barely had time to squeeze in Sunday church and dinner with her family, much less any kind of social life. She received promotions and raises as quickly as anyone else who started with her. But then things stopped happening so fast for her. At first, she thought she had just reached a natural plateau before she advanced again. Then she heard that Greg Bard had just received a promotion. "Greg Bard," she thought to herself, "why, I've done lots better work than he has ever since we both started together!" When, one day over a quick lunch, she casually asked her boss about Greg's new job, he just shrugged his shoulders and said, "Yeah, that Greg is a real family man; the boss loves him and his wife." After that, Anita took a long look around her company and noticed that while there were a lot of women at her level, doing really fine work, very few could be found in the levels above them.

That Sunday in church, Anita's minister preached a sermon on the "Song of Miriam," Exodus 15:20–21. "Just think," the minister enthused, "these two verses, according to the scholars, were probably sung at the very event of the crossing of the Red Sea itself, and it was a woman who sang them![3] Who says women don't play important roles in the Bible!" "Remember," the minister continued, "Miriam was the sister of Moses. She first appears in Exodus 2, as

---

[3] See Bernhard W. Anderson, *Understanding the Old Testament*, 3rd Edition (Englewood Cliffs: Prentice-Hall, Inc., 1975): 72.

the baby Moses' guard when his mother put him in a basket in the river. When Pharaoh's daughter rescued Moses, it was Miriam who volunteered to get as a nurse for the child the Hebrew woman, who unbeknownst to Pharaoh's daughter was the baby's mother. In this episode, she doesn't have a name, but we can be sure that girl was Miriam. She doesn't come into the story again, however, until the singing of these verses when, just like a man, she is called a prophet, and she leads all the women in rejoicing. "Thus," concluded the minister, "we can see from this illustration, that women, like men, can and should rise to positions of power and influence in the church, and in the world."[4]

Anita was comforted by the minister's confidence in women, but nagging doubts about what was happening to her and to other women in her company continued to bother her. So, one evening, she pulled out the concordance that her pious aunt had given her when she was baptized, blew the dust off it, and began to trace Miriam's story through the Bible.

Anita discovered that Miriam plays no other part in the rest of Exodus. She reappears in Numbers, in a much more unflattering light than before. In chapter 12, Moses married a Cushite woman, and, for some reason not given in the text, that marriage displeased Moses' siblings, Aaron and Miriam. So they spoke out against Moses, saying, "Has the Lord spoken only through Moses? Has he not spoken through us also?" God heard what they had said and summoned all three into God's presence. There, in a pillar of cloud, God spoke of the superiority of Moses over them and, in anger, rebuked Miriam and Aaron for daring to question Moses' actions.

When God departed, "Miriam had become leprous, as white as snow." Aaron then turned to Moses, saying, "Oh, my lord, do not punish us for a sin that we have so foolishly committed." (Anita could not help but wonder why Aaron was saying "do not punish *us*," when Miriam was the only one afflicted.) Moses, in turn, cried out, "O God, please heal her!" God then decreed that Miriam would be cut off from the camp for seven days, at which time she would be healed of her leprosy. The text also adds, "and the people did not set out on the march until Miriam had been brought in again."

Not a word is said, thought Anita, about why Miriam received such a drastic and visible punishment and Aaron received nothing.

---

[4] Although Anita is unaware of this fact, a number of scholars argue that the long poem attributed to Moses in Exodus 15:1–18 may be a later embellishment of Miriam's song, made up and inserted before her song, perhaps, to subvert the tradition that continued in Israel concerning her leadership. See Phyllis Trible, "Bringing Miriam out of the Shadows," *Bible Review* 5 (1989): 34.

Nor, mused Anita, does this passage say anything about why speaking one's mind, even against God's elect, merits such harshness. When she asked her minister about the episode later, he responded, "Well, maybe we just don't hear about Aaron's punishment in this story. But I'm sure he got what he deserved as well." Anita was not so sure about this, and she began to see that women, no matter what people said, were not just like men, and were not treated just like men.

Miriam is not mentioned again until her death and burial in Numbers 20. With the help of her concordance, Anita discovered that Miriam is named only four other times in the Bible. In Number 26:59 she is found in a list of Israelite ancestors with her mother's other children, Aaron and Moses. In Deuteronomy 24:9, as a warning against leprosy, she is held up as a negative example. The other two citations are quite positive. In 1 Chronicles 6:3, in another ancestor list, the pattern, "the *sons* of Levi,…the *sons* of Kohath" etc., is broken with the inclusion of Miriam among the offspring of Amram. There, she is the only woman named in a long catalog of descendents of Levi. Finally, in Micah 6:4, God reportedly speaks to the people about what has been done for them, including the bestowing of the leadership of Moses, Aaron, and Miriam, without mention of the unpleasant episode of Numbers 12.

Although she may not have been a sophisticated biblical scholar, Anita was an intelligent, thoughtful woman who could observe that Miriam is portrayed both positively and negatively in the Bible. Sometimes, just like her brothers, she is remembered with respect as a member of a powerful triumvirate. Even after she has been cast out, the people will not leave her behind, maybe as a sign of their regard for her. Moreover, traces of her are found in the New Testament in the name "Mary," which is the Greek transliteration of "Miriam." Yet, at other times, for no reason given in the text, she is singled out for harsh treatment, unlike her brother Aaron. Women, Anita was learning, were just like men, only different, both in the Bible, and in real life.[5]

"Woman as Victim"

Revelation 12; 17; and 21:9–14

Rebecca had the dubious distinction of being known as the "easiest girl" in her high school class. She remembers as clearly as if they

---

[5] For a provocative treatment of Miriam, see Phyllis Trible's remarks in Cullen Murphy, "Women and the Bible," *The Atlantic Monthly* 272/2 (August 1993): 50.

had happened yesterday the events that gave her this reputation. It all began late one Friday evening, when everyone was hanging around the local park, shortly after Rebecca had moved with her family to town. A new friend had invited her to go out with some other friends and Rebecca had excitedly accepted the invitation. She desperately wanted to belong with a crowd. Together they all went to a nearby park, where a lot of kids from their school spent the week-end evenings. Soon after they arrived, amid the chatter and laughter of the group, Jack Brady, one of the most popular boys in the senior class, began to pay attention to Rebecca. So when he invited her to take a walk with him, she went along eagerly. When he began to kiss her, she returned his ardor. But when he began, as kids say, to move the action along, she tried to resist. Jack Brady, though, rarely took "no" for an answer from anybody, and he certainly was not going to take it that night. When he finally let her up off the ground, he told her she had been great. Then he said that he would call her and walked off. Rebecca spent the rest of the weekend waiting for a phone call that never came.

Monday morning did come, however, and at school Rebecca reso-lutely confronted Jack with his neglect. "Why didn't you call me?" she demanded. "Oh," he responded, "I just didn't have time. Be-sides, I already got what I wanted from you and I figure you already got what you wanted." "You're the only one who wanted that!" whispered Rebecca frantically, "I didn't want it!" "Oh yes, you did," claimed Jack, in a louder voice. "I could tell you did. There are only two kinds of girls as far as I can see—those that want it and those that don't. And you definitely wanted it. I gotta go." As Jack walked off down the hall, whistling, Rebecca stood there, embarrassed, no, panic-stricken, wondering how he knew that there were only two kinds of girls and, more important, what kind she was. By late Mon-day afternoon, his version about what she had done Friday night with him had spread through the school. Rebecca spent the rest of her senior year fending off boys who were always saying, "Come on, Rebecca, you did it with Jack. Why won't you do it with me?"

To compensate for her high school reputation, Rebecca worked hard to keep herself away from the sexual relationships that were offered in college. She succeeded, for the most part, in portraying herself as a nice girl, the kind of girl that boys might want to marry, if not stay out with all night. Since her one sexual encounter was so frightening, she did not want a repetition of that experience. At the same time she was convinced that she had to do *something* to keep boys interested in her, so she took to doing the kinds of caretaking things that mothers do and, she thought, that wives do. For her boy-friends she sewed buttons on shirts, straightened dorm rooms, typed papers, and fussed about eating habits. Rebecca's strategy paid off, or so she thought: she dropped out of school to marry a fellow student and tried to make him happy enough to keep from leaving her.

She continued to work after their marriage, both at home and in a fairly unsatisfying job as a secretary. She ran the household and the office to suit the men in her life—her husband and her boss. When her husband complained about her lack of interest in sex, she dutifully got some interest, with a little help from Marabel Morgan's *Total Woman*. When her boss complained about things undone, she dutifully stayed late to finish them. So the time went by as Rebecca worked hard at her job and even harder at her marriage. Of course, she sometimes resented her situation, but she did not know what to do about it other than to pretend not to notice that she was the one in the office fetching all the coffee and she was the one at home wearing the Saran Wrap.[6] Ten years after their wedding, her husband left her anyway.

At that point, Rebecca finally got angry enough to do something about what was happening to her. After taking a long, hard look at herself and her life through the help of a pastoral counselor, a woman she came to trust and admire, she reentered college to complete her degree and to find a career. There, in a place she never expected, in a Bible class that was required in her small church-related institution, she found confirmation of Jack Brady's claim that there were two kinds of women. A term paper was assigned on any biblical topic of interest, and Rebecca chose to focus on the portrayals of women in the book of Revelation. Although the professor did not think it was a particularly interesting or important topic, she doggedly set to work.

Rebecca found three female images in the book. Two, she noticed, were set in opposition to each other, almost in direct support of Jack Brady's division of women. At the beginning of chapter 17, an angel says to John, the revealer, "'Come, I will show you the judgment of the great whore who is seated on many waters, with whom the kings of the earth have committed fornication'" (17:1–2). John is then shown a horrible picture of a woman who is dressed in purple and scarlet, adorned with jewels, and drunk on "the blood of the saints and the blood of the witnesses to Jesus" (17:6). Rebecca saw in her mind's eye a drunken sorority girl at the end of a spring formal, giggling and falling down, pretty silk dress now awry and stained. Upon the woman in this text is blamed much of the evil of the world. She is a temptress, a seductress, luring kings and nations to their

---

[6] This, or course, was one of Marabel Morgan's most famous suggestions for keeping a husband happy and in charge of the home. See Marabel Morgan, *Total Woman* (Old Tappan, N.J.: F. H. Rowell, 1973).

destruction. But she will get her just deserts, says the angel, for "the ten horns that you saw, they and the beast will hate the whore; they will make her desolate and naked; they will devour her flesh and burn her up with fire" (17:16). The revealer uses similar imagery in describing a real woman, dubbed "Jezebel," in the church at Thyatira (2:20–23). These, Rebecca thought, were women who, as Jack Brady would say, wanted it—and got it, in spades.

The polar opposite of the whore is found in chapter 21. The same angel who showed John the whore returns and says, "Come, I will show you the bride, the wife of the Lamb" (21:9). The revealer now sees the holy city Jerusalem, "coming down out of heaven from God," like a radiant jewel (21:10). Elsewhere this same bride is described as being dressed in "fine linen, bright and pure," and ready to be married to her groom (19:7–8). Rebecca saw this time the woman on the cover of last month's issue of *Bride's* magazine, a flawlessly made-up creature dressed in white silk and lace covered with seed pearls. This woman was so beautifully perfect that she was untouchable. She was pure and spotless, aloof from the cares of life. She radiated an awareness of her perfection and of her exact compatibility for her absent mate. She was the other kind of woman, the kind that Rebecca had spent most of her adult life trying to be.

The more Rebecca thought about these two contrasting images, the more infuriated she became. Why, she wondered, are women usually presented in such polarities?[7] Why is this polarity practically confirmed in the Bible, the book about God? After all, the same angel says the same words each time he shows one of these female images to John, placing them in clear opposition. Though her professor pointed out that these two images were not "real" women, but just symbols of a larger reality that had nothing to do with femaleness, Rebecca was not placated. She thought that even if they were symbols of another "larger" reality, they were still problematic for real women. They seemed to her to be archetypes, categorical models, used too often for describing the nature of real women. And, Rebecca believed, surely there was more to being female than these two choices.

So she explored the third alternative presented in the Revelation. In chapter 12, John sees in the heavens "a woman clothed with

---

[7] Peter J. Rabinowitz makes this same observation when he writes, "In our culture, we have a number of categories in which to place women, but they tend to fall into pairs of binary oppositions: Madonna/whore, good girl/bad girl, victim/villain....Men, in other words, can be rich as characters; women, on the whole, have the choice of being pure or being monstrous." Peter J. Rabinowitz, *Before Reading* (Ithaca: Cornell University Press, 1987): 207.

the sun, with the moon under her feet, and on her head a crown of twelve stars. She was pregnant and was crying out in birth pangs, in the agony of giving birth" (12:1–2). As the story unfolds, there in the heavens, a terrible and mighty red dragon appears who wants to devour the woman's child as soon as it is born. When the child, a boy, is born, however, he is snatched away from the dragon up to the throne of God. The woman, in turn, flees to the wilderness "where she has a place prepared by God" (12:6). Thereupon, the dragon engages in battle in heaven with Michael and his angels until he is thrown down to the earth. He then returns to his pursuit of the woman, but she is constantly rescued from his efforts to get her. The episode concludes with the words, "Then the dragon was angry with the woman, and went off to make war on the rest of her children..." (12:17).

The woman is never named, noted Rebecca, but she looks suspiciously like Mary, the mother of the Messiah.[8] Because this Mary-figure of the Revelation is a victim, totally out of control of what is happening to her, Rebecca readily identified with her. She had also felt out of control of her life, a victim, first of Jack Brady, later of her husband's demands and abandonment. In an effort to make sense of this female image for her own life, Rebecca concluded her paper with some personal remarks about its effects upon her. "Like the woman of chapter 12," she wrote, "we women are victims, always hunted and pursued, never determiners of our own fate, dependent upon God, or something, to protect us. This woman, this victimized Mary-figure, is the only image that accurately reflects women's reality as women themselves might describe it. Thus, she is the only appropriate image for women in the whole book of Revelation."

Later, after she turned in the paper, Rebecca began to wish she had not written that statement. It did not bother her that the professor had not thought it was real biblical scholarship and gave the paper a B-. Rather, she began to question whether the image "victim" was any better for women than the images of "bride" and "whore." It may depict the reality that many women experience, but it should not be held up, almost fatalistically, as a model for female life. Rebecca came to believe that if women always thought of themselves as helpless, then they might never take control of their lives. "What we need," she thought, "are images of women who are powerful and in charge of their own lives. What we need is to name ourselves and to de-

---

[8] In the Gospel accounts, however, Mary is pursued only once by a dragon-like figure. This occurs in Matthew's version, when Mary and Joseph and their baby boy must run away from Herod, the baby-killer.

scribe who we are in our own terms. The question is, how are we going to do that?"

"Women-Centered"
Luke 1:26—2:20

When Yolanda was three years old, her parents were killed in an apartment fire. So she went to live with her grandmother, a strong woman who had buried a husband and a daughter and endured a great many other difficulties. At a time when people of her race were generally denied admission into the local public colleges, she had gone to a small private college to earn her degree. Now she was a schoolteacher and, as matriarch of a large extended family, she supported financially a host of children, nieces and nephews, grandchildren, and friends. Her meager resources did not stretch very far, but she gave what she could and more. Yet more appreciated than her gifts of money were her gifts of wisdom, compassion, and love. She was determined to make life better for the people that she loved, one way or another.

Yolanda hardly noticed the hardship around her when she was growing up because her grandmother was careful to keep it a secret from her. When she wanted a new dress, her grandmother stayed up to make it; when she wanted a birthday party, her grandmother threw the grandest affair for the whole neighborhood. And if she could not do whatever Yolanda needed or wanted, her aunts surely could. For Yolanda, the orphan child, was the darling of the women of her family, the focus of their hopes and dreams, and they were trying to give her what they wanted for all their children—a better life. Only occasionally would they let Yolanda see that the world was not so rosy for everyone, that they were treated with less than respect in most circles, that members of their gender received less than their share almost everywhere.

One would think that Yolanda would have become spoiled and dependent with all this attention. But with every gift, every act of support, came the admonition, "To you much has been given; of you much is expected" and she took it to heart. Since Yolanda was bright and talented, she was encouraged to stretch herself like her grandmother stretched their money. When she did well at something, everyone celebrated; when she did not do so well, everyone, in his or her own way, showed support. "It's OK, honey; you'll do better next time," was a constant refrain in her life. So Yolanda learned, at a very early age, to appreciate women and to value the things they offered—nurture, encouragement, resilient strength. She learned that life happened not just in grand events and in decisions made by important persons, but in everyday cares and concerns, in the struggle to stay alive with dignity and self-respect.

These lessons grew less and less important for Yolanda as she grew up. Like her grandmother and her aunts before her, she joined the struggle for civil rights for her people. She worked her way through college, and then law school. Yolanda finally became a lawyer, respected in her community for the battles she waged in court for justice and equal rights. When she arrived at this point in her life she also began to sense a kind of denigration of the gifts and strengths she brought as a woman to her work. At home she had been taught that responsibilities should be shared, that the talents of each individual should be nurtured and celebrated by all the members of the family, that nothing that was painful was too insignificant for the family to care about. But in the workplace, none of these things mattered. In fact, if she was seen as too compassionate or too nurturing, she was either laughed at or taken advantage of by her coworkers. She learned that in her professional world, the "men's world," she would be most successful if she kept herself impassive, uninvolved, and disconnected from the daily life around her. Unlike Anita, who had not seen many women advancing in their careers, Yolanda saw them, and herself, get promoted. What she seemed remarkably oblivious to, however, was the way in which she and the other women were required to check their "female-ness" at the door of the office and assume a kind of "male-ness" in order to get ahead.

Yolanda reflected little on all this as she pursued her career, until her grandmother died. As the family gathered to mourn her passing, an aunt told her how proud they all were of her. "Still," she continued, "it's a shame you had to get so hard-boiled to get what we all wanted for you. I remember when you were such an open, loving little girl." That night, in her old bedroom, as she considered that remark, Yolanda remembered a conversation she and her grandmother once had years ago about what it meant to be a woman.

One Christmas Eve, when the eight-year-old Yolanda was already in bed, her grandmother came in to tuck her in and say good night. Like most children on Christmas Eve, even those who no longer believed in Santa, she was not sleepy and she wanted to talk. Her grandmother obliged her and started chatting about the church service they had attended earlier that evening. "You know," said her grandmother, "I like the story of the baby Jesus being born and the angels singing and the shepherds visiting, but what I really love is the part about Mary and Elizabeth. Now there were two women you could really admire, because they knew what was what and they did what was needed." And she opened Yolanda's Bible, as she tended to do on occasions she considered important and worthy of a word from God.

All these years later, Yolanda, sitting there on her old twin bed, saw her Bible on a shelf and opened it to the same place, Luke 1:26. "In the sixth month," she read, "the angel Gabriel was sent by God to a town in Galilee called Nazareth, to a virgin engaged to a man whose name was Joseph, of the house of David. The virgin's name was Mary" (Luke 1:26–27). Mary, of course, was surprised by this unexpected, unbelievable visit, and even more startled by the news the angel gave her. "You are the favored one of God," the angel said, "and so you are going to have a baby, the Son of God, and you will call him Jesus." As Yolanda read, she could hear again the conversation between her grandmother and herself about Mary. "I think having a baby without being married is a funny way to be blessed by God," Yolanda had commented on that Christmas Eve years ago. And her grandmother had replied, "Having a baby should, in just about every case, be regarded as a favor from God."

Their conversation about how Mary graciously accepted the news and the job of bearing and rearing God's child had continued. "Do you think she could refuse?" Yolanda had asked. "Of course," her grandmother had said. "You always have a choice with God and God will still love you, no matter what." Then came her grandmother's favorite part. After the angel's announcement, Mary went to visit her cousin Elizabeth, who was also pregnant. Unlike Mary, Elizabeth was not so young; she was, in fact, "getting on in years" (1:7). Yolanda heard again her grandmother muttering under her breath, "Well, maybe being pregnant at her age wasn't such a great favor."

Not only was Mary worthy enough to receive a heavenly emissary, she was also worthy enough to sing with her own voice a song that generations after her were also to sing. "My soul magnifies the Lord, " Mary began in a song of God's concern for the poor and the hungry, the weak and the lowly. "Her song," her grandmother had remarked, "is just another version of the song Miriam sang way back on the shores of the Red Sea about the triumph of God over those who think they are so high and mighty."

Mary stayed with her cousin about three months, before she went back to Nazareth. "What do you think they did all that time?" asked Yolanda naively. "Well," said her grandmother, "I guess they got ready for their babies. And they talked a lot about what they were going to do for those babies and how their lives were about to change. And they cared about each other, like your aunts take care of each other." In due time, Elizabeth gave birth to her baby and named him John, against the advice of her friends and neighbors who wanted to name him after his father, Zechariah. It was at that point that Zechariah, who had been struck dumb for his disbelief over the news that he was going to be a father, wrote a note to confirm Elizabeth's choice of names. "Immediately his mouth was opened and his tongue freed" (1:64), and he began to speak words much like those Mary had already spoken.

In this way, Yolanda and her grandmother had told each other the story of the birth of two babies. Then, at Yolanda's prodding, they read again Luke's account of the journey of Mary and Joseph to Bethlehem. They talked about how miserable Mary must have been riding a donkey when she was ready to deliver her baby. Yolanda had asked if giving birth was really as easy as the Christmas songs made it sound and her grandmother had emphatically answered, "Not at all! Having a baby is hard work, regardless of how special it is! You push and push and push, and finally, when you don't think you can push anymore, that baby comes out. And then, just when you think you can rest, it's hungry and you're the only one who can feed it." "What do you think Joseph was doing all that time?" wondered Yolanda. "He was just doing what he was told to do. And if more men would follow his example, the world would be a lot better place!" her grandmother had railed. Then they remembered, one more time, the angels, the shepherds and Mary, who "treasured all these words and pondered them in her heart" (2:19).

Now that she had grown up, staring at her Bible as she sat on the edge of her bed, Yolanda also pondered about herself and who she had become. She thought about the tough outer shell she had developed in order to be successful and the fact that her grandmother, also successful in her own way, had never been accused of being hard. Of course, her grandmother had not been a lawyer, a profession that might require more toughness, but Yolanda knew women in other professions who were seemingly as unfeeling and as coldly analytical as she had become. It occurred to her that women seemed to play a prominent role in the Gospels only at events surrounding birth and death, at the edges of life. Maybe it was only at these edges that the gifts she had always especially identified with women—a warm concern for the people around them, sensitive and intuitive kindness, empathy—were appreciated and needed. "Is there a way," she asked herself, "to bring these gifts in from the edges to other arenas of life?" Was there a way to bring the happy completeness she knew at home as a child into her office? What would it mean to embrace the "femaleness" of her personality and allow it to be a part of her professional identity? Yolanda didn't know the answer that night, but she was determined to find out in the coming years of her life.

Everyone Must Be Included

John 20:1–18

Ming-li is only six years old and most of her story has yet to be lived. Like Yolanda, she bears the hopes of generations of women before her and around her who dream of a time when all people, female and male, of African, Asian, European, and Native American ancestry, will, in the apostle Paul's words, be truly one in Christ Jesus (Galatians 3:28). Her parents are working for a time when distinctions between genders and among races and ethnic groups will no longer be the yardsticks by which individuals are measured and sorted into various roles and categories.

Perhaps Ming-li may be spared some of the pain that older women have experienced, a pain that has sometimes been intensified as they read the Bible and reflected on the nature of their lives in its light. Margaret, in her reading of Matthew's account of the birth of Jesus, discovered that often in the Bible, women are portrayed as props to be moved around the stage and placed in the scene according to the demands of the stories of the men around them. Their feelings, thoughts, hopes, concerns are as invisible and unnecessary to the story as Margaret had come to believe herself to be in her own life. "Where are the women?" she asked; and in the text she read she received a very uncomfortable answer from the Bible.

Anita found the women in the Bible, or, at least, one woman. And she found that woman, Miriam, in a position of power and authority in the wilderness community of the Israelites. For no reason offered in the text, however, Miriam is forced to bear more than her share of the punishment for an offense that Anita thought minor at best. Anita could only conclude that the story is told in such a way because Miriam is a woman. Like Anita, she may have had an abundance of talent and ability, but those things became unimportant in light of her gender. Anita learned that even when women are depicted as strong, powerful people in the Bible, they are not always treated just like men.

Rebecca, forced by the circumstances of her life to play roles she did not choose or like, found confirmation of those roles in her reading of the book of Revelation. There women, albeit as female symbols, were sorted into stereotypes that have been used to describe real women for centuries. A woman is either "whore," threatening in some way to male authority and power structures and described almost exclusively in terms of sexual promiscuity, or "bride," adored for her aloof, unreal perfection. Rebecca rejects both images as inappropriate stereotypes of real women. When she discovers a third alternative, woman as victim, she rejects it as well in spite of its closer parallel to her reality and that of many other women. She is angered by these stereotypes and begins to look for images of "female-ness" that represent more closely ideals that women might choose and value for themselves.

In the lives of her grandmother and her aunts, and in the story of Mary and Elizabeth told by Luke, Yolanda is taught those ideals. She is surrounded by a circle of women, celebrating "women's things" such as birth and new life, supportive relationships, and the values of sharing, nurturing, loving. Yet Yolanda finds herself unable to take these things with her into her workplace. These "women's things" must be left at home, she believes, in order for her to succeed at her job. The recognition that she must divide herself in this way is painful.

Ming-li's parents hope that she will be able to integrate in all facets of her life the gifts that have been typically associated with women with "male" attributes such as analytical ability and assertiveness. They made this hope more concrete by the name they gave her at her birth. When asked by a neighbor about the two Chinese characters that comprise her name, her mother responded, "The *ming* means 'bright' or 'clear' and the *li* means 'reason' or 'principle.' Together the characters signal one who has understanding or who is reasonable." "That's more like a boy's name," replied the neighbor. "You should use the *li* character that signifies 'politeness' or 'decorum.' Then everyone will know she's a girl." "No," said her mother, "we have no need to send out advance signals of the gender our child is. Let her be known by who she is and what she does with her life, not by stereotypes that may constrict her." Even as she said this, however, she hoped that Ming-li would learn to treasure the particularities of her life: her femaleness, her cultural heritage and the struggle of her people that it reflects, and her Christian faith.

Because Ming-li is just now learning to read, she has had very little experience reading the Bible for herself. So her mother reads it with her, in an effort to teach her to read it carefully, with an awareness of what she brings from her own life to her reading, and then to interpret her own life through its lens upon the world. One story they have recently read together is the story of Mary Magdalene at the tomb of Jesus, as told in the Gospel of John. This is how her mother is teaching Ming-li to read this story.

According to this Gospel, Mary Magdalene is the first person to come to Jesus' burial place on the first day of the week. When she finds the tomb empty, she hurries to Peter and the unnamed beloved disciple to tell them about her discovery. They come running to look for themselves, enter the tomb, and, seeing only the burial wrappings, leave. Mary, however, remains and weeps over the loss of the body and life of Jesus. "As she wept," says the Gospel, "she bent over to look into the tomb; and she saw two angels in white, sitting where the body of Jesus had been lying, one at the head and the other at the feet" (John 20:11–12). Unlike the male disciples, Mary sees angels, but apparently she does not recognize them for what they are. They ask her why she is crying and she replies, "They have taken away my Lord, and I do not know where they have laid him" (John 20:13).

After saying this, she turns from the tomb and sees Jesus himself, without recognizing him. Instead, Mary takes him to be the gardener. Like the angels, Jesus also asks her for whom she is looking and again she replies that she wants the body that was in the tomb. Then Jesus calls her by name: "Mary." The Greek New Testament preserves the Aramaic form of her name, "Mariam," perhaps a form of the name "Miriam." She turns and instantly recognizes him, calling him in Aramaic, "Rabbouni," which, as the text says, means "Teacher." The use of their Aramaic names invokes an aura of intimacy, a moment in which Jesus and Mary recognize and accept each other fully, addressing each other by their true and proper names. Moreover, perhaps Mary's turning, first away from the tomb and then to Jesus, represents in this passage far more than a physical movement of her body. Her movement is a turning away from the past and its previous rules and regulations and a turning toward a new life. It is a conversion from old strictures and structures for being faithful to God into new ways of living out her faith.[9] Ming-li and her mother might also think of such a turning as a turning away from the old hurts, from the old images of and claims about women that force women into unacceptable molds, to a new reality in which we are known and called by our true names.

Upon her recognition of him, Jesus tells her, "Do not hold onto me, because I have not yet ascended to the Father" (John 20:17). There may be in this statement an implicit claim that one cannot hold onto Jesus' physical body as if he were present only in it. Rather, he is present now in the community of those who follow him—they just do not know it yet. Jesus then instructs Mary to go his brothers and tell them, "I am ascending to my Father and your Father, to my God and your God." These words sound like an echo of Ruth's words to

---

[9] Sandra M. Schneiders, "John 20:11–18. The Encounter of the Easter Jesus with Mary Magdalene: A Transformative Feminist Reading," Paper presented in the Johannine Literature Section at the Annual Meeting of the Society of Biblical Literature, Washington D. C., November 19–23, 1993. Much of what follows in this interpretation of this passage is inspired by her remarks.

Naomi, "Your people shall be my people, and your God my God" (Ruth 1:16). So Mary Magdalene goes and announces to the disciples, "I have seen the Lord" (John 20:18). In doing this, she becomes the first person in the Gospel of John to receive a personal commission from the resurrected Jesus, and the first evangelist after the death and resurrection of Jesus, the first to proclaim the good news of the risen Christ. Because Jesus gives Mary, a woman, such an awesome responsibility, we can think of her proclaiming this news not just to the brothers, but to the sisters as well.

Ming-li, of course, cannot yet read this story by herself in this way, since she is, after all, a child. Who knows how she herself will grow up to read the Bible, what questions she will bring, and what she will learn? She may explore her Asian heritage more fully in light of the witnesses in the Bible; she may learn to appreciate the unique perspectives women of other cultures and races bring to their reading. We do know that when she reads with her mother, however, she will not be required to leave her gender or her cultural heritage or her own unique personality on the shelf in order to assume someone else's. Her way of reading the stories will be valued, at least at home. At the same time, if her mother is a good teacher, she will learn to listen to and to value other people's readings of biblical stories. She will also learn to evaluate those readings, those interpretations, in light of other portions of the Bible, in light of its context as a first-century document, and in light of the contexts of its interpreters. Most important, building upon the work and reflection of women who have gone before her, she will know that there are "women's things" in the Bible and that the stories in which they are found offer powerful words about and for the women who read them.

Works Consulted

Anderson, Bernhard W. 1975. *Understanding the Old Testament*. 3rd Ed. Englewood Cliffs: Prentice-Hall, Inc.

Murphy, Cullen. 1993. "Women and the Bible." *The Atlantic Monthly* 272/2 (August): 39-64.

Rabinowitz, Peter J. 1987. *Before Reading*. Ithaca: Cornell University Press.

Schneiders, Sandra M. 1993. "John 20:11–18. The Encounter of the Easter Jesus with Mary Magdalene: A Transformative Feminist Reading." Paper presented in the Johannine Literature Section at the Annual Meeting of the Society of Biblical Literature, Washington D. C., November 19–23, 1993.

Trible, Phyllis. 1989. "Bringing Miriam out of the Shadows." *Bible Review* 5: 14–25, 34.

Theology
Section II

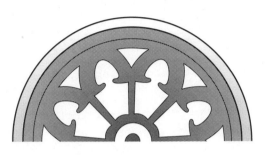

Introduction

to Section II

Serene Jones

In Section II of this book, four Disciples women theologians share their thoughts on topics that have traditionally fallen under the category "theology." Although the title "theology" may make it appear as if this section will be overly abstract or academic, if one thinks about the topics being covered—God, Jesus Christ, the church, language—one will recognize that they are topics that Christian women and men reflect on in the course of their everyday lives.

Defined in simple terms, the word *theology* refers to this activity of thinking about God: it is thinking, in an imaginative, responsible, and critical way, about what we as Christians believe concerning who God is, how God relates to the world, and what God wills for our lives. In the eleventh century, the theologian Anselm of Canterbury coined a wonderful phrase to describe this kind of thinking when it is done in the context of the church: he suggested that theology is best understood as "faith seeking understanding"—as thinking done by faithful persons who seek to understand God better and thereby to understand themselves better. In this section we offer you a series of reflections on the imaginative and critical paths that women theologians from the Disciples tradition have traveled as they "seek to understand faith" in our contemporary world. It is our hope that by traveling with us along these paths, you too might come to new insight and reach new understandings of the faith that shapes us all as members of the Christian community.

It is unfortunate that this lively and inclusive definition of "faith seeking understanding" has not been, in recent years, the main definition that society has given to the enterprise called "theology." With the rise of the North American university system and its concomitant interest in training men and women in the skills of scientific expertise and efficiency, the church has increasingly let its view of "knowledge of God" become shaped by these same modern standards of technical know-how. When God becomes subjected to such standards of investigation, at least two problems can and have occurred. First, the richly dramatic story of God's ongoing relation with creation risks being reduced to an analytic calculus often void of image, complexity, and significant personal/communal meanings. Second, the technical expertise needed to render such calculations becomes viewed as the special province of a few "professional theologians" who, because of their training, are qualified to do theology and thus understand faith. As a result of this emphasis on technical expertise, the average person in the Sunday morning pew is seen as unqualified to offer judgments about the content of Christian faith.

While this view of theology does have positive aspects, such as its insistence that faith can be sustained and even flourish under the most rigorous standards of intellectual assessment, it also has its dangers. Indeed, in many churches today one can see the troubling repercussions of such a view. In some instances, this view of theology has led people to think that the language of scientific fact is the only way to talk about God; and hence much of the richness of God's story goes unexamined as does the richness of faithful Christian lives whose complexities cannot be exhaustively covered by scientific categories. It is also the case that this view of theology often makes people feel that if they do not have the training or expertise needed to engage in theology, they should give up on the task of thinking about faith and turn the whole enterprise over to a small group of persons who have the required seminary degree. When lay and clergy persons avoid "doing theology" for these reasons, the whole church suffers: it suffers because it is not allowed to learn from the many rich voices of faith that—although they are not professionally trained—have been highly educated by the reading of scripture, by years of service to the church, by many an hour of prayer and reflection, and by lifelong experiences of Christian witness and struggle. It also suffers because in its failure to listen to such voices, the church allows these many rich experiences and seasoned wisdoms to go untested, unchallenged, and unsharpened by the insights that can follow from lively theological conversations.

Fortunately, in the Disciples tradition we have long been wary, at least in principle, of such a restrictive view of theology and we have tried to work against it by charging *all members* of the church to see themselves as fully empowered, well-equipped, and highly educated theologians simply by virtue of their faith. This means that in our tradition, one will find theologians in second-grade Sunday school classes when a child asks why God would let her mother get sick, in weekday workplaces when a colleague ponders the usefulness of prayer, in evening deacons' meetings when an AIDS group is invited to meet in the building, as well as in the more traditionally recognized minister's pulpit where hopefully theology is done in an ongoing manner. This broad definition of theology thus means that no one gets off the hook of having to thinking critically, responsibly, and imaginatively about faith because all the faithful are considered theologians. It means as well that by requiring all persons to think about faith, we create an environment in the broader church community that similarly encourages the ongoing struggle to be responsible, imaginative, and self-critical about how the church fulfills its mission as God's people in the world.

In this section of the book, our four writers are particularly interested in listening to the voices of a specific group of persons who are highly educated theologians. They are educated in terms of the time they spend reading scripture, praying, struggling to do justice, and serving both church and neighbor. Yet they are also persons who traditionally have not been considered "experts" or "qualified enough" to speak theologically about God, Christ, the church, and its language. The group I refer to is, of course, Christian women, a rather large "group" within the church to say the least. By listening to these voices, drawing together their wisdom, imaginings, and criticisms, and by then testing and sharpening them in the context of lively theological conversation, these articles all attempt to offer a Disciples theology done from the perspective of its tradition's women. While the perspectives offered here by women theologians do not represent what every woman in the Disciples tradition thinks or should think about God, they represent an attempt to open up a whole arena of theological reflection that has been historically overlooked. Given the long-standing ecumenical commitments of Disciples theology, their voices represent as well a new perspective on the Protestant tradition in general and North American theology in particular.

As Rita Brock so vividly explained in the introduction, the views represented here are not only by Disciples women but they are also "feminist" in character. This feminist orientation is reflected in the way each article explores two subjects: first, how our traditional talk about God, Christ, the church, and language has been at times oppressive for women; and second, how our tradition and its language of faith has been at times powerfully liberating for women. These articles also claim the title "feminist theology" because they each attempt a third task, that of imagining new ways of thinking about the Christian faith, ways that will continue to let God's word shape and direct the church's future contribution to this ongoing process of empowering women. This last task, that of constructing new theological possibilities for enlivening our talk about God, Christ, and the church is the area where we, the authors, believe that the Disciples tradition has much to offer the church at large, for our heritage not only encourages the best in imaginative creativity but also demands responsible, critical thinking about the faith we proclaim.

Let me take a brief look at these three words that I have used to describe the activity of doing theology thus far: *responsible, imaginative,* and *critical.* What more do they tell us about theology in general and the Disciples tradition in particular? To begin with, when one says that theology must be done in a responsible manner, it implies that there is something *to which* one is responsible in this process of theological reflection. In the Disciples tradition, there has been a multilayered view of that to which one is responsible as one endeavors to think theologically.

In the first place, Disciples have long affirmed that when one does theology responsibly, one seeks to give an account that is shaped first and foremost by our knowledge of God. In this sense, it is considered "God-given knowledge" and not just a knowledge that one imagines or makes up. It is a knowledge that has its ground in the life of the Divine. The tradition adds a further claim to this confession of Divine object and source of our knowledge, namely, that it is in the life, death, and resurrection of Jesus Christ that human beings are invited to know God most fully and intimately, that in Jesus we meet God in the flesh as a person who walks among the people, who dies from the force of human hands, and who is resurrected in the midst of history in order to both tell us and show us "who God is." When theology is done responsibly, it is done, therefore, in the context of a faith which is normed and shaped by the reality of this life, this story, this person. This Christological affirmation—that Jesus Christ should be the norm of Christian life—has been captured in the well-known Disciples saying: "No creed but Christ."

In addition to this assertion of the Christological center of theological reflection, Disciples next affirm that not only is there no creed but Christ, but also "no book but the Bible." What this often deceptively simple claim suggests is that when theology is done in a responsible manner, it will allow itself to be shaped by scripture. This canonical book we call the Bible has been passed down through the ages to the church as a recorded narrative about the history of God with us: the story of God and the people of Israel, the history of God incarnate in Jesus Christ, and the narrative of God present to the emerging church of the early apostles. As a way of acknowledging the centrality of this book in the shaping of faith and theology, the opening section of the present book is devoted to exploring what is meant by scripture or the Bible and how this book serves to shape our identity.

It has also been the case that the tradition has taken very seriously the degree to which theological thinking must be responsible in a third way: it must be responsible to the church as well as to scriptural witness to the reality of Jesus Christ who is God in our midst. What does it mean to say that theological thinking must be responsible to the church? It is simply a reminder that one's theology has been shaped dramatically by the Christian community where one learns what it means to be a Christian, where one learns how to worship, where one hears scripture interpreted and thus learns how to live into its stories; it is, in short, the place where one learns how to believe in God and how to be shaped by faith. To say that one is responsible to the church is a further reminder that not only does the church socialize persons into the faith, it also continues to be the audience and context of one's theological reflection. This means that in doing theology, one needs to be always asking, How does a particular view of God, Christ, and the church relate to and affect the life of the Christian community? It should be added here as well that thinking theologically with the church as context and audience also involves thinking about the world in which the church finds itself and to which the church is called to minister. This notion of theology's being responsible to the church and world as both its context and audience is often linked by theologians to reflections on the Holy Spirit. As the following essays make clear, recent works in feminist theology have focused a great deal of attention on the power of God's spirit as it moves through community, creating communion and communicating grace.

Added to this notion of theology done in a responsible manner is the claim that theology is an inherently imaginative enterprise. As the reader will no doubt discover in reading the following articles, it is precisely from the realm of imagination and creativity that Disciples women theologians draw much of their strength. Why do we need to speak of the imagination as a part of the theological enterprise? Quite simply because "imagination" refers to that place in each individual/communal life of faith where Jesus Christ, the world of scripture, and the insights of the church begin to meet, mix, and mingle with the rich storehouse of experiences (stories, events, encounters, images, histories, languages, memories, relationships, rituals, landscapes, and the list could go on) that make us who we are both personally and in our complex networks of relationships. In recent writings of feminist theologians, the realm where all this meeting and mixing occurs has been referred to often as the realm of "human experience." Feminist theologians have further argued that when one is raised and socialized as a woman, one is disposed to having in her rich storehouse of experiences a number of events, memories, images, etc. that have not been on the whole a part of the mix and mingle out of which the traditional male theologian has written. Recognizing this, the challenge of feminist theology has been to describe, analyze, and articulate what faith looks like when it emerges out of the mix and mingle of women's experience.

As the following articles make clear, describing women's experience and then ascertaining how it influences theology are parts of a complex process that involves doing analysis at several levels. At one level, it involves the difficult process of naming the varied *oppressions* that women have experienced historically and asking how these experiences of oppression affect the way one understands God. As we shall see in the pages ahead, the results of such an analysis can be profoundly unsettling as well as empowering, as it requires us to reexamine some of the tradition's most valued views of how God should be named and imaged and how human creatures are called to respond to Her.

In addition to analyzing how women's experiences of oppression often lead to a critical challenging of certain aspects of the tradition, imaginative theology also explores how women's experiences allow them to identify and explore aspects of the faith that historically have been overlooked or under-emphasized. For example, women's diverse experiences in the assigned role of society's "caretakers"—those who care for children, the sick, and the elderly—have often led us to see the complexity of human relationships, human emotions, and human interdependency in ways that traditional male theologians have not. This storehouse of experiences with the work of caring has allowed feminist theologians to imagine new forms of community, new textures of relationships, and new configurations of ethical values in the context of faith. Thus, from this collective storehouse new images for God are beginning to emerge—a new vocabulary is starting to unfold for describing how God loves and cares for us, and a new lens for discerning how, as Christians, we are called to love and care for ourselves and our neighbors.

Women's experiences bring imaginative resources to the doing of theology in a third way as well. This third way is perhaps not as dramatic or painful as looking at how oppression affects the way women do theology, or as creatively constructive as naming how experiences of such things as women's caretaking work shifts the character of our theological vocabulary, but it is nonetheless a critically important aspect of how the experiences of women influence the doing of theology. This third aspect involves exploring the ways that our *everyday* experiences as women, in their dazzling diversity, in all their often mundane and common rhythms, and in their messiness and ambiguities (often neither oppressive nor particularly constructive), form the ongoing contexts of our reflections as theologians. In the four essays that follow, many of the insights that emerge, as each author struggles to articulate the ways women's experiences mix and mingle with language about Christ, the church, and God, are insights born out of the material of their own everyday lives as women scholars (and as sisters, mothers, friends, teachers, etc. as well) in the Disciples tradition. It may not always be obvious how these experiences stir into the language of their theology, but their resonances run deep, just as they do in the life of anyone who engages in theological reflection. And when theologians thus confess the imaginative edge of their faith as it seeks understanding, the invitation is extended to all to imagine vividly out of the common, the different, and the ambiguous stuff of each moment.

The last term I use to describe the activity of doing theology is "critical." What does it mean to do theology "critically"? It does not mean, as it might first appear, that doing theology critically requires that one only do it negatively or oppositionally. While it can mean this, the sense of critical that I want to invoke here is larger. It refers to the measuring or testing aspect of theology or to the evaluative or questioning moment in the process of faith seeking understanding. In other words, it refers to the challenge that every feminist theologian faces when she makes a claim about God, Jesus, language, or the church, namely, the challenge of testing whether she is making a faithful, true, and meaningful claim. Anyone who has experienced either the shock of realizing that one's view of God is dramatically flawed or the exhilaration of awakening to a new insight born of close study will recognize the importance of this critical moment. It is, in short, the moment where one steps back and tests her position, asking, *Am I giving this my best thinking, my most faithful reflection, or am I seeing only dimly, perhaps confusedly or even wrongly? Am I being responsible and creatively imaginative as I do theology? Am I contributing to the upbuilding of the church or am I tearing it down? Is my theological vision empowering or does it oppress or harm others? Is it true to the life, death, and resurrection of Jesus, or does it represent a false claim, a distorted position? Is it a vision driven by the Holy Spirit, filled with the liberating power of God, or is it the product of misguided imaginings?*

In order to begin the process of finding at least minimal answers to such grand questions, theologians have many "testing" tools at their disposal. For example, as the theologians writing the following articles will demonstrate, one can use the tools of critical scholarship such as language analysis, historical reflection, and philosophical insight to test the intelligibility and coherence of a theological claim. One has at her disposal as well the practical tools of experience and the communal tools of dialogue and inter-subjective debate. As a theologian one can also measure one's claims against scripture, against the work of past theologians, and against the possible future one's theology carves out for the next generation. And most important, in the Disciples tradition, we affirm that the critical moment in theological reflection involves a testing by the Spirit, a testing that asks, does this theology bear witness to the gospel? Is it a theology that proclaims good news?

In each of these moments—the critical, the imaginative, and the responsible—the theologian is engaging in an enterprise that is at once exciting and daunting. And most important, because it is an enterprise that cuts to the heart of what one believes about God, Christ, and the church, it is a very risky enterprise. It is risky because one may find that age-old beliefs are challenged, that deep commitments are tested, and that new ways of living are called for. It is risky because one may find as well that the faith one is already living, with great integrity and wisdom, is a faith that is true and abiding and calls for ever deeper rest and joy in grace. For women in particular, this resting in grace and taking joy in the integrity of one's faith is something that is often hard to accept. In such a case, the risk that imaginative and responsible theology confronts is the risk of knowing oneself to be loved, good, and complete in God.

In the four chapters that follow, you are invited to follow the paths that our authors have walked as they have undertaken this risky theological enterprise in a critical, imaginative, and responsible manner. In the first chapter by Jane McAvoy, we jump right into one of the most risky and controversial areas of contemporary theological reflection as we enter into conversation about the character of the language the Christian community uses to talk about God. Beginning with the question, "What is the link between the words we use to describe our relationship with God, the church where we speak those words, and the practices of that church regarding the leadership of women?" she embarks upon a complex analysis of the reasons why feminists have pushed for nonsexist, inclusive language in liturgy. Lifting up a variety of models that feminist theologians have used in their struggle to inclusivize language in this manner, McAvoy explores the theological reasons for pushing these questions as hard as we can. She also invites the reader to experience the fruits of this labor in her closing inclusion of an example of feminist Disciples liturgy taken from *Table Talk: Resources for Communion Meals.*

From language and liturgy we next move on to the topic closest to the heart of Disciples theology, the person and work of Jesus Christ. Offering the reader both a concise summary of traditional themes in Christology and a powerful analysis of present issues being raised by feminist theologians, Sondra Stalcup's article draws together the best of classical views of Christ and the most compelling pieces of current scholarship on Jesus. As she travels through both worlds, she visits such topics as "sin," "the cross," "the maleness of Jesus," and the power of Jesus "the Christ"; and at each stop along the way, she uses responsible, imaginative, and critical tools for opening up the resources the tradition has to offer to present conversations about the inclusivity of Christology.

Following this discussion of feminist Christology, Rita Nakashima Brock begins a provocative analysis of the concept of "God" that broadens the discussion of Christ to include topics related to the creation and sustenance of the world. Using images of the "greening of the soul" and the "web of life," Brock suggests new ways of figuring the complexities of our relationships with God, creation, and one another. Again, borrowing both from the rich resources the tradition has to offer and from the best insights of present-day feminist theory, Brock weaves for the reader a paradigm for imagining God where connectedness, openness, differences, and gracious affirmations define the contours of terms like *salvation, healing,* and *liberation.* Similarly, her work to redefine the notion of sin with an emphasis on its social and relational dimensions brings added depth to a concept that has both troubled and liberated the Disciples theology for many years. Adding to this rich mix of theological categories, Brock brings in the concept of "covenant" and the image of "Christ our mother, God our mother" to complete her theological web and concludes with a call to understand the notion of "friendship" with God and with one another in new and empowering ways.

With this notion of friendship and its emphasis on mutuality in community, we move on to the final essay of this section, Kristine Culp's powerful reflection on the nature of Christian community. Taking up the topic usually referred to as "ecclesiology" (*ekklesia:* assembly; *logos:* discourse), she addresses a number of issues related to how the Christian community understands the shape, mission, and character of the church. Using models of community drawn from sources such as Toni Morrison's *Beloved*, the stories of Salvadoran Christian mothers, and Anglo-American women's religious work of crafted care, Culp opens up her discussion of the church by encouraging us to think creatively about the nature of community and the historical role that women have played in imagining and constructing its contours. Focusing on two models in particular, the model of the "body of life" and the "testimonies of survival and resistance," the former a holistic, inclusive model and the latter a protest, prophetic model, Culp suggests ways in which the church needs to understand its identity as formed in the tension between gracious welcoming and the righteous, often rupturing struggle for justice. And in this suggestion lies once again the sense of possibility and struggle that ties together the reflections of each author in this section.

5

God with Us

From Language to Liturgy

Jane McAvoy

What is the link between the words we use to describe our relationship to God, the church where we speak those words, and the practice of that church regarding the leadership of women? The answer to this question has been a major concern of Christian feminists and has led to a number of answers and strategies that apply to theology, language theory, and liturgy. Among these are the development of nonsexist and inclusive language, female metaphors for God, and reinterpretations of traditional understandings of divine power and presence.

Realizing this link between language and liturgy usually comes through some kind of trigger event. Recently, one of my students said to me, "It's so unfair." The previous Sunday she had been struck for the first time by the sexist language in the worship service. She noticed that the hymns were filled with references to mankind who worships the Lord and King, and the scriptures and prayers were read by men who described the relationship of the brethren and their Father. Prompted by her newfound knowledge about the history of religious women, she asked her husband why women did not have a leadership role in the worship service at their church. "They just can't," was his reply. While unable to explain the reason for his opinion, he adamantly held to his views and the practice of their church.

She however, was not convinced. "I have discovered one more topic I can't discuss with my husband," she lamented. So begins another woman's awareness of the relationship between language, the church, and injustice, as well as the difficulty of questioning the use of language in the practice of Christian worship.

Prelude to Consciousness:
Concern for Nonsexist Language

The first insight about language used in liturgy is that women are absent not only from roles of leadership but from the words spoken in worship. Behind this insight is the realization that words matter and that the use of words such as "mankind" and "brotherhood" are harmful because they inaccurately name the human race with words that refer to only half its members. As the women's movement has begun to question the use of these and other "generic" terms, Christian feminists have understood this concern for truthfully naming human experience as a matter of Christian justice. This prelude is the beginning realization that corresponds with the first strategy of women's consciousness, observing that women are not named in language. The solution is an insistence that language become nonsexist, which corresponds with the second strategy, declaring that women be treated equally, just like men.

What is behind the call for nonsexist language is the understanding that language is formative of attitudes, thought, behavior, even the very character and quality of life. As the editors of the book *Womanspirit Rising* state, "It is through naming that humans progress from childhood to adulthood and learn to understand and shape the world around them" (Christ and Plaskow: 7). As we name people and things we give power to them and influence the way we think about them. The ancient world understood this power and expressed it in the belief that in naming one had power over that which was named. In the Genesis creation story, for example, it is the power to name every living creature that shows the power of humankind as the steward of creation. Likewise, the fact that Adam names Eve symbolizes the power of man over woman.

One of the first Christian feminists to realize the power of language is Valerie Saiving. In her article entitled "The Human Situation: A Feminine View," she writes, "I am no longer certain as I once was that, when theologians speak of 'man,' they are using the word in its generic sense" (25). She raises the provocative possibility that while there are significant differences between masculine and feminine experience, theologians base understandings of the human situation, especially the definition of sin as pride and redemption as sacrificial love, on male experience. The result is a false naming of the human situation and correspondingly inaccurate understandings of sin and redemption for women who struggle not with pride and self-less love, but with lack of self and confidence.

The first response to this false naming is to eliminate the use of words that perpetuate the myth that male experience equals human experience. The practical application of this principle is the change of words in Christian worship such as "mankind" to "humankind," "men" to "men and women." These changes can be seen in the liturgical resource *Everflowing Streams* (Duck and Bausch). Hymns such as "Good Christian Men, Rejoice" are changed to "Good Christian Folk, Rejoice." In other examples a text is rephrased. In the familiar hymn "Blest Be the Tie that Binds" the phrase "the fellowship of kindred minds," becomes "the unity of heart and mind." Rather than changing the words "Faith of Our Fathers" a second verse is added which begins "Faith of Our Mothers." The editors note that the motivation for these changes is a concern for justice. "We must be intentional in reflecting justice in the way we worship, as well as in the way we live."

The Trigger Event: Critique of God the Father

As Christian feminists have become more aware of the power of language, we have begun to notice that false naming of humankind results not only from words that name the human situation but from words used to describe God. The power of this naming is doubly damaging. Not only does it reinforce the absence of women, it falsely names God. This third strategy realizes the way traditional names for God victimize women and calls for the critique of names for God drawn from male experience.

No book has been more influential in raising consciousness about the power of the names we use to refer to God than *Beyond God the Father: Toward a Philosophy of Women's Liberation*. Its central claim is that "if God is male, then the male is God" (Daly: 19). What is meant by this assertion is that the dominant use of male references for God (such as the pronoun "He" and titles such as "King") reinforces the valuing of males (but not females) as worthy of comparison with God. Furthermore, the predominant reference to God as "Father" serves to give divine sanction to a system of father rule that oppresses women.

Daly notes that critics have countered her argument with the claim that "God is not male, He is Spirit" (17–18). If this is the case, then why do so many people argue that it is inadequate to use the feminine pronoun to refer to God? Daly concludes it is because Christians do not understand God as a genderless Spirit but as male (Our Father). This exclusive identification of God and Father is idolatry; it is the valuing of men as like God and implies the devaluing of women as less like God than men. Like all idolatry it leads to false worship. It is seen in the biblical claim that the husband is the head of the house as Christ is the head of the church, and throughout Christian history when kings claim that their rule over women, children, and servants is an extension of divine rule. The logical extension of this idolatry is the claim that only men can serve as religious leaders.

Daly argues that to correct this idolatry there must be a new understanding of God "beyond the Father." It requires more than just eliminating references to God as "Father" and "He." Daly suggests a moratorium on using any nouns to refer to God because they will lead to idolatry, projecting human experience onto God. Instead God should be understood as a verb, the power of being, the "Eternal thou from whom, in whom and with whom all true movements move" (28). It is the hope experienced by those working for justice, such as in the women's movement. It is the power that summons women to work toward a world free from patriarchy. The naming of God happens not through descriptive nouns, but through active participation in the power of divine being. "The unfolding of God, then, is an event in which women participate as we participate in our own revolution"(40).

This critique of male references to God can be seen in liturgical resources such as Jane Parker Huber's *A Singing Faith*. In the preface she writes, "I do not use male terms and words as if they were generic because I no longer think they are inclusive. I do not use third-person singular pronouns for God because God is neither female nor male"(18). While not eliminating all nouns for God it does strive for nonsexist nouns. For example, the hymn "Creator God, Creating Still," refers to the Creator God, Redeemer God, and Sustainer God. Likewise, some churches change the familiar refrain of "Father, Son, and Holy Ghost" in the doxology to "Creator, Christ, and Holy Ghost." Another strategy is to avoid using the pronoun "He" by using second person pronouns to refer to God, such as in the United Church of Christ Statement of Faith that begins, "We give thanks to you, O God, Eternal Spirit" (Duck and Bausch).

Singing a New Song:
Reclaiming Female Metaphors for God

While many Christians agree on the need for nonsexist liturgical language, some question Daly's suggestion of understanding God as Verb. Feminist scholars such as Carol Christ question the effectiveness of a noun-less naming of God. Christ argues that while sex-neutral language may eliminate the direct offense to women created by male God symbolism, it will not necessarily force people to change their understanding of God. As we have seen, one can use sex-neutral language and still imagine that God is male. For example, it is possible for people to name God as the power of being and still imagine that power as like a Father's power. Therefore we need language that forces us to think about the "positive inclusion of the female in the nature of God and to rethink our prejudices about women's roles in society" (Christ: 246).

This women-centered mode of feminist consciousness has led to a discovery of female names for God that have been buried in biblical texts and Christian tradition as well as the reclamation of a whole prior history of Goddess traditions. Advocating use of female names for God in theology and worship builds on the religious truth that male and female are created in the image of God, and understands this naming as a necessary step in correcting the idolatry of exclusive use of male names for God.

A wide variety of approaches to this renaming exists. One approach is a recovery of feminine names for God that draw upon typically feminine characteristics and roles. Examples include scriptural references to Sophia/Wisdom and examples from the Christian tradition of naming God as Mother (See Mollenkott; Bynum). These names are seen as complements to the dominant masculine names for God and emphasize feminine characteristics such as divine compassion. Another approach is to recover resources from ancient traditions that describe the Goddess as Gaia or the Great Mother, who brings forth and nurtures life. These resources suggest an alternative understanding of God's presence as immanent, symbolized by the Spirit within, not the Father in Heaven. (See Gimbutas.) As Alice Walker writes, "God is inside you and inside everybody else" (103).

Another approach is to bring together sources from the Christian and Goddess traditions for a women-centered theology as exemplified in Rosemary Radford Ruether's *Sexism and God-Talk*. From ancient traditions Ruether recovers the understanding of God and Goddess as equivalent names that express the totality of divine presence and power. This is combined with the Christian tradition's emphasis on God as redeemer and liberator, and the prohibition of blasphemy, the use of God's name to promote injustice such as patriarchy. Ruether suggests language for the Divine "as redeemer, as liberator, as one who fosters full personhood and, in that context, speak(s) of God/dess as creator, as source of being" (70). Ruether explains that God/dess is an unpronounceable name that describes our understanding that God is beyond gender yet promotes the full humanity of men and women. This naming of God/dess leads to a reevaluation of our understanding of every aspect of Christian life and belief, including the conception of ministry, so that women as well as men will be included at the center of the Christian community and the world.

The result of these various approaches is the development of worship resources that include female names for God. One example is *An Inclusive Language Lectionary*, which strives to translate biblical texts so that the church "is not overwhelmed by the male metaphors, but is also allowed to hear the female metaphors for God." Ways to achieve this balance include highlighting biblical texts in the lectionary, such as Isaiah 42:14 and Luke 15:8–10, which describe God as a woman, adding names of biblical women to texts so that "the God of Jacob" is read "the God of Jacob, [Rachel, and Leah]," and changing references to "God the Father" to read "God the Father [and Mother]." It also substitutes the title "Sovereign" for "Lord" and changes references to Jesus as the "Son of man" and "Son of God" to "the Human One" or "Child of God." While admitting that this first attempt to make scripture inclusive is provisional, the changes are guided by the insight that the translation of scripture needs to reflect an inclusive understanding of God. The editors of the *Inclusive Language Lectionary* write, "Scripture is written in patriarchal language, but God is not a patriarch."

Seeking Divine Community:
Models of God

The desire for religious language to be truly inclusive has led to the realization of the way in which names for God impact not only the valuation of gender, but race and class as well. Moreover, learnings from women representing a variety of race and class constituencies have challenged white feminists to enlarge the understanding of what is needed for liberating God-language. From these encounters has come an effort to look again at the classic Trinitarian language of Christianity as a model that expresses divine and human diversity and community.

One thing white feminists have learned is that not all groups consider the fatherhood of God to be the central problem or concern of Christian belief and worship. Kelly Delaine Brown has argued that while white feminists tend to deemphasize the centrality of Christ, for the black church "God is as Christ does." Therefore, the central issue for African-American women is understanding Christ as God incarnate who affirms their struggle to survive and be free while rejecting the claim that being male like Christ is a necessary precondition for ordination in the black church.

Likewise, Latin American women write about the need to apply feminist criticism and concern for female names for God to understandings of all persons of the Trinity. Maria Clara Bingemer writes, "We believe that there is a special need in Latin America for careful reflection on the theme of the Trinity from woman's experience" (56). She argues that since the Trinity is understood as a way of naming God's unity within plurality and difference it provides the ultimate possibility for integrating the masculine and feminine aspects of divinity. Also, because the Trinity expresses the truth that individual identity is lived in a community of mutuality, it suggests a way of living in community that critiques the marginalized status of Latin American women.

A number of white feminist theologians have also written about the Trinity because of its suggestion of divine community, the possibilities for gender inclusivity, and a focus on the person of Christ. Catherine LaCugna has done extensive research on reclaiming the intent of Trinitarian language to express the church's understanding of God's presence with and for us. Elizabeth Johnson has written about the mystery of the Trinity as the power of "totally shared life at the heart of the universe." Sallie McFague has suggested a renaming of the Trinity as Mother, Lover, and Friend to name God's creating, saving, and sustaining activity in relationships of justice, healing, and companionship. Carter Heyward, while not focusing on the Trinity per se, has suggested an understanding of God's power as power-in-relation (118–122). What all these theologians share is an awareness that the Trinity is the Christian expression of God's mystery-in-relation, a radical presence and power that transforms all human institutions of exclusion and oppression.

This effort to include everyone's insights and concerns into liturgical language has just begun. How can white feminists respond to African-American feminists' concern to reaffirm the centrality of Christ as God? In response to Latin American suggestions about Trinitarian language, should the naming of God as Father be reintroduced in North American worship? One response to this dilemma has been the introduction of hymns from a variety of cultures in worship. For instance, the recently released *Chalice Hymnal* includes hymns such as the African-American spiritual "My Lord, What a Morning" and the Mexican song "Somos Uno" which includes the words "un solo Dios, un solo Senor, Una sola fe, un solo amor, un solo bautismo, un solo Espiritu y ese es el consolador" (only one God, only one Lord, only one faith, only one love, only one baptism, only one Spirit, which is the Counselor).

Another approach is to incorporate ideas associated with Trinitarian theology in worship. One example is this prayer from the worship resource *When We Gather* that begins, "Mystery of mysteries, whose wisdom surpasses the farthest reaches of our imagination, whose compassion comforts us when shadows lengthen and our busy lives are hushed, whose mercy restores us when we stray, we give you thanks" (13). Another example is a prayer written by Elisabeth Schüssler Fiorenza that begins, "Holy One invoked with a Myriad of Names, God our Mother, God our Sister, God our Goddess." After references to Christ and the Spirit the prayer continues, "You are neither Father nor Mother, You are neither Male nor Female, You are neither God nor Goddess. Our language is insufficient" (209–210).

But what about the name Father? Is there a way to use this name in Christian worship that critiques its power in a patriarchal context? One implication of a Trinitarian understanding of God is that the name "Father" should be used as a parental name only in context with the other persons of the Trinity, not as the only name for God. One way of critiquing the identification of the fatherhood of God and patriarchy is to combine the name Father with feminine pronouns. For instance, the traditional doxology could become "Glory be to the Father and to Her Son." Such a change shocks people into recognizing the limitations of the name Father while preserving its Trinitarian function. Another possibility is to name the Trinity using three women's names such as the women who went to the tomb of Jesus (Mary Magdalene, Mary the mother of James, and Salome). This possibility highlights the social character of Trinitarian names.

The Road Ahead:
Reviving Disciples Worship Around the Table

On any given Sunday morning all of these strategies might be incorporated into Christian worship. Hymns are printed in the bulletin to eliminate sexist language, the worship leader carefully constructs his invocation so that male pronouns are not used for God, the minister centers her sermon on Luke 15:8–10, the congregation joins in praise to "God the Father and Her Son," and the service closes with the hymn "O Somos Uno."

These are strategies that draw from a number of Protestant resources and are applicable to any Christian denomination. But a true inclusion of women in the church will not be accomplished until this understanding of religious language is applied to communion liturgy. Communion is the moment in the worship service that most profoundly celebrates God's mystery-in-relation, yet ironically it is also the act of worship that women are prohibited from leading in some Christian denominations. As Marjorie Proctor-Smith notes, "the traditional theological emphases of the eucharist offer places where feminist memory and imagination can expand the meaning of the eucharist so that its emancipatory potential can be fully realized" (160). In order to realize this potential, communion liturgy needs to faithfully name the character of God's presence and power as remembered in Jesus Christ with the hope that this true naming will lead to the transformation of women's exclusion from serving at the communion table.

The most powerful words in the worship service are "This is my body, This is my blood." They name the profound mystery of divine presence that is with us and for us in bodily form. The impact of these words is that God is with us in all our physicality, our joy, and our pain. The liberating nature of this presence is embodied in Jesus' ministry with all people, even the Samaritan woman. The ever-abiding nature of this presence is felt in Jesus' words of agony on the cross.

These words also name the character of divine power as a power-with rather than power-over others. It is the power of blood, a life force that flows within our veins. It is the healing power of Jesus that flows to the bleeding woman through her touch. It is a reciprocal power that can be thwarted by those who reject the vision of peace and goodwill for earthly possession and privilege (the tragedy of the crucifixion), but not overcome (the victory of the resurrection).

Because of their tradition of lay leaders who weekly pray for the bread and the cup, Protestant denominations such as the Christian Church (Disciples of Christ) can make a specific contribution to the development of language and liturgy by developing communion meditations and prayers that realize the full meaning of communion. By naming the pain of remembering the presence that suffers with the world and the joy of celebrating the power that works through the world, communion liturgies will be remembering the inclusive nature of God's presence and transforming hierarchical understandings of power.

One such example is the communion resource, *Table Talk: Resources for the Communion Meal*. An Advent litany names the pain of our day, cancer, AIDS, and violence, followed by a prayer for God's presence. "Our lives cry out for a savior. Gather us, O God, around the table, of hope and salvation... In communion with Christ and with one another, may we claim your power coming into the world" (McAvoy: 13). A prayer for the cup describes the character of divine power. "O Spirit, who bursts forth in our lives, filling us as this cup is filled, with the sweetness of perfectly ripened fruit....You enter us and fill us, and we enter again the womb of life" (83). Implicit in these worship resources is a prophetic denouncement of practices of exclusion because, as one meditation reminds us, "you are what you eat" (91). If the church eats of the presence of God with us and drinks of the power of God with us, how can it continue practices that exclude anyone from any aspect of the Christian community?

The hope is that such liturgical practice will be the trigger event for an ever-growing number of people within the Christian community. For as we name God, we name and give value to ourselves. False naming is the painful reality of language, liturgy and the church, and the emancipation of naming is women's hope.

Works Consulted

An Inclusive Language Lectionary: Readings for Year A. 1983. New York: National Council of the Churches of Christ in the U.S.A.

Bingemer, Maria Clara. 1989. "Reflections on the Trinity." *Through Her Eyes: Women's Theology from Latin America,* ed. by E. Tamez. Maryknoll: Orbis Books. 56–80.

Brown, Kelly Delaine. 1989. "God Is as Christ Does: Toward a Womanist Theology." *Journal of Religious Thought* 46/1: 7–16.

Bynum, Carolyn. 1982. *Jesus as Mother: Studies in the Spirituality of the High Middle Ages.* Berkeley: University of California Press.

Chalice Hymnal Sampler. 1993. St. Louis: Chalice Press.

Christ, Carol. 1987. "Symbols of Goddess and God." *Laughter of Aphrodite: Reflections on a Journey to the Goddess.* San Francisco: Harper and Row.

Christ, Carol, and Judith Plaskow, eds. 1979. *Womanspirit Rising.* San Francisco: Harper & Row.

Daly, Mary. 1973. *Beyond God the Father: Toward a Philosophy of Women's Liberation.* Boston: Beacon Press.

Duck, Ruth, and Michael Bausch, eds. 1981. *Everflowing Streams: Songs for Worship.* New York: Pilgrim Press.

Gimbutas, Marija. 1989. *The Language of the Goddess: Unearthing the Hidden Symbols of Western Civilization.* San Francisco: Harper & Row.

Heyward, Carter. 1984. *Our Passion for Justice: Images of Power, Sexuality, and Liberation.* New York: Pilgrim Press.

Huber, Jane Parker. 1987. *A Singing Faith.* Philadelphia: Westminster Press.

Johnson, Elizabeth.1992. *She Who Is: The Mystery of God in Feminist Theological Discourse.* New York: Crossroad.

Kirk, James. 1984. *When We Gather: A Book of Prayers for Worship: Year B.* Philadelphia: Geneva Press.

LaCugna, Catherine. 1991. *God for Us: The Trinity and Christian Life.* San Francisco: Harper & Row.

McAvoy, Jane, ed. 1993. *Table Talk: Resources for the Communion Meal.* St. Louis: Chalice Press.

McFague, Sallie. 1987. *Models of God: Theology for an Ecological, Nuclear Age.* Philadelphia: Fortress Press.

Mollenkott, Virginia Ramey. 1984. *The Divine Feminine: The Biblical Imagery of God as Female.* New York: Crossroad.

Proctor-Smith, Marjorie. 1990. *In Her Own Rite: Constructing Feminist Liturgical Tradition.* Nashville: Abingdon Press.

Ruether, Rosemary Radford. 1983. *Sexism and God-Talk: Toward a Feminist Theology.* Boston: Beacon Press.

Saiving, Virginia. 1960. "The Human Situation: A Feminine View." *Journal of Religion* (April 1960). Reprinted in *Womanspirit Rising,* ed. by Carol Christ and Judith Plaskow. San Francisco: Harper & Row, 1979. 25–42.

Schüssler Fiorenza, Elisabeth. 1993. *Discipleship of Equals: A Critical Feminist Ekklesia-logy of Liberation.* New York: Crossroad.

Walker, Alice. 1983. "God Is Inside You and Inside Everybody Else." *Weaving the Visions: Patterns in Feminist Spirituality,* ed. by Carol Christ and Judith Plaskow. San Francisco: Harper & Row. 101–104.

6

What About Jesus?

Christology and the Challenges of Women

Sondra Stalcup

I *believe that Jesus is the Christ, the Son of the Living God, and I* *accept him as personal Lord and the Savior of the world.* These are the words I professed aloud at the age of ten before my entire congregation of the East Dallas Christian Church in 1964. These traditional words, spoken in one form or another by so many who had gone before me and by so many since, were my "confession of faith," the Great Confession, which in the Disciples of Christ precedes baptism and signifies formal membership in the church universal through a particular home congregation. In denominations that practice infant baptism, a similar confession of faith is made at the time of one's confirmation, providing a sign of conscientious decision for membership in the body of Christ with an acceptance of the responsibilities. Further, sharing in communion or eucharist, which Disciples do every week, involves symbolically a recalling of one's baptism, an affirmation of the faith expressed in that first profession. In addition, when new members join a local congregation, they are often asked to reaffirm their confession by responding again to the question: Do you believe that Jesus is the Christ?

In my home church, the people there were the ones who had nurtured, taught, and embraced me since birth. I cannot remember a week that went by when we were not at church two or three times, sometimes more; the community of faith was the focal point of my life. Church was the primary setting where the reality of God's love that prompted my confession was made known to me. As I grew through adolescence and into young womanhood, I continued to be active in church work, yet nagging questions about the place of women in the church grew, as well. Together with women friends from church, I came to an increasing awareness of our exclusion. We saw men heading meetings, men at the lectern, men at the Table, men passing communion and men in the pulpit. Where were the women? Our "feminist consciousness" grew in a way similar to the five stages spelled out in chapter 1. Not only did we notice the absence of women, we were not content merely to "add a few women and stir." We began to understand the church's own role in the subordination of women, not only within the church, but in every aspect of society. Exclusion, limitation, subordination, oppression, and for so many, violence. Feminist theology was born of "woman-vision" and born of "woman-pain," stemming from an ever-growing, critical feminist consciousness of the secondary status of women under patriarchy and the suffering it brings, highlighted by the role of religion in reinforcing the pain.[1]

This awareness became such a part of me that I could no longer separate it from any level of my living, action, or reflection. My feminism and my Christianity became inextricably intertwined, with my feminism influencing my Christian identity and my Christian commitment coming to bear in my feminist perspective. And as women of the church who continue to confess the Christ, we find that fostering the full humanity of women—and the changes that implies—is a demand of the gospel itself.

But what does it mean to confess Jesus as "the Christ"? What is the force behind the words spoken, behind the culturally influenced words of the confession? Is there not more to it than a decidedly patriarchal reflection of male language and hierarchical imagery? Is there really something there so that those concerned with the suffering caused by patriarchy might remain in the church, and thus continue to profess a genuine connection to the Christ? Or further, might you, with conviction, commend Christianity to your women friends?

In the Gospel accounts, Jesus poses the question "Who do you say that I am?" The assertion that he is "the Christ" is a way of trying

---

[1] I employ *feminist* in a broad sense to designate the perspective of those committed to promoting the full humanity of women and girls. As a white North American, I use the word *feminist*, but *womanist* and *mujerista* are the terms chosen by African-American and Hispanic women for their theologies.

to formulate the significance of the experience or the encounter with "him" or the witness about him. When one is committed to being a "Christian," a member of the Christian community, this usually means that one confesses or believes in some way that Jesus Christ is the decisive factor in one's life, indeed, the true or authentic meaning of human existence—in very traditional Christian terms, our "salvation." While this has been expressed through the centuries in many different ways, Christians have intended to convey that this encounter or experience of Jesus as Christ is the authentic understanding of oneself in relation to God.

This self-understanding is not simply a piece of information or a collection of certain important facts to believe, but rather an orientation of one's entire being. This existential understanding is a response of the whole self as one discovers the true self in light of the Source and End of everything that is. In other words, to ask who Jesus is, is to ask at the same time who we are and who God is. As Christians, we can say that this experience of Jesus, or of the witness about Jesus as the Christ, provides the answer to our deepest human questions: *Who am I? Who is God? Who am I in relation to God? Who am I in relation to others?*

These interrelated questions seem to be raised by all human beings, at some level of consciousness[2]—questions about our very existence, the meaning of life, how to act, the purpose of acting, especially in light of suffering. Very simply put, we are creatures with an intuitive sense of a "whole" of being of which we are a part. We have a primal perception, a very "basic faith" that we somehow matter, a fundamental trust that life has meaning that enables us to go forward. And yet this foundation is constantly challenged, called into question, and threatened as we experience our limits. We are finite beings, we must one day die, and we realize the inevitable deaths of our loved ones. We also come face to face with horrible suffering, which is sometimes daily for so much of the human race. Because this is so, in our living and being, we tend to ask ourselves again and again who we are and what we're to be about.

While these ultimate questions are shared in common by all humanity, they are questions that are nevertheless raised and answered

---

[2] There is a long history to the perspective I am conveying here, stemming from work in philosophy, theology, anthropology, and sociology. This group of interrelated, simultaneous questions — Who am I/Who is God/How do I relate to God/How do I relate to all others? — is often called the human "existential question." The existential question is raised in some way by all human creatures, and an answer to it is developed by every human society. In the nontheistic religions that do not use the term *God*, there are functional equivalents to refer to the Ultimate Reality.

in the particular context of each one's life. Christianity, with its witness of faith about Jesus as the Christ, offers a specific answer to the human existential question. And in offering an answer, one we presumably would commend to others, Christians are also called upon to make sense of the claims they make. This sense-making, explaining and validating of claims, is the "formal" task of Christian theology, the heart of which is Christology.

As Christians in the world today, we are pressed to ask again with fervor, "Who are we as women?", as female human beings in relation to God and others, when that God is so consistently worshiped as male Father, male Son, and supposedly male Holy Spirit. Who are we as women when God is said to be revealed in one who is designated in masculine and patriarchal terms as Son of God, Son of man, Lord, King, Master, Groom, Head? Where do women stand with a God who is mediated in much of the visible church through a male priesthood (and still "re-presented" predominantly by male ministers)?[3] What are women to be in the midst of a scriptural tradition recorded and edited and canonized by males, and in a theological tradition shaped and perpetuated by males, one in which women have been regarded primarily as peripheral and "the other," helpers at best and cause for original sin at worst? How do we feel as women when we are presumably unable to achieve the "perfection" of full and authentic humanity since that has been identified the historical male Jesus? And what do we do when our efforts to break out of molds of mere servitude at the expense of self are suppressed and criticized as self-centered, thus, "sinful"?

So, what can it mean for women to confess Jesus as the Christ today? What is there in the Christian witness to suggest that we as women can be in meaningful and authentic relationship with God that is truly decisive for our lives and for our relationships with others?

It is still my conviction, and that of many other women, that there *is* something in the Christian witness of faith that is definitive for our lives, which means for our relationship with all others. We believe the encounter with God's love through the gospel of Christ has the capacity to meet our deepest human needs, our yearnings for love and purpose and the fullness of being human. As women, we

---

[3] I refer to Roman Catholic, Eastern Orthodox and certain Anglican and Episcopal communions, as well as to various "fundamentalist" denominations, in which ordination is still denied to women. And in those churches who do ordain women as ministers, there are still obstacles for women in being appointed to or called by congregations with anything close to parity with men.

may sense our authentic woman-ness in the depths of that divine love. Yes, it is all too true that we as women have so often experienced hurt, devaluation, and disrespect in the context of the church and in elements of scripture and its interpretation; indeed, some of us have been brutally assaulted in the name of Christian teaching—and we cannot excuse even the least offense, lest we participate in allowing it to continue. But this is not the whole picture. We as women have also been affected in a redeeming, liberating way as we experienced the biblical witness and the living witness of those in the church who nurtured and sustained us. The church has been a place of women gathering, talking, singing, helping, and nurturing each other through births and deaths, amid all the ups and downs of life. It has been a place of education, leadership training, and organization of outreach beyond its doors. From teenage girls to eighty-year-old women, ordained and lay, businesswomen and homemakers, this dual experience of the community of faith has been expressed time and again in recent years.

In other words, the church has been a place of hurt for the majority of its membership and has contributed to the oppression of women in family and societal structures, politics, law, and economics. Yet the church has also been the primary setting where the reality of a loving God has been made known and vividly experienced, the very encounter that underlies the confession that Jesus is the Christ. The church has been for women the locus of both oppression *and* liberation. How can we understand what seems to be a contradiction?

It is with this predicament that we find ourselves right in the middle of the fascinating arena of *Christology*. If to be a "Christian" is to be connected in a true and viable way to one called "Christ," then we of necessity become engaged with Christological questions. We Christians become so used to saying things about Jesus, repeating phrases we grew up with, and making claims about the Christ, without realizing what we're saying—and if we really wish to be saying that after all! The women's movements have taught us well how extremely important it is to pay attention to the historical and cultural contexts that shape our religious language, beliefs, and practices; this is especially crucial when it comes to Jesus Christ. It is my hope to acquaint the reader with a few of the "whys" and "whats" and "hows" of Christology, broadly and generally, so we may better understand what is at stake. But moreover, we will move into specific concerns in Christology in light of feminist questions.

Just What Is Christology?

When so many women have made the difficult decision to leave the church, we find ourselves understanding their decision to move on and away from the limitations, hurts, and oppression. Yet at the same time we hurt for them, we can't bear to see them leave (or be run out of) what is their own church, their own "home" (we feel a big dose of "Stage Three" anger). How can we help? Perhaps these women saw only traditional orthodox Christianity as "Christian." Perhaps they lost hope that church and theology can be transformed. But many of us are seeking ways and means to understand and express our Christian faith anew, with truth and integrity. We are finding viable ways to be both feminist and Christian; in fact, in our own contemporary world, one may see that seeking the full humanity of women and doing justice for women is an imperative for Christians. By getting to the heart of what it means to confess Jesus as the Christ in our own day—by doing Christology—we find vindication that we may express that truth in the words of women.

We are doing things in some new and different ways, but we are also joining in a long conversation. Christology, in the very broadest sense, is *logos* about *Christos*; that is, thought and speech about Christ, or even more accurate historically, thought and speech about Jesus who is said to be "the Christ." It is what we do when we confess, proclaim, think about, and share with others who Jesus Christ is and what that means to us. But there is a narrower, stricter definition of "Christology," which refers to the more intentional critical reflection on this thought and speech. This level of Christology asks more formally what it means to assert Jesus' decisive significance for human life and how it can be true or valid that he is the one in or through whom God is known. It is an act of critical interpretation, analysis, and assessment that asks about the conditions necessary for truthfully making such claims, as well as the implications for our living.

So then, if Christology asks what it means to say Jesus is the Christ, and whether or not it is true, where do we begin? The Christology in the New Testament is the obvious place. Jesus was confessed not only as "Christ" or the Messiah, but also Lord, the Son of man, the divine Logos, God's Sophia (Wisdom), the Son of God, and even God. In the New Testament we find these and other honorific titles attributed to Jesus from the various Christian communities, many of them rooted in Jewish culture (such as the apocalyptic notion of a Messiah), with others notably more Greek (such as the Logos). Also in the New Testament, we find testimony or witness about Jesus in narratives we have come to understand as either mythological or legendary. For example, there are stories about his conception and birth, his preexistence and destiny, his earthly life as one uniquely wise, perfect and sinless, and so forth.

In light of the range of titles and narratives of this type from many different communities, we see that "Christ" came to stand not as a mere title but as a "proper name" to designate the significance of "Jesus," indeed his decisive significance. From the earliest times and in many different ways, Christians proclaimed a message of "salvation," claiming Jesus as the one in whom humanity's existence is summed up, the one through whom human beings are "saved" or "redeemed" or "brought to new life" by God.

Already in the New Testament writings there is Christology taking place in both the broad and narrow senses we have discussed. There is witness about Jesus being borne, and there is interpretation and reinterpretation going on within and across communities and as time passed. Biblical scholarship has well illustrated the basic development of Christology. In the earliest strands of witness about Jesus, discerned in parts of the Synoptic Gospels, the focus was clearly upon Jesus' message, especially on what he proclaimed about God's reign being at hand. Thus, the earliest reconstructible witness about Jesus only *implies* a Christology, without mention of Jesus as divine. This early form of witness, with only an *implicit* Christology, soon developed into the varying forms of *explicit* Christology such as we have mentioned, e.g. in titles, mythological narratives, and legends about Jesus himself. And what seems to have occurred is this: *The proclaimer became the one proclaimed!* How can we understand this change, this development of Christology? The explicit formulations reflect the followers' attempt to square the decisive or "saving" significance experienced in Jesus and his message with the fact well understood by both Jews and Greeks, that *only God saves.*

This points us to the fact that in the New Testament we also find an overlap of the questions about the "what" and "who" and "how" of the encounter with Jesus or the message about him. In other words, since there is a decisive event or "salvific action" (work) experienced in the encounter with Jesus (person), there are attempts made to understand or justify the action in terms of who Jesus is, his "essence" or "nature," his own self-understanding, special attributes, or unique relationship with God. New Testament narratives and formulations already suggest that Jesus is a figure who is both human *and* divine. One way of approaching this was expressed in an "Adoptionist" model, as seen, for example, early in the Gospel of Mark, when Jesus is appointed by God at his baptism to be Messiah. The other prominent Christological model is "Incarnational"; we may think immediately of the divine conception and infancy stories, as well as John 1:1: "In the beginning was the Word [Logos], and the Word was with

God, and the Word was God." The naturalness of this tendency to talk of Jesus as both human and divine may be understood along these lines: If it is only God the divine One who saves, then Jesus must be in some sense divine.

But again, realize that there is in the New Testament witness quite clearly an interrelationship of person and work, i.e.: "in or through Jesus, God saves us." It is difficult to even talk about one without the other—salvation is in or through Jesus, God saves us through Jesus, in Jesus we are saved (by God), and so forth. Work and person; person and work. Even though they came to be discussed separately later in Christian doctrine, logically there is no such separation.

From the implicit Christology of the earliest strata of witness, through the explicit formulations of other New Testament traditions, and on through the Trinitarian and Christological controversies of the fourth and fifth centuries, the church struggled to define itself and to interpret its professed faith. As the church evolved from its status as a persecuted sect into the official religion of the empire, its identity-shaping stemmed from Christians' own experiences of the testimony about Jesus as the Christ, as individuals and as communities of faith in many different locations. Just as in its earliest days, the church's identity and interpretations were being shaped by the words and concepts and practices of the cultures surrounding it.

Discussions about the nature of the Christ were naturally informed by Greek philosophy and classical "metaphysics" (which is the philosophical term for a theory of experience as such, a general theory of concreteness, an unpacking of reality).[4] The Greek "worldview" envisioned not only a three-tiered universe, but also assumed a separation between the ideal world and the typical world of matter, which tended toward the elevation of mind over body, and other dualisms. This worldview informed discussions about the character of the divine Logos or Wisdom, its relation to God, how to protect the unity and transcendence of God while not denying the real humanity of Jesus, and other puzzlements.[5]

---

[4] You may have seen in recent times a shelf in your local bookstore called "Metaphysics," which has been erroneously adopted to indicate New Age materials and current mystical offerings. I am using metaphysics in one of the traditional ways it is employed in philosophical theology, to indicate the theory of being, or reality as such.

[5] Please see Richard Norris' excellent book *The Christological Controversy* for a clear and helpful discussion of the issues raised in the debates that led to the Chalcedonian Definition, and the condemnation of various "heresies." It is actually a fascinating piece of history, filled with both political infighting and passionate faith.

After years of debate between competing "parties," from east and west, both political and theological, with popes and emperors, theologians and laypeople involved, an official christological "Definition" was finally adopted. The Council of Chalcedon in 451 set forth what we may designate "orthodox Christology," and all other alternatives were condemned as heresies. In short, the "Chalcedonian Definition" was a formulation that identifies Jesus Christ as "one hypostasis" or entity or subject, but existing "in two natures."

> [Christ is] the one divine Son who possesses at once complete deity and complete humanity. At the same time, however, it insists...that Christ exists in "two natures" which are neither divided from each other or confused with each other....that is, he is a single reality, the divine Logos, existing as such, and at the same time existing as a human being. (Norris: 30)

This orthodox formulation of the person of Christ was accepted and assumed in Christendom for the next thousand years. Even through the period of "scholasticism" in the late Middle Ages, the Chalcedonian Definition prevailed, although Thomas Aquinas and others tried valiantly to "make sense" of the given formula of Chalcedon in terms of metaphysics. Moreover, even with the radical theological changes of the Protestant Reformation and the embracing of "justification by grace alone through faith alone," Luther and the other reformers of the sixteenth and seventeenth centuries were not interested in challenging the particulars of Christology.

But there were, of course, other powerful factors operating in Western civilization that came to affect long-held teachings of the church. The Age of Enlightenment, initiated by Descartes, Newton, Kant and others, was dawning. Different standards for determining truth evolved, standards based not simply on the authority of the early councils, the pope, or any church teaching, but on human reason and experience. The rise of this new enlightened perspective with its stress on the autonomy of reason initiated a radical shift in worldview. An acceptance of the general "cause and effect" nature of the universe influenced every field of inquiry; in turn, the metaphysics of the Chalcedonian Definition were deemed untenable. A heightened awareness of the human capacity for reason and a basic confidence in the ability of humans to resolve the inherent questions and problems in life became the rule of the day. As Kant stated it:

> Enlightenment is humanity's emergence from its self-imposed nonage [immaturity]. Nonage is the inability to use one's own understanding without another's guidance. ... *Dare to know! (Sapere aude.)* "Have the courage to use your own understanding," is therefore the motto of the enlightenment (1072).

A notable aspect of the Enlightenment perspective, as Rita Nakashima Brock points out in the introductory chapter, is feminism's own roots in the drive toward autonomy and freedom, away from "nonage," especially as women realize the means and courage to use their own minds and to act "without another's guidance," (i.e. without male guidance).

The Enlightenment emphasis on self-autonomy and the dismantling of classical metaphysics acted as a catalyst for a new phase in theology and biblical criticism, utilizing the new standards of knowledge. A reexamination of the Bible's history, sources, meaning, and purpose was taken on with increasing interest and excitement. It became evident that the four Gospels of the New Testament were not "biographies" of Jesus or "histories" per se. One need only glean the many obvious differences—and even contradictory accounts— between the four books to notice that there was something going on other than the recording of simple facts or the promotion of a particular worldview. A fairly wide consensus evolved as to the general development of the Gospels. They came to be understood as representing the traditions and faith stories of different Christian communities, in different contexts, with different needs, and different ways of expressing the gospel of Jesus as the Christ effectively in their own time and place.

Inevitably, the question of the meaning of confessing Jesus as the Christ came to the forefront with urgency in the "modern" era. The Gospels were understood in a new light, and theology could no longer appeal to an understanding of Jesus' significance based on a Christology that depended upon authority alone or on the metaphysics of a bygone age. Criticism was directed toward the superstitious and mythological manner in which people used the concept of incarnation to point to the metamorphosis or transmutation of a divine being into a human being, which is actually a common theme in polytheistic religions. Furthermore, it became clear that something crucial was being neglected in orthodox Christology: the *humanity* of Jesus. Despite the words, Jesus' humanness could never quite be sustained in the old Christology.

A new phase in Christology was launched and the "divinity" of Jesus was sought in the unique quality or character of his life on earth. The foundation for Christology was now to be rooted in the human "self." From the time of the work of Friedrich Schleiermacher (1768-1834), "revisionary Christology" began to focus on Jesus as the model, example, or representative of moral perfection and compassion which we as humans could emulate. Thus, for example, Jesus of Nazareth is said to be the human who uniquely lived the fullness of "God-consciousness"; and because he did this, we are able to live that way as well, helping to "usher in the kingdom," so to speak (for further details on revisionary Christology, see Bultmann, 1958; Tillich, 1957; and Ogden, 1982, etc.).

In order to discover the words and deeds and thoughts of the "real" Jesus, so we might better understand our own human potential, many and various "quests for the historical Jesus" were embarked upon. And it is fascinating how often these quests yielded a "Jesus" who held views much like the people from the culture of the author. By the early twentieth century, it was clear that a message of Jesus as a "moral leader whom we can be like" is simply not to be found in the Gospels (see Schweitzer). Although the Jesus of the Gospels surely can provide us with guidance for our morality, a mere "example" is not the meaning of "the Christ" in the New Testament.

Further, there was an obvious disjunction between thinking of Jesus as an example we could attain and the fact that we as human beings continually fail to do so. The horrible evidence in our own century of our inhumanity to humanity initiated necessary shifts in theology. The havoc wreaked by World War I, followed so closely by World War II and the unparalleled atrocities of the Holocaust, were stark and appalling reminders that humans continue to do evil, despite their wondrous reasoning capacity, despite any "model" of Jesus Christ (indeed, many outrageous acts were committed in the name of Christ).

Confidence in the ability of human beings to emulate Jesus Christ was utterly destroyed, and Christological thought had a profound awakening. Different accounts of the meaning and truth of the Christ had to be developed. There arose a renewed appreciation for two traditional understandings of the New Testament: first, that human beings do "sin"; and secondly, that Jesus Christ is an "eschatological event," one who makes a radical difference to the world and for the world. This event is not to be understood as a timeless truth or simply a historical event of the past, but an in-the-present encounter of God's acting grace, of God's love here and now. Revisionary Christology continued along the lines of various schools of thought, which are still influential today. Among these are: Karl Barth, dialectical theology, and neoorthodoxy; Rudolf Bultmann, demythologizing and existentialist interpretation; Ludwig Wittgenstein, linguistic inquiry and functional analysis; and also process theology, process philosophy, and revisionary metaphysics. There are, of course, Paul Tillich, the Niebuhrs, Karl Rahner—we could go on and on. Furthermore, over the last twenty-five years, the theologies of liberation that have come out of Latin America, Africa, and Asia, and from African Americans have had a tremendous impact on contemporary theology worldwide; no longer is theology just a Euro-American male enterprise. And, as this book testifies, feminist/womanist/mujerista theologies and the voices of women around the globe are gradually being heard. Revisionary Christology continues in full force. All of us are still in the process of discovering ways to understand and to live out of our confession of God's unconditional love for all, as we experience it in Christ.

If you take only *one* thing away from this brief unfolding of Christological thought, please note this: in every time and place and situation, since the earliest days of the New Testament witness up to the present, Christians have used different words and concepts to express the same truth found in the assertion implied by "Jesus is the Christ." The expressions or formulations may change, but the point never does. The living word of God happening here and now and in every new present is the same word experienced in the earliest witness of the New Testament, the word of love proclaimed again and again in many different words.

This does not mean, however, that every expression or formulation is appropriate to the gospel, reasonable, or fitting to a situation at hand. For example, it would hardly be an expression of love to say to a woman lying in a hospital bed with injuries from a beating by her husband, "Be subject to your husband, as is fitting in the Lord" (Colossians 3:18), or to say to an African American, "Let all who are under the yoke of slavery regard their masters as worthy of all honor..." (1 Timothy 6:1). The validity of the gospel of Christ is not limited to or reducible to moral codes, worldviews, and ideologies of other times and places; and when certain expressions are no longer effective, if they "block" a genuine encounter with the living Word, then we should not use them. The love of God we say we encounter in Jesus, or in the message of Jesus as the Christ, is to be expressed ever anew.

Feminist Challenges to Christology

If the truth of God's love as experienced in Christ is not to be limited by the systems of other places, times, and situations, then it is quite clear that patriarchal and sexist traditions are not an essential part of Christian witness. As a matter of fact, when so many women find these traditions not only a block to encountering God's love but directly harmful, it is high time to let go of them. It is also quite clear that the voices of women belong to the theological conversation.

We as women are talking from our experiences about what Jesus as the Christ means to us. In a vast variety of ways, we are trying to do so in terms that are in keeping with the point of the gospel, intellectually and experientially credible, as well as spiritually satisfying. You have seen from this book's section on the Bible that significant feminist efforts have been devoted to rediscovering and reclaiming the biblical stories about women, especially in connection with Jesus; there is a clear sense that for women, the Gospels convey a Jesus who loves "even women," thus revealing a God who does. Further, feminist theologians have sought to reconstruct Christian origins in light of the early women followers of Jesus, as well as the apostles we read of in Paul's letters, such as Prisca. There have also been efforts to unearth and illuminate the few writings of women in Christian history, such as the medieval women pointed out in this book by Lahutsky (see also Amy Oden, ed., *In Her Words: Women's Writings in the History of Christian Thought*). It is exciting to discover threads of the witness and work and experiences of millions of silent/silenced women in each generation, including the traditions of African-American women drawn out by womanist theologians. We are strengthened by a sense of our foremothers and foresisters. We realize once again that it has always been a church of women; women have proclaimed the Christ in their own ways; and we join that great cloud of witnesses as we weave our own testimonies and interpretations. Firsthand experience is respected in feminist theology and always informs it, because women find their individual and collective "voice" in sharing together. In the broadest sense of Christology, we are "doing Christology" in every aspect of our Christian witness, study and contemplation.

Further, just as there is not one definitive "feminist theology," as Brock points out in chapter 1—or one feminist opinion or feminist strategy—there is no singular "feminist Christology." Writings about Christology by feminist theologians are as varied as writings among theologians generally. There is a diversity and richness in feminist Christologies, reflective of differing circumstances, contexts, races, cultures, experiences in church and life, and—we must admit—of differing degrees of oppression and suffering.

While there is no one feminist Christology, there is a "core" agreement or central focus among them: *an appreciation of questions of power and privilege raised by gender awareness.*[6] In fact, there is near-consensus that the following issues need to be taken into account by anyone doing theology in today's world: (1) the reality of gender injus-

---

[6] In the view of womanists, a Christology of black women includes not only gender analysis, but analysis based upon their tridimensional experience of racism/sexism/classism. "To ignore any aspect of this experience is to deny the holistic and integrated reality of Black womanhood" (Grant, p. 209).

tice in the church and its role in colluding with culture; (2) an uplifting of the gift of embodiment, which includes our sexuality (as opposed to pointing out the pitfalls of our bodyselves); (3) an emphasis
on "relationality" as constitutive of existence. In addition, and especially pertinent in understanding the significance of Jesus as the
Christ, feminist Christologies usually involve addressing these issues: (4) concerns about "sin" as self-love when "woman's sin" may
well be self-denial, and problems with the whole notion of being
"saved"; (5) difficulties with "self-sacrifice" or "servanthood" as
models of discipleship; (6) questions about the significance (or lack
thereof) of Jesus' maleness; and, in turn (7), the relation of Jesus to
"the Christ."

The Reality of Gender Injustice

Perhaps the most critical question in theology today centers on
the immense amount of *avoidable* human suffering in our world. And
that suffering is most often the direct and indirect result of the policies and actions of those with power and privilege—nations, institutions, structures, classes, and individuals—which includes the church.
For so many in our world, one's daily question is sheer *survival*. And
within the wide-ranging concern of suffering and survival, earlier
theologies simply do not exhibit an awareness of power and privilege it raises, *especially not in connection with gender*.

Much of this chapter—and most of this book—has tried to illustrate some of the realities of gender injustice in church and theology,
as well as pointing to the differences found in the experiences of females and males because of sociocultural roles, expectations, and
opportunities. We have also directly and indirectly pointed to the
church's role in reinforcing the continued subordination of women
and, at its worst, colluding with culture in the abuse of women—
actively through its teachings, and also passively by its silence. Aspects of traditional Christology are especially problematic in women's
own willingness to condone mental and physical abuse.

In the many feminist challenges to Christology, the depth of injustice to women and the church's role in abuse is a key theme underlying virtually every other issue. Transformation or elimination
of all theology, liturgy, and practices that glorify or help perpetuate
suffering is a requirement of any feminist/womanist interpretation
of the ultimate significance of Jesus as the Christ.

Embodiment

Feminists have been concerned to counter negative views of the
human body and sexuality—particularly women's bodies and sexuality—that have prevailed more or less in Christian tradition through-

out its history. The reasons and needs for this counter include several things, a few of which we shall mention here. First, and obviously, there is an important part of Christian witness that calls one to honor the body as a gift from God. Second, as we mentioned already in connection with Greek philosophy, there has been a tendency in the history of the Western philosophical and religious traditions toward dualism and the equation of woman with body/nature, and man with spirit/reason. This split often resulted in elevating maleness and subordinating femaleness as well as the rest of nature. Third, there is a history of religious taboos regarding menstruation, childbirth, and even lactation, as well as a total lack of worship rituals celebrating the various changes and lifestages in female lives. Further, there is a long history of fear and suspicion about sex, a confused complicity between sexuality and sin. This confusion is contributed to in no small part by a "mixed" male view of women—as an evil seductress, on the one hand, and as a virginal mother figure placed upon a pedestal, on the other. These factors, reinforced by patriarchal structures that objectify women, reveal how generally we have learned to devalue our bodies, devalue ourselves.

Based on women's own interpretations of embodiment, there is a movement toward women's reclaiming our bodies as our own, as integral to our selfhood, as the centers of personal activity. This reclamation of the body-self means not only taking our bodies seriously, even sacredly, and living holistically; it also means refusing to yield control of our bodies to men, individually and institutionally.

The celebration of embodiment also means that in feminist Christology, the humanity of Jesus, which became downplayed in orthodoxy, is fully realized and appreciated. His unjust crucifixion is not glorified at all, but rather understood as an unbearably painful and violent act. Any notion that Jesus died "for us" cannot be understood in terms of blood sacrifice or atonement or restitution; instead it could point only to God's genuine participation with all humans who are suffering—which, for women, has meant especially God's presence with them even in the midst of abuse.

Relational Existence

In most feminist writings, relationship with others is prominently featured in describing our humanness, our womanness. Rather than abstract autonomous individuality, relationality provides a more accurate picture of existence. "Interdependence" is highlighted instead of strict dependence or independence. Humans are essentially relational, able to know and be known, to love and be loved—and to hurt and be hurt. Our relationships with others are part of the concrete reality of our lives, not merely accidental to our selfhood, but a very part of our humanness. This does not mean that the concept of autonomy is useless—feminists also affirm the importance of freedom and uniqueness. The emphasis on relational reality simply means that there is no "pure" autonomy, no truly separate individuals. The focus is on the interdependence of human communities and the interconnectedness of all creation.

While women have generally positive feelings about community and relationality as the context and essence of life, we are also more than fully aware of the implications of this social dimension of human striving. The individual, the autonomous self, is not simply free to enact decisions independent of other considerations. We are all impacted by the influence of our immediate families and circumstances, but we are also dependent on the social factors which surround us. There are biological, psychological, sociological, economic, and political "powers" operative and effective in individual decision.

Relationality informs an understanding of God, as well. Feminists find that the one-sided notion of an absolute, omipotent deity acting upon creation like a master puppeteer isolated above, feels too much like the way men have ruled women's lives. That is not love. Love, if we understand it all, is always found in mutual relation, in both giving to and receiving from. Feminists often resonate with process theology and neoclassical theists by insisting upon the relationality of all existence, indeed reality *as* social process. This understanding of existence is in keeping with a concept of God which posits God as literally relational, not just symbolically. This means that God both gives to us and receives from us, our joys and sorrows, our pleasures and pain, such that the confession of the words "God with us" are given substance. In this view, the encounter with Jesus as the Christ reveals that God's love for us is a deeply intimate, boundless love because God not only relates, but God's relating encompasses *everything* that is or even could be.

One of my favorite ways of expressing God's love as made known in Christ is "the unlimited love that calls forth love." When we experience this neverending love, we can do nothing less than respond by loving others. This love, this radical and universal relatedness, suggests our authentic human existence in connection to God and others.

Woman's "Sin"

As early as the 1960s, pioneer in feminist theology Valerie Saiving raised the question of whether the "sin of man" as often portrayed in Christian teaching was an accurate depiction of the human condition, or indeed refers to the state of males. (Also on Saiving, see Miller-

McLemore's chapter and Brock's introduction to Section III in this book.) Think about it. If sin is described as excessive "self-love," how many women do you know who fit that description? Is not the opposite problem more likely true, since women are generally socialized to put themselves last and taught in church that subservience and self-sacrifice are true discipleship? There has been much discussion in feminist circles of just what "woman's sin" is, and what the "condition" is from which women need to be redeemed.

In the Judeo-Christian tradition, sin refers to *hubris*, which means the state or condition of "trying to be like God," that is, attempting to take on a status and/or power that is inappropriate for human beings. Sin, of course, has also been called *idolatry*, or putting the self above God and others. It has also been called *estrangement*, or separation from our essential created goodness. All of these terms for sin refer to the matter of not being one's true self, not living one's authentic human existence, not being who God created us to be—living in "unfaith."

Theologians of the past have tended to dwell on the state of sin and descriptions of living out of sin as "pride," or putting one's own self above God and others. But is there not another "pole" involved in an understanding of idolatry? In women's experience, we are more likely to fall into self-negation, having no self at all to offer to God or any other. We could rightly say that the manifestation of woman's sin is putting *others* above God (and self). Understanding this, we see how the condition from which women may need to be redeemed or saved is indeed inauthentic existence, an inappropriate state for human beings, an untrue self. But what of sacrificial theology that promotes her "sin"? What of Christian traditions that reinforce her "idolatry of others" at the expense of self, which also allows those others to abuse her sacrifice for their own ends, thus living out of their own sin as "idolatry of self"?

Feminist explorations of human sin and salvation seek to account for the very goodness of every living thing and our need to recognize that goodness. At the same time, we acknowledge and account for the human estrangement from God, ourselves and one another, as not at all a *necessity* of our existence, but as nevertheless a *fact* of our existence. Some of us live it out by harming others, failing to live in our true relatedness to them as beloved by God. Others of us live it out harming ourselves, failing to live as though we are essentially a good part of all being, beloved by God. Either end of the spectrum reflects a condition of sin or estrangement.

Although essentially good, we too easily live estranged from God, the ground of our being; from other beings, humans and other creatures; and from ourselves, which is more likely the symptom of sin in women. Even though it is still important in Christianity to decide to put someone else's needs above one's own, there is a moral and theological limit to that kind of sacrifice. One could easily argue that we cannot in love even give ourselves to others if we have no "self" to give. If someone sacrifices herself entirely, she is still estranged from her true self, still in sin, unreconciled to God, herself, and others.

The Cross: Problems with Self-Sacrifice and Servanthood

A woman can literally sacrifice her self, her very selfhood or humanness, in serving and attending to others. A predominant theology of self-sacrifice is hardly good news to women in that state. One cannot help but note the evidence that a call for sacrifice in the name of Christ serves quite well those in power in patriarchal structures of households, governments, and religious institutions. Womanist theologians have been quick to point out that the theologies of servanthood and the encouragement to be "slaves of Christ" have been used by whites (including white women) to keep Africans in their place. When one's heritage and life include actual slavery, household service, field labor, yardwork, and so on, where is the redeeming, liberating message of love in servanthood?

Feminists and womanist theologians are by no means the only ones to raise serious questions about doctrines of atonement and sacrificial theories of salvation. Many in theology since the Enlightenment have pointed to the inconsistencies in positing an all-loving God with a required execution of an innocent person. But we might say they raise them with a new fervor, based on women's immediate experience of just how harmful such notions can be in perpetuating human suffering—in particular, the subordination and abuse of women.

> Women are acculturated to accept abuse. We come to believe that it is our place to suffer...and the ways in which we have become anesthetized to our violation is a central theme in women's literature, theology, art.... [And here is] the deep and painful secret that sustains us in oppression: We have been convinced that our suffering is justified....Christianity has been a primary...force in shaping our acceptance of abuse. The central image of Christ on the cross as the savior of the world communicates the message that suffering is redemptive....Self-sacrifice and obedience are not only virtues but the definition of a faithful identity.... (Brown and Parker: 1-2)

Let us return for a moment to the question of "from what do we need to be saved?" Those in the early Greek church wanted to be saved from death and error. In the Roman Catholic church, often salvation is from guilt and its consequences in the afterlife in purgatory and hell, while classical Protestants express the need to be saved from the law, the anxiety it produces and its power to condemn. In pietism and revivalistic traditions, being saved is the overcoming of a "godless state" through conversion and transformation. Ascetics hope to conquer special sins, and liberals want progress toward moral perfection (Tillich, 1957: 166f.). Some liberation theologies equate political liberation with salvation.

But remember for a moment the root meaning of salvation, from the Latin word *salvus*: healed. In the present situation of humankind, we may best interpret salvation as "healing." Some feminist Christologies suggest that sin is "damage" and that the salvation we seek and need is indeed healing (e.g., Brock, 1991). While we can talk about our estrangement from God that needs to be reconciled, we must also talk about the need for healing from the manifestations of that estrangement in our lives—from hatred and war and subjugation of others, from all the pain we cause each other. In Christ, we say we find the power of salvation, the very healing we seek. Again we notice that the person and work of Jesus Christ are not "split." As Christians, we never really separate our talk about the Christ and salvation, because each one implies the other. And the power of that salvation is nothing less than the power of God's love that is always ours, if we will but live out of it.

As a matter of course, it is not too strong to say that "the only legitimate reason for women to remain in the church will be if the church were to condemn as anathema the glorification of suffering" (Brown and Parker: 4). And this is especially hard when the cross is the central visual symbol in most churches, and when communion is so often centered on Jesus' "broken body and spilled blood." For alternative visions of "nonsacrificial" communion meditations, let me commend the roundtable discussion found in the last chapter of this book.

The Significance of Jesus' Maleness

Rosemary Radford Ruether's now classic question, "Can a male savior save women?," points to several difficulties for women, many of them interrelated: maleness came to be the generic sex of the human species; maleness came to be equated with wholeness, or holiness; women have had problems in being able to personally identify with a male, or connect with male symbols at the deepest level; women have struggled with the whole notion of needing to be "saved," or defined by a man; and they have questioned whether any empirical facts whatsoever about Jesus matter at all theologically (a question not only for women, but for all Christians).

Certain Christological traditions, both orthodox and revisionary, have suggested that the full perfection of human potential is summed up in Jesus. Not only is there some difficulty for women in closely identifying with a man, there is a clear inference that women, not being male, cannot achieve full humanness, or authentic human existence as we've called it.

Further, one may say that in our contemporary world, part of womankind's growth and journey involves development of a reliance on herself, a trusting of her own perceptions and judgments in defining her life and purposes—rather than definition by the men in her life (i.e. father, husband, father-in-law, priests, male officials, etc.). How helpful is it to this growth and journey to think in terms of the *necessity* of a man Jesus in one's life? Indeed, there is a question of needing to be "saved" by anyone.

However, in African-American tradition, it is important to note that the name of "Jesus" is quite significant, and black women are not eager to adopt the white woman's more gender-neutral reference of simply "Christ." In womanist Christology, black women identify their own struggles and pain with those of Jesus and, in turn, it is believed that Jesus as God identifies with them as well. It is the *humanity* of Jesus that is relevant, not his maleness; and further, it is the presence of God in that humanity. Jesus is the "Black Christ," the divine co-sufferer, truly with them in the bondage of slavery in the past and amid the racism and poverty of the present. As one slave woman expressed her love for Jesus: "Come to we, dear Mass Jesus. We all uns ain't got no cool water for give you when you thirsty....But we gwine to take de 'munion cup and fill it wid de tears of repentance, and love clean out we heart" (quoted in Grant: 213f.).

Much of the history of the doctrine of Christ clearly denies the relevance of Jesus' maleness, uplifting only that Jesus is a human being. Yet, it is in fact the *maleness* of Jesus that has been used by the official church to continue the subordination of women by limiting their roles—most obviously, by denying women ordination to the priesthood or representative ministry. Feminists did not create the problem of Jesus' maleness, the official church did by using it inappropriately as a barrier, as a dividing line against women. Even with the changes in many churches in recent years, there is still a solid wall for the majority of women in the world. Women's secondary status and "natural deficit" is clear in Pope John Paul's latest restatement prohibiting the ordination of women, which said in effect that it is even a matter of "unfaith" even to disagree or discuss it.

"I declare that the church has no authority whatsoever to confer priestly ordination on women, and that this judgment is to be definitively held for all the church's faithful....[Christ] acted in a completely free and sovereign manner" in selecting only men as his apostles—the first priests....Despite an all-male priesthood unbroken across two millennia, "in some places it is nonetheless considered open to debate." No more....The pope's views are not to be regarded as new, or as opinion, or a matter of discipline, "but as certainly true." "Therefore, since it does not belong to matters freely open to dispute, it always requires the full and unconditional assent of the faithful, and to teach the contrary is equivalent to leading consciences into error" (from the apostolic letter and commentary, "On Reserving Priestly Ordination to Men Alone," as it appeared in *The Dallas Morning News*, 5/31/94).

When Jesus' own maleness or the maleness of his apostles is elevated for theological warrant, then empirical facts are being given a false significance. Theologically, in the matter of understanding the redemptive experience of Jesus as the Christ, there is no material significance in Jesus' biological makeup, or in any fact about him in the past. As an event of God, as the eschatological event in every new present, Jesus' sex—or Judaism or race or marital status or any fact of what he said or did in and of himself—is not relevant in confessing him as the Christ.

Nevertheless, even if we acknowledge that Jesus' maleness is theologically irrelevant, we still have a potential problem with the impact of male symbols. In most churches today, the reliance on traditional and historical language and imagery makes it quite difficult to "get around" the maleness issue. The significance of religious symbols and images has been much explored in the work of feminists, particularly as it relates to women's need for those to be more woman-identified in order to be meaningful, to touch the heart and grab the mind, to stimulate feeling and motivate action. This is part of the effort to reclaim the stories of biblical women as part of our heritage and in the worship experience. It points to the move toward imaging God in female terms in thought and worship in order to incorporate the womanness of the Divine One into ourselves. And this recognition of the importance of symbol also comes in creating new stories, new rituals, and new liturgy. This innovation must include the heart of Christian teaching—Jesus is the Christ—which is part of what we are up to in doing Christology, formally and informally.

The Relation of Jesus to "the Christ"

As feminist Christians, while disheartened and discouraged with the church, we find meaning in Christian life important and vital enough to keep pursuing ways to validly understand how Jesus is the Christ for women today. While theologies in the modern era insisted upon demythologizing scripture and tradition, the various theologies of liberation have insisted that scripture and theology be "de-ideologized" as well (i.e. sorting out culturally bound ideology and perspectives, such as anti-Semitism or sanctioning the status of the poor). In parallel, feminist Christians insist upon "de-patriarchalizing" texts and theologies. Indeed, the need to name patriarchy for what it is is perhaps even more crucial for human well-being than was the initial step in the modern era of demythologizing; the cost in human pain, especially women's pain, is so great. Patriarchy is perhaps the most extreme form of "objectifying" thinking, seeing, acting, and being, which existentialist interpretation seeks to overcome. As much as mythological language and various ideologies obscure the possibilities of understanding authentic human existence, so do patriarchal and sexist traditions blur and block woman's (and man's) understanding of her true relationship to God, herself, and all others. Moreover, patriarchy is not merely one ideology alongside others—not even alongside imperialist or class oppression; patriarchy includes an underlying assumption about one-half the human race in a system of domination/subordination that is part of virtually every aspect of life, with its impact cutting across the lines of culture, socioeconomic class, race, nationality, and so on.

Feminist efforts to depatriarchalize Christianity have of course included Christological reinterpretations, although Christology has only fairly recently come to the forefront in feminist theology. After years of attempting to identify the problems, find our voices, and name the pain, we are more able to go about the business of constructing alternatives. And as we already pointed out, there is rich diversity and difference in feminist Christologies.

One model in feminist Christology may be seen, for example, in the work of Ruether, and is in keeping with the revisionary strand that understands Jesus as moral leader or example for humanity. Jesus is part of the prophetic-liberating tradition found in the scriptures, and as "the Christ" is a significant Prophet, a "Liberator" of the poor and oppressed. Jesus' ability to liberate is not to be found in his maleness, "but, on the contrary, in the fact that he has renounced this system of domination and seeks to embody in his person the new humanity of service and mutual empowerment" (Ruether, 1990: 56).

Another prominent Christological model has been offered in the work of feminists such as Elizabeth Johnson and Elisabeth Schüssler

Fiorenza. This type involves what we might call a "sophialogical approach" in which Jesus is interpreted in connection with the Sophia/Wisdom and Logos traditions. Jesus' redemptive action or messianic work is seen as identical to that of Divine Sophia; Jesus is Her messenger, sage and prophet (e.g. Schüssler Fiorenza: 131-163 passim). The model stemming from these sophia traditions are "theologically significant because they assert the unique particularity of Jesus without having to resort to exclusivity and superiority" (157).

A third model in feminist Christology relies on relational images and affords a shift away from the centrality of Jesus himself, on to the community surrounding him. Brock offers a Christology that finds incarnation as the power found in relationship—erotic power, *eros*, love and interdependence. This model seeks to affirm Jesus' particularity in diverse forms as an aspect of God/dess and the world in him. This allows us to acknowledge both how Jesus differs from us and how we ourselves and our world also incarnate God/dess. The Christ—the revelatory and redemptive witness of God/dess' work in history—is "Christa/Community." Christa/Community emerges from, reveals, and recreates erotic power (52-69, passim).

Finally, there is the alternative Christological model out of which I have operated in this chapter. The resolution to the tension in theology created by theologies of self-sacrifice and the emphasis upon empirical facts about Jesus in and of himself can be resolved in an existentialist-feminist perspective. In this perspective, Jesus' liberating significance is understood not in the material aspects of his sacrifice or material aspects of his being or life in the past, but in the basic existential significance for humanity, for *us*. Jesus is "the Christ" insofar as we encounter in the witness about him the reality of God for us and our authentic understanding as human beings. Jesus is the specific, definitive "re-presentation" of God and God's love that is always and already available to all. In this way, we understand the expressions of Jesus as Black Christ, Jesus Christ as Mother, Jesus as Sophia-God, Jesus as "Christa," and any number of conceptions.

Extremely significant—especially for Disciples of Christ—is that the earliest reconstructible witness in the Gospels does not conceive of the redemptive experience in terms of the metaphysical divinity of historical Jesus, as Logos or Sophia or anything else. But please note, nor does the earliest witness convey that this redemptive experience depends upon any factual details of what Jesus said and did and understood as a human being, not even his relations with others.

To talk about the existential significance of Jesus is what we are doing when we confess that Jesus is "the Christ." It is to understand Jesus (or the witness, spoken or acted toward others, about him) as the decisive re-presentation of the meaning of ultimate reality for us, of *God* for us. And that means discovering in that witness the answer to life's deepest questions—the ones we referred to at the beginning of this chapter: *Who am I? Who is God? Who am I in relation to God and to all others?* It is the unlimited love that calls forth love. According to the New Testament, to experience this love, to respond in faith, is always faith enacted in love. And in our day, faith enacted in works of love means seeking justice. And seeking justice, in turn means nothing less than the liberating praxis required by a feminist theology. This liberating praxis is individual, social, and political, requiring all our contemporary knowledge and resources. It is transformation of church and world.

Many believe we are in a new "Reformation" and, as the bloody battles of the sixteenth and seventeenth centuries showed, that is always a difficult path. We are often weary. We sometimes feel impatient, sad, hurting. But we are uplifted by the love of God experienced in the community of faith. And we will continue to bear living and loving, justice-seeking witness to the world, in the name of the Christ.

Works Consulted

Arendt, Hannah. 1958. *The Human Condition*. Chicago and London: University of Chicago Press.

Aulen, Gustaf. (1960 ed.). *Christus Victor: An Historical Study of the Three Main Types of the Idea of Atonement*. Trans. A. G. Hebert. New York: Macmillan.

Brock, Rita Nakashima. 1991. *Journeys by Heart: A Christology of Erotic Power*. New York: Crossroad.

Brown, Joanne Carlson, and Rebecca Parker. 1989. "For God So Loved the World?" In *Christianity, Patriarchy, and Abuse: A Feminist Critique*, ed. Joanne Carlson Brown and Carole R. Bohn. New York: Pilgrim Press. 1–30.

Bultmann, Rudolf. 1934 and 1958. *Jesus and the Word*. New York: Charles Scribner's Sons.

—. 1958. *Jesus Christ and Mythology*. New York: Charles Scribner's Sons.

Cannon, Katie G. 1985. "The Emergence of a Black Feminist Consciousness." In *Feminist Interpretations of the Bible*, ed. by L. Russell. Philadelphia: Westminster. 30–40.

Carmody, Denise Lardner. 1982. *Feminism and Christianity: A Two-Way Reflection*. Lanham, MD: University Press of America/Abingdon.

Carr, Anne E. 1988. *Transforming Grace: Women's Tradition and Experience*. San Francisco: Harper & Row.

Case-Winters, Anna. 1990. *God's Power: Traditional Understanding and Contemporary Challenges*. Louisville: Westminster/John Knox Press.

Chopp, Rebecca S. 1989. *The Power to Speak: Feminism, Language, God.* New York: Crossroad.

Chung, Hyun Kyung. 1990. "Who Is Jesus for Asian Women?" In *Struggling to Be the Sun Again,* by Chung. Maryknoll: Orbis. 55–73.

Davaney, Sheila Greeve. 1987. "The Limits of the Appeal to Women's Experience." In *Shaping New Vision: Gender and Values in American Culture,* ed. by Clarissa Atkinson, Constance Buchanan, and Margaret Miles. Harvard Women's Studies in Religion Series. Ann Arbor: UMI Research Press.

Fabella, Virginia and Mercy Ambab Oduyoye, eds. 1988. *With Passion and Compassion: Third World Women Doing Theology.* Maryknoll, NY: Orbis.

Farley, Margaret A. 1984. "Feminist Consciousness and the Interpretation of Scripture." In *Feminist Interpretation of the Bible,* ed. by Letty M. Russell, Philadelphia: Westminster. 41–54.

Fulkerson, Mary McClintock. 1994. *Changing the Subject: Women's Discourses and Feminist Theology.* Minneapolis: Augsburg Fortress.

Grant, Jacquelyn. 1989. *White Women's Christ and Black Women's Jesus: Feminist Christology and Womanist Response.* Atlanta: Scholars Press.

Hampson, Daphne. 1990. *Theology and Feminism.* Oxford: Basil Blackwell.

—, and Rosemary Radford Ruether. 1986. "Is There a Place for Feminists in a Christian Church?" From the Catholic Women's Network and Women in Theology conference, London.

Hartshorne, Charles. 1948. *Divine Relativity: A Social Conception of God.* New Haven: Yale University Press.

—. 1984. *Omnipotence and Other Theological Mistakes.* Albany: SUNY.

Heyward, Carter. 1989. *Speaking of Christ: A Lesbian Feminist Voice.* Ed. Ellen Davis. New York, Pilgrim Press.

Johnson, Elizabeth A. 1992a. *Consider Jesus: Waves of Renewal in Christology.* New York: Crossroad.

—. 1992b. *She Who Is: The Mystery of God in Feminist Theological Discourse.* New York: Crossroad.

Kant, Immanuel. "What Is Enlightenment?" trans. Peter Gay, in *Introduction to Contemporary Civilization in the West* (1954), I. 1071–76.

Lerner, Gerda. 1986. *The Creation of Patriarchy.* Oxford: Oxford University Press.

McFague, Sallie. 1993. *The Body of God: An Ecological Theology.* Minneapolis: Augsburg Fortress.

Norris, Richard A., Jr. 1976. "The Ordination of Women and the 'Maleness' of Christ." *Anglican Theological Review,* Supp. Series, 6: 69–80.

—. 1980. *The Christological Controversy.* Philadelphia: Fortress.

Ogden, Schubert M. 1961. *Christ Without Myth.* New York: Harper.

—. 1979. *Faith and Freedom: Toward a Theology of Liberation.* Nashville: Abingdon.

—. 1982. *The Point of Christology.* New York: Harper.

Pelikan, Jaroslav. 1985. *Jesus Through the Centuries: His Place in the History of Culture.* New Haven: Yale University Press.

Plaskow, Judith. 1980. *Sex, Sin and Grace: Women's Experience and the Theologies of Reinhold Niebuhr and Paul Tillich.* Washington, D.C.: University Press of America.

Ruether, Rosemary Radford. 1990. *To Change the World: Christology and Cultural Criticism.* New York: Crossroad.

Russell, Letty M., ed. 1985. *Feminist Interpretation of the Bible.* Philadelphia: Westminster.

Saiving, Valerie. 1960. "The Human Situation: A Feminine View." *Journal of Religion* 40: 100–112.

Schleiermacher, Friedreich. (1963 ed.) *The Christian Faith.* Ed. H.R. Mackintosh and J.S. Stewart. New York: Harper. *(Der christliche Glaube,* 1821–1822.)

Schüssler Fiorenza, Elisabeth. 1994. *Jesus. Miriam's Child, Sophia's Prophet: Critical Issues in Feminist Christology.* New York: Continuum.

Schweitzer, Albert. (1962 ed.) *The Quest of the Historical Jesus.* New York: Macmillan. (Trans. by W. Montgomery from the 1st German ed., 1906.)

Soelle, Dorothee. 1974. *Political Theology.* Trans. John Shelley. Philadelphia: Fortress.

Stevens, Maryanne, ed. 1994. *Reconstructing the Christ Symbol: Essays in Feminist Christology.* New York: Paulist.

Thistlethwaite, Susan and Mary Potter Engel, eds. 1990. *Lift Every Voice: Constructing Christian Theologies from the Underside.* San Francisco: Harper.

Tillich, Paul. 1957. *Systematic Theology, II: Existence and the Christ.* Chicago: University of Chicago Press.

Tong, Rosemarie. 1989. "Existentialist Feminism." In *Feminist Thought: A Comprehensive Introduction,* by R.Tong. Boulder/San Francisco: Westview Press. 195–214.

Williams, Delores S. 1989. "Womanist Theology: Black Women's Voices." In *Weaving the Visions: New Patterns in Feminist Spirituality,* ed. by Judith Plaskow and Carol Christ. San Francisco: Harper. 179–186.

Young, Pamela Dickey. 1990. *Feminist Theology/Christian Theology: A Search for Method.* Minneapolis: Augsburg Fortress.

—. 1992. "Diversity in Feminist Christology." *Studies in Religion/Sciences Religieuses,* 21/1: 81–90.

7

The Greening of the Soul

A Feminist Theological Paradigm of the Web of Life

Rita Nakashima Brock

Introduction

A pastor once reported that when his congregation introduced inclusive language into its worship services—for many of the reasons discussed in Jane McAvoy's essay—one of those most resistant to changing language about God was a feminist elder of his congregation, whom I will call Mary. When asked her reasons for resisting, she gave vague replies about not tampering with tradition, even though it had been demonstrated to her that female images for God were found in the tradition and the Bible. He was surprised at her resistance. Eventually, she confessed that she believed God *had* to be male because no mother would do to her son what God did to Jesus. Mary knew it was not a very sophisticated reason, but her gut feeling was that something was wrong with the idea of a loving parent who had the power to save a child and did not, or who sent the child to suffer. The idea of such a God offended her deeply.

A quick glance through the theologies of the tradition have made not a few feminists allergic to, if not downright appalled by androcentric definitions of God, human nature, salvation, and love. What we have been told to believe often does not reflect the needs and life experiences of many women. But we have not been satisfied to see ourselves simply as victims of theology. We have sought instead to create women-centered, as well as inclusive, theologies.

What sorts of theology might emerge if a variety of women wrote it out of our experiences of life and of God? Fortunately, we have examples, both from the past and from current work in feminist/womanist/mujerista theologies. Listen to Hildegard of Bingen, an eleventh-century abbess, scholar, and mystical visionary.

> Glance at the sun. See the moon and stars. Gaze at the beauty of earth's greenings. Now, think. What delight God gives to humankind with all these things.
>
> There is no creation that does not have a radiance. Be it greenness or seed, blossom or beauty. It could not be creation without it.
>
> God says: I am the supreme fire; not deadly, but rather, enkindling every spark of life. I am the breeze that nurtures all things green. I call forth tears, the aroma of holy work. I am the yearning for good.
>
> Good People, most royal greening verdancy, rooted in the sun, you shine so finely, it surpasses understanding. You are encircled by the arms of the mystery of God. And so, humankind full of all creative possibilities, is God's work. Humankind alone, is called to assist God.
>
> The first seed of the longing for Justice blows through the soul like the wind. The taste for good will plays in it like a breeze. The consummation of this seed is a greening in the soul that is like that of the ripening world. Now the soul honors God by the doing of just deeds. The soul is only as strong as its works. (Uhlen: 26, 31, 45, 90, 106, and 123)

Hildegard seems startlingly well grounded in the beauty, generosity, and power of earthly creation. She regards human life positively, as good. Yet, only recently has Christian theology begun creating ideas that highlight this concept of "greening," of respect for God's creation of the natural world and its goodness. For example, the World Council of Churches' call to affirm the goodness and integrity of creation came in the 1980s, a time when eco-feminism became strong. Until that decade, much contemporary theology was influenced by the development of Enlightenment science, with its ideas about rationality, objectivity, and human progress. Hence, theologians had done little reflection on and promotion of life-sustaining relationships with the natural world because it was seen as a machine, like a clock, that could be worked on, manipulated, and controlled for human progress. And, like nature with which we were associated, women were relegated to an inferior status. In addition, the mid-twentieth-century revival of Reformed Protestant theology in the neoorthodox movement emphatically split revelation from nature (partly as a response to the Nazi use of genetics and "nature") and was deeply suspicious of any theology that emphasized the immanence of God or that was called "natural." Yet, a woman's voice from the eleventh century speaks of a deep love and respect for creation, as well as for humankind as part of that creation and as caretakers of love and justice. I find in her voice an echo of my own deep love for nature, in its beauty and its sometimes frightening power, and a basic sense that human life is a gift and rare opportunity. Such values are of bedrock importance in East Asian cultures and reflect the first six years of my life in a Japanese family in Japan and Okinawa. These values are found in many non-European cultures and are also profoundly biblical, as Hildegard knew.

If we begin with Hildegard's fundamental affirmation of life as a blessing and of the responsibility given to us to nurture and protect it, where might our theological musings lead us? In the following paradigm of feminist theology, I suggest one direction our musings might lead, if the starting point of our theology is this "greening," this affirmation of the web of life, the verdancy created by God. To begin with creation and human participation in creativity means we begin not with the fall or doctrines of sin, but with interconnected life—with the goodness of living and our responsibility for loving care. This hearkening back to Hildegard is an important reminder to Protestant women of our legacy from Catholic women in our tradition, a legacy that continues today in Catholic feminist theologians such as Rosemary Radford Ruether, Elisabeth Schüssler Fiorenza, and Elizabeth Johnson, who continue to bring much to the feminist theological table.

While the exact ideas below are mine and no one else's, many of their themes, images, and issues reflect a movement within feminist theology away from traditional fall/redemption or sin/salvation theologies. These traditional, atonement-based theologies focus on the fall or sin and our need to be saved from sin. They begin with a negative assessment of human nature as the central point for theological systems. The central focus of my theology is the affirmation of creation as good, the beginning point of the Bible, given to us in the first story of creation.

This deep intuition that creation (the natural world) is good and that human beings are not born sinful may come more easily to women who feel a responsibility and commitment to nurturing life and caring for families. Women with such responsibilities often find ourselves affirming life as we are immersed in daily life-giving tasks: fixing dinner for a family, wiping the fevered brow of a son, washing the old frail body of a grandmother, holding a weeping friend, making love to our life-partner, or teaching words to a toddler. We respect especially the life-giving survival skills that women have developed while living under adverse circumstances such as slavery, poverty, racism, and domestic violence. The appreciation for the natural world also runs deeply in the history of women in the U.S. The diaries of nineteenth-century women crossing the prairies of the Western frontier, despite the hardships and dangers of travel, mention the beauty of the natural environment more often than any other subject. They were awestruck at the sight of so much natural splendor.

Many feminist/womanist/mujerista theologians share these beginning life-affirming premises, which move us to ache for justice and liberation for all the suffering people of the world and to work for more whole relationships to each other and to the earth, which we depend on for life and which gives us so much beauty. While I am focusing on North American theologies, these new women's theologies also point us toward the suffering of the Two-Thirds World, especially our sisters there, and to the poor in our midst as we struggle to create a just and safe world for all.

The theological picture of the web of life described below will, I hope, provide a framework for understanding how theology might work from some women's perspectives and prompt readers to explore other models. To illustrate how this web works in a new way, the second part of this chapter uses the framework to reflect on how we might understand our relationship to God in the image of the birther of creation. As one way of experiencing God's creativity and care, I propose we examine the image of God as Mother.

A Feminist Theology: The Web of Life

Visualize the theology below as a great, intricate web. The power that creates and repairs it is the love of God. "God is love" is the central affirmation of Christian faith without which divine grace and creativity cannot be understood. We affirm that God creates the world out of this love, just as human life is conceived and nurtured in loving relationship when we live at our best. Without love's power, nothing could exist. Without the web, the weaver has no embodied self-expression, no incarnate manifestation of beauty and shimmering energy. In other words, God loves and needs the work of creating. The world and we are the complex weavings of divine love, found in our works of caring in the world. We need each other to be able to express love fully, and the fullness of God's love is made incarnate in our daily living.

The Web's Central Knot: The Goodness of Creation

The first strands of the web are interlocked into the central knot through which the whole takes shape and is bound together. These fundamental, core strands weave together the goodness and integrity of creation. The love of God is described as *Ruah*, the hovering Breath or Spirit of God in Genesis 1 that creates the world from the waters of the deep. She (*Ruah* is a feminine noun in Hebrew) breathes life into matter, creates the rhythms of time, and quickens the many beings, animate and inanimate. The first principles of this creating are love, beauty, and joy, which are the spiritual core of life and the sources of blessings. This Spirit of creating is later identified as the *wisdom* of God (*Sophia* in Greek and *Hokmah* in Hebrew), who exists at the first moment of creation (Proverbs 8:22–31).

Humankind is inspired by that divine Spirit. We are made in the divine image, female and male as equals, not as opposites, but as beings of like spirit, called by Wisdom to be wise and loving. We are the helpmates of God for creativity and for caring. Through our connection to creating, we find Hildegard's greening of our souls.

If we live, as many Americans do, in suburban and urban dwellings, we are often lulled into a false sense of independence and separation from the natural world. Yet our theological and biblical heritages insist that we are bound to this creation by the very substance of our bodies, by air, water, and sunlight. We live, irrevocably interdependent with the physical universe. Our physical body depends on the environment around us. We are, as Genesis reminds us, made of the earth, of humus, from which we take the word humble. Through care of this earthly body we sustain the dwelling place of God's love and receive the love of others.

Everything that exists, the Bible proclaims, is created by God—even, as the character Shug in *The Color Purple* reminds us, things and people we don't like. When the Bible says all creation is good, it is not speaking of good in a moral sense. There is much violence and struggle in life, so we use "good" to mean that everything that exists is valuable because it exists as part of God's creating. Christians often focus on light, mind, and eternity. We forget that darkness, flesh, and the changing cycles of time are also gifts of life, that light cannot exist without darkness, love without flesh, or beginnings without endings. The delicate balance of the forces of life, not the overwhelming presence of one aspect, gives life a sense of struggle worth the effort, of harmony achieved by the balance of conflicting forces, of wholeness made from healing brokenness, and of creativity born of sweat and work. This sense of creative wholeness, even in the midst of pain and brokenness, reminds us that creation is good and beautiful in its own ways, even when these ways may be mysterious to us.

When we get too focused on light and on a one-sided view of things, we tend to view death as a problem. Yet to be physically alive means to live one's life from the death of living things. As a part of the activity of the world and the rhythms of life, physical death is part of life. Our difficulties with death lie in the thoughtless taking of life and in loneliness and the often painful suffering that accompanies dying. Elderly people abandoned to die alone on our city streets or under the cold, impersonal tools of technology are a judgment about our inability to maintain humane ways of living and dying, not a judgment about death itself. Death is often painful and tragic, but the reality of death is not separate from life and its ongoing, creative process, a process that transcends personal death. Death can come as deliverance from incurable suffering, just as it can feel like the appropriate ending of a long, well-lived life that has finally reached its completion and reward. The tragedy of death is to die alone, unloved, unremembered, without a legacy and without people who care. The evil of death comes from the loss of balance, when violence and poverty inflict death out of time. We balance the sorrow and losses of death and counter its tragedy by our acts of loving and of creativity and out of our work for justice, which show the constant, regenerative work of God's Spirit in our lives and our faithful response.

The Radiating Strands: Affirmation as Response

The strands of the web that radiate from its center sustain our response toward life. Our faithful response to life is gratitude for God's grace and generosity, and with gratitude comes the call to live by grace and generosity toward all that is. And generosity translates into an attitude of affirmation toward the diverse and complex lives given to us. We are invited to celebrate God's gift of love to us and of us to each other, a love that casts out fear. In loving fearlessly, we embrace the vast diversities of life. Because the many creatures who live on this earth are evidence of the creating and loving Spirit, we are called to be open to life and to be generous toward even that which we neither understand nor control.

We are called to receive the offering of creation with open hearts and minds and to approach life not in fear or bigotry, but with affirmation, in truthfulness and in respectfulness. Through such openness "radiance is uncovered," and our "greening lives" illumine the meaning of our faith. If we think about how love works in our lives, we know that our transformation comes through the presence of others. Life-renewing joy comes when another is fully open and present to us, when we are trusted enough for others to be their honest selves with us. Through such openness we are able to be transformed by our love for another, which is also why the absence of such love is so painful to us. In knowing such wondrous transformation, we learn the many ways human beings find to love each other. We make such love manifest when we take the risks to be open and trust, when we refuse to be hidden, closed, and hostile.

To live in gracious openness toward others allows us to affirm the differences and diversities among us, which in turn enhances our creativity and capacities to care. Because we know we are loved by God, we are empowered to expect grace and generosity from others. That love helps us detect and withstand disrespect and hate from those who wish us harm. However, living graciously and generously is neither easy nor uncomplicated. The mystery of life often stretches the limits of what we know, and if we are unable to trust ourselves, to know we can rely on our own capacities for renewal and resiliency, we will be unable to open our arms to the world. New experiences unsettle the safety and security of our conventional attitudes, as the prophet Jonah's reaction reminds us when he cannot accept God's forgiveness of the Ninevites.

Cherished habits of thought and behavior are challenged when we are confronted with realities that we have not been prepared to understand. For example, when I left for college in 1968, I naively assumed all human beings were heterosexual. I did not know what the word homosexual meant. That fall, when a good friend of mine, Jerome, revealed that he was gay, I had to ask him to explain what that meant. The whole idea sounded a little strange to me. It had never occurred to me that people could love others of the same sex intimately. But I knew Jerome was a good, caring person. I struggled with my own assumptions and decided that, if love was the evidence of God's spirit in the world, it should not be limited by my imagination.

In the intervening years, I have had to engage in the painful process of examining my heterosexist view of the world because persons who did not fit that view were invisible to me. My own journey away from heterosexism is like many of my straight friends whose children, parents, and/or friends have come out to them as lesbian, gay, or bisexual. In that journey, I have learned to think more discerningly, honestly, responsibly, and carefully about my own sexuality. I have discovered a whole new world of loving friends who are patient with my biases and who care deeply about making justice for all people. I have been taught by gay, lesbian, and bisexual friends what mutual love between equals can be and to expect such love in intimate relationships. Learning to love fearlessly is a lifelong process and, finally, a rewarding one.

Struggling with my heterosexism brought me back to the Genesis text of the creation of humankind, where I had always been taught to see the creation of opposites, male and female. But as I looked at it more carefully, I saw that it speaks deeply of sameness in the midst of diversity, of how we are created *humankind*, the same spirit in God's image, even when we are different. Could it be that the focus on opposites (not individual uniqueness and cultural differences, but opposites) lies at the roots of both the subordination of women as a group and of homophobia? I have increasingly come to think so. Our tendency to set up opposites teaches us to think in terms of conflict and to fear differences in others because their unlikeness threatens our identity—as if knowing who we are requires us to set up fences around ourselves. We are led to believe that if loving them makes us too like them, our loving takes something away from us, rather than enlarging us, which may be one reason why intimate relationships between male and female are often viewed hierarchically and are charged with power struggles.

Theological visions that emphasize grace and generosity, rather than encouraging us to think in opposites, offer the church "include everyone" theologies. They invite us into positive visions of differences and diversity. They show us how embracing differences can expand the capacities of faith to be healing and to nurture life. Our affirmation of the differences among us opens doors to new insights and ideas that emerge from those who have suffered deeply from oppression and dominating powers. The complexity of the world and of human beings is bewildering and fascinating. In that complexity is the creativity of God, acts of creating we cannot fathom—a mystery of endless new life and a continuing challenge to our ability to love and to understand the incarnation of God in this world. Through that mystery, I believe we are constantly renewed and made alive through our experiences of loving. In being open and affirming, we embody our belief in God's generous grace. When we live in openness, affirmation, and self-respect, we are truly free to love and live without fear. But loving fearlessly also requires careful discernment about the sources of our pain, which leads us to another set of strands.

The Interweaving Strands: Healing and Liberation

The strands that weave the cross patterns in the web and intersect with the radiating strands are healing and liberation. They give strength to the web to withstand both the everyday sorrows and struggles from death and pain, which show us our human limits, and the powers of willful destruction in the world, which are strong. Withstanding deliberately inflicted violence especially requires courage, vision, and a supportive community. The powers of the world that willfully prevent or destroy the fullness of creation must be named and exorcised, for they are legion. Evil is not simply the absence of good, but the active presence of hatred, fear, abuse, and destruction. The Bible uses the image of the casting out of demons to signify liberation, an appropriate metaphor to depict how forces— demons—of destruction can permeate our psyches deeply.

When the demons possess us we are overcome with feelings of powerlessness, and personal healing is crucial to the return of our selves and our powers to care. For example, we know from recent research by psychologists such as Judith Herman that when children are severely abused, especially sexually, they develop important survival mechanisms that disconnect parts of their memory or personalities from conscious knowledge, a process also found often in victims of torture. A person with multiple personality disorder is helpless to know or control all the personalities she or he uses to cope with the evil that has afflicted her/him. And many people are haunted by fears or self-destructive behaviors they cannot locate in any conscious memory of their past. For those so afflicted, healing begins with the return of memory, with safe places to remember, and with the support of those who are not afraid of the suffering of those they love.

Our works to heal each other are the means by which God's love is affirmed and restored to a suffering world, a world often afflicted by pain that we cannot prevent and that comes from injury and injustice. The limits of our human ability to control our lives often become vivid to us in the face of the impersonal fury of hurricanes, floods, earthquakes, hailstorms, tornadoes, and fires. When we know the injury inflicted is deliberately caused, we often feel outrage and fury, which, along with the pain of our injury, may also eventually be healed when *kairos*—when the ripe moment—comes. We struggle to heal together because it gives us hope in the midst of pain and tragedy, which constantly eat away at our capacities to care. Our works for healing open doors for grace and generosity to return.

For the fullness of God's creation to be made manifest—for the greening and ripening of creating—all beings must be provided a chance to fulfill their potential to create, to celebrate, and to care. For our lives to be lived at their fullest, human beings require a just, peaceful, and whole world, and a safe, healthy environment. For this, we work and hope in the face of despair and destruction. As the prophet Micah reminds us, we are to do justice, to love mercy, and to be humble when God walks with us. We commit ourselves to healing and liberation because we know the brokenness of human life and its injustices. We are called by God to commit ourselves because we know that through healing and liberation we are led to know grace and generosity. As Hildegard reminds us, "the soul honors God by the doing of just deeds. The soul is only as strong as its works." The works of love and justice that we leave behind are the measure of what we have done with the gift of life bestowed on us.

Our commitments to healing and liberation require risk because the love and trust required to love fearlessly opens us to injury. To remain open and to receive the world's gifts requires us to maintain a capacity for vulnerability, and the tragedies and limits of human life can weaken our trust so that we move from love toward fear and withdrawal. Our vulnerability means we are not completely immune to the forces of evil. Research on human beings under conditions of extreme abuse, torture, imprisonment, and war has taught us that virtually all of us have a breaking point, a point at which we succumb to evil. For those brought to such a breaking point, death can come as mercy and relief; for evil is not simply death per se, but is rather the consequence of misused power and unjust death. Evil is created by powers that cause violence, that create unnecessary suffering and death, and that seek control as an ultimate value; evil is to refuse to help another in pain, to create hatred of others, or to exploit another's vulnerability. Evil is to foster contempt for life, to live by deceit, to choose despair, to separate people from relationships of love and care, and to live by supporting or benefitting from unjust systems while doing nothing to change them. Sometimes, in fact, evil comes from within ourselves because we reproduce our own history of being abused by hurting ourselves or others, we succumb to despair, or we simply fail to help when we should. Wherever we encounter the forces of control, of violence, domination, exploitation, oppression, passive despair, and abuse, we must do what we can to restore the goodness of creating.

To commit ourselves to the work of God's love and justice means taking enormous risks in order to keep healing and liberation alive in the world. We must be aware that the forces of oppression, hate, and violence are strong and canny. They are organized to resist relinquishing their power. In our communities of struggle, we must remain ever alert, open, and careful because sources of evil may not come simply from an external enemy. They may also come from within our communities, from our families, or from within ourselves. We require courage—strength of heart—to challenge evil, even as we remain suspicious of our most self-righteous polemics and defensive postures. Courage enables us to cherish our anger at injustice at the same time we are attuned to the opportunities to heal the pain that lies below anger.

The Christian tendency to focus too narrowly on personal sin and redemption often blinds us to the evil found in organized systems that misuse power to control and destroy. We forget that the greatest forces in our lives, from birth to death, are social forces because love, a social reality, is essential to our survival. Personal sin can pale by comparison to the political and economic forces of injustice in our world that destroy people and relationships. And often, personal behavior is closely tied to the power of such systems. Those forces crush God's creating. In the face of those forces, we are called to work for liberation.

An example of such devastation happened in Argentina in the 1970s when the new military government "disappeared" citizens. Thousands of idealistic young adults, who worked with the poor or were critical of the government's policies, were kidnapped and murdered. Pregnant women were forced to deliver, then killed, and their babies given away to military families and their friends. Many parents and grandparents, ignored by the government, felt desperate and powerless when they tried to get information about their children. But a group of women refused to be intimidated. They started a weekly demonstration in front of government buildings in the capital. They were called the Mothers of the Plaza Del Mayo. By the time the government began to notice the activity of this group of "crazy old women," the world press knew of them and the human rights violations they protested. It became impossible to disappear them all without other governments noticing. When the reign of terror ended, the bones of thousands of tortured and murdered women, men, and youth were found around the country. The Mothers had become a symbol of the conscience of the country, and their activism in solidarity with writers and other activists helped to bring down the government. (To this social role of mothers we will turn in the last section of this chapter.) There are now Mothers groups in many countries in the world where governments torture and kill citizens.

For their sake, for the sake of all the world's mothers, for the sake of all those who suffer now, for the sake of our bruised and poisoned creation, and for the sake of our own desire to live in God's grace and generosity, we are invited by the gospel—by the ever-abundant love of God—to commit our lives to the work of healing and liberation. In our commitment, we must, however, be aware of the ways we benefit from structures of injustice in our own lives. We must seek to make right what we can at the same time we work to heal ourselves. We make right what we can, not because we are to blame or are guilty, but because we commit our heart, mind, soul, and strength to the work of God, to the renewal of God's spirit in our lives. Out of the empowerment of that spirit and of our love, we remain attuned to the suffering of others and to the terrible consequences of injustice. Where we can make a difference, we are called to do so, even when it means an uncomfortable examination of our own lives, our attitudes, our behavior toward others, our lifestyle, and our personal goals. We often miss the mark because of the limits of our lives. However, we continue because we know we are loved, and we seek to increase the work of God's love in the world. And through our just deeds we find the greening of our souls and the renewal of life on earth.

The Web's Anchor: Covenant

The gossamer and resilient web of life—creation/incarnation, grace/generosity, and healing/liberation—are anchored to the covenant we make with God as the source of life and our community. As human beings and as Christians, we cannot live a creative, gracious, liberating life without a commitment to each other, to our communities, to our history as a religious people (as complex and ambiguous as that is), and to God. We do not commit to a particular creed, a particular statement of faith or formula, to a book, or to a human authority, but to covenant, to relationships—to God and to each other as the body of the risen Christ, the embodied Holy Spirit, which has made us one in our baptism. There is no more powerful or important embodiment of that commitment than the communion table. At that table, the creative love of God joins the elements of nourishment and joy, produced by the earth, with our human lives. The suffering of the world is brought to the table to be embraced by a vision of justice and openness that empowers our hopes for its fulfillment. This incarnational vision affirms the body of Christ as the people of God in brokenness and in resurrection. At the table, we recommit ourselves to loving each other, to remembering our ambiguous and hopeful history, and to working for the healing and liberation of ourselves and those to come.

If we affirm the web of life and images of God as nurturing life, the communion table, where we celebrate the covenant that anchors us, may move us beyond betrayal and sacrifice. The Table may call our attention instead to covenant and the life of Jesus, who worked for healing and justice, as well as to remembrance of his very real death. If the words of institution and invitation to the table were to affirm the kind of theology sketched out above, they might say something like the following:[1]

> We remember that on the evening before Jesus was killed by those who feared him and his ministry, he sat at table with his friends, women, men, and children. They shared in the meal of the Passover, which celebrates the liberation of God's people from slavery. Remembering the brokenness of lives destroyed by the principalities and powers and the risks he took in challenging those powers, Jesus took bread, broke it, and passed it to his friends saying, "This is my body broken for justice, a sign of our work together to make whole a broken world, our body of struggle. Take it all of you and eat. Whenever you break bread together, please remember me."
>
> After dinner, Jesus took a cup of wine and passed it to them, as it is passed to us saying, "This is my life with you and our hope for a renewed creation of healing and love. This cup is for all. In partaking, we affirm our love for each other and our hope for peace and the liberation and healing of God's people throughout the world. Drink it all of you and do this remembering me."
>
> Each time we celebrate this meal together, taking the bread and the cup, we remember the life of Jesus and the lives of all who have risked much for God's love and creation. In taking this meal together, we participate in the Body of the Risen Christ, in the hopes of the cloud of witnesses who have gone before us, and in the hopes of this Community. As we partake, we re-create the Body of the Risen Christ in our work together for Shalom—for justice, healing, and peace.
>
> This is the table of God set for all the people of God. We share an inclusive communion, which means you do not have to be a member of this or any faith community to join us at the table. We believe that Christ sets this table and with Christ we welcome everyone. Come, for the table is ready.

In our words at the table, we affirm that our fragile and strong web remains solidly anchored in its life with God. As it is torn and rewoven, it is continually made new by God's love, which, as its center, radiates outward to all creation.

---

[1] This version is paraphrased from worship at Spirit of the Lakes UCC, Minneapolis, Minnesota. The liturgist for the day develops words of remembrance similar to these, which are adapted as new theological insights are learned by the pastor and congregation.

Christ Our Mother, God Our Mother

In thinking about the image of God who weaves the web of life, I want to return for a moment to the story I told at the beginning about Mary and her difficulty with changing God language. At an important theological level, her doubts point to the question of how nurturing love relates to power and responsibility. She insisted that God had to be male not because Jesus calls God Father, which he does sometimes, as well as other titles. Rather, Mary thought of God as male because of the doctrine that God's plan for salvation requires Jesus to die for human sin. Many in the Christian tradition cling to the image of God as Father based on the kind of ruling power and authority a male image conveys—not an image of nurturing comfort and care. The image of father has traditionally been related to punishment, judgment, obedience, and controlling power, especially as such power judges sin. The Christian tradition has assumed, following Paul, that obedience is the right relationship of Christians to the Father because it has accepted the idea of our inherent sinfulness. In relating to human fathers, as we are supposed to relate to God, children are traditionally expected to obey paternal authority, rather than to listen to their own feelings, bodies, and needs—a process that often makes children unable to recognize when they are being hurt.

Children, we are taught, are supposed to be controlled by the superior will of adult authority, which is often how traditional fathers are depicted as dispensers of discipline. That kind of relationship has been extended to describe Jesus as subject to the will of his Father. This protection of authority creates a power system whereby any action by an authority is deemed right and, if children are disobedient, they deserve their abuse, i.e. the disobedient deserve to suffer. If we isolate God in a special category, as the only reliably good authority we obey, the authoritarian structure of obedience and punishment still remains and is used as a model, by Paul and the tradition, of how we are to relate also to human authorities. We are told that the divine father is good and loving, which is one of the images conveyed by Jesus' use of *Father*. Yet we are also told that this same loving father sent his son to be killed and the innocent, obedient son went without complaint. This union of love and violence is the false trap for women and children created by battering relationships in which, for centuries, the church preached acquiescence to abuse and forgiveness of perpetrators without accountability. Patriarchal fatherhood and the hierarchical family are extensions of this theological set of images. Jesus, depicted as an innocent lamb taken to slaughter for us, reinforces the idea that abuse is all right for a good reason. Structures of oppression and violence become acceptable, if they serve a good purpose.

If divine child abuse, to save humanity, is acceptable, and human parents are to obey the example set by the Father, then violence against children and women can be justified on the same grounds, as has been the case in the Christian tradition. Images of God the creator become distant and abstract as they are linked to judgment, distant and remote like the traditional meaning of the term "fathering a child." The emphasis on the punitive, judging aspects of God belie the generosity and freely given nature of divine grace, the goodness of creation and humankind, and the hovering, intimate presence of the Spirit. Both Philip Greven and Nel Noddings have challenged the ethical assumptions of theological claims about divine punishment, which rests on the idea of human sinfulness. Abuse and the demand for blind obedience to authority snap the strands of the web of life.

In moving to an image of God as Mother, I hope we do not fall into the tendency to idealize mothers or to universalize the image. Not all mothers are good and, for some people, the image of mother is as problematic as father is for others. I would like us to play with the image of God as Mother, to explore what good mothering might tell us about nurturing love and what the virtues required of mothering may suggest to us about alternative ways to think about our relationship to God. We may, through such exploration of human experiences, find new ways to discern what a faithful life requires of us.

To move in a different direction does not mean we must assert that human beings are always good. Rather, we are faced with the ambiguities of human life. Parent-child relationships are ambiguous because children are not always good, but parents, who have greater power, have greater responsibility to be ethical. And to be ethical requires self-knowledge and self-reflective honesty, as Sara Ruddick insists in her work on maternal thinking. Children can provoke intense frustration and anger, and parental feelings about children involve a great deal of ambiguity, but the unrestrained expression of parental anger and abuse should not be blamed on children, even when they act unreasonably. At issue is not the guilt or innocence of children. Children of even a very young age are capable of making demands that are often quite difficult for adults to meet, even in societies that support and respect mothering. Infants are capable of provoking highly ambiguous feelings in their caretakers, including those who love them deeply.

Instead of focusing on the nature or state of children or victims, I propose we explore the ethics, behaviors, and responsibilities of authority and power as a way to explore how we relate to God. We must ask how commitments to love can be held even under the most

trying of circumstances and within the experience of the most conflicting feelings. Love requires us to prevent abuse, not inflict it. Appropriate uses of greater power and authority include preserving
through love, fostering growth, and teaching conscience. The work
of power is to create greater respect and empowerment, so that power
can be shared and equalized as much as possible. The goal is to enable friendship, not obedience.

If we are to honor love, then we must recognize the integrity and
self-respect of the other, especially of those with less power, just as
our embracing of the web of life includes the lives of those not like
ourselves, who may trouble or puzzle us. To honor the capacity for
profound love and openness in children, we must nurture self-respect so that a child gains the knowledge and self-confidence that
enables her/him to assert her/his will in the world, sometimes in
opposition to a parent's desires. Ruddick describes the ambiguous
irony of parenting that is trustworthy so that a healthy suspicion of
authority is encouraged.

> If, when their mothers fail them, as they inevitably do, children
> deny their hurt and rage so that they can continue "trusting,"
> they are in effect giving up on their mother. By contrast when
> they recognize and protest betrayal, they reaffirm their expecta-
> tion that their mother has been and can again become worthy of
> their trust....Proper trust is one of the most difficult maternal
> virtues. It requires of a mother clear judgment that does not give
> way to obedience or denial. It depends on her being reliably
> good willed and independent yet able to express and to accept
> from her children righteous indignation at trust betrayed.
> (Ruddick: 118f.)

Such willfulness is nurtured, not by attempting to maintain obedience in children or to control them, but by encouraging them to
gain greater knowledge of good and evil in themselves and others,
including their own parents, and by parents supporting the right of
their children to be disobedient at times. In other words, teaching
children to live well means letting them learn to negotiate the full
range of human experiences we are likely to have. Adult responsibility means setting appropriate boundaries for their behavior, rather
than dictating to them what they ought to feel or shielding them
from ambiguity. Hence, to be happy, a child is not always "good."

We must remember that power is part of a relational process and
rarely remains permanently fixed. Children who grow into their own
wisdom and maturity are able to become our friends when they no
longer need us to care for them, or when we need them to care for us.
The ultimate goal of parenting is to nurture a virtually helpless child,

who has few alternatives but to submit to adult power, and to create a caring relationship of honesty and trust, such that when that child reaches maturity, she or he will choose to remain connected, to befriend those who nurtured it. And when that choice occurs, friendship beyond obligation flourishes.

To interpret God through this image of nurturance and respect, rather than obedience and punishment, points us toward an old idea. What would theology look like if we envisioned a nurturing, life-giving God who encourages willfulness, self-knowledge, and self-respect?

> But you too, good Jesus, are you not also a mother?
> Are you not a mother who like a hen gathers her chicks beneath her wings?
> Christ, my mother, you gather your chickens under your wings;
> Warm your chicken, give life to your dead one, justify your sinner.
> *—Anselm of Canterbury, eleventh-century bishop*

> Jesus is our true Mother in whom we are endlessly carried and out of whom we will never come. In Jesus we have the skillful and wise keeping of our Sensuality as well as our restoring and liberation; for He is our Mother, Brother, and Liberator. Just as God is truly our Father, so also is God truly our Mother.
> *—Dame Julian of Norwich, fourteenth-century anchoress*
> (Doyle: 99, 101, 103)

While the Protestant tradition has focused mostly on the father, Jesus refers occasionally to God in female images and to himself as mother, a fact unknown perhaps to Paul, but not lost to medieval Christian mystics, including the theologian Anselm, who saw in maternal images protection, warm life, and renewal.

Brendan Doyle, in her translation of Dame Julian's work, discusses the anchoress' use of mother. Julian develops the image especially in relation to the Trinity and, more thoroughly, in relation to Jesus (a medieval lack of obsession with gender roles discussed in Nadia Lahutsky's essay in Section III). Julian focused on the image and role of mother in a time when any attention to mothering was rare. Even images of Mary in the fourteenth century showed her as distant and disconnected from her son. Julian lived at a time when the plague, known as the Black Death, killed two out of three children and a mother's bonding with her children was ambiguous and more likely painful than rewarding. In addition, many of the poor were forced to abandon their children at locations in town squares or city cathedrals specifically established for abandoned children. Julian's strong mother images make me wonder what kind of mother she had. Did she create these images out of a sense of absence and her need for a mother in God, maternal love she missed in her real life, or did she create them in tribute to the rare mothering she experienced? Christian feminists today have looked to her work as an early harbinger of images that emphasize the love, rather than the controlling power, of God. In exploring this less common female dimension of imagery for God, I believe we come to a different understanding of the demands of God's love and our relationship to Her because we have an intimate, organic sense of God's work to create life.

If we envision the love of God as like that of love from mothers, the power of God takes on a different quality. If we take as a starting point for our theological reflections, the struggles of mothers to keep their children alive, to protect them from harm, to teach them willfulness, to foster friendship and mutuality, and to pass on their knowledge and wisdom to their grandchildren, what can the experience of mothering teach us about the necessary elements of a nurturing, empowering love in social relationships when our powers differ in scope and responsibility?

This may be an odd question for me to pose, since I am not a mother. But most women, whether or not we actually raise children, are socialized to think of ourselves as potential mothers, as I did when I played with dolls, watched my mother take care of my younger siblings, babysat, and especially when I helped raise my infant brother who was twelve years my junior (which cured any tendency I might have had to romanticize mothering or think of it as a natural gift). The consciousness and skills I have learned through such socialization and activity manifest themselves in the other nurturing relationships of my life, including the role of teacher, and they indicate to me that a nurturing, empowering love is something we should *all* work to develop, men and women, not just mothers.

Love, as a mutually enhancing and nurturing process, must struggle to empower others, even when the choices of those we love may frustrate us and even when we might need to protect ourselves from harm. To be gracious and generous means we affirm the basic goodness of creation and of human life and seek in love to allow the greatest possible freedom for everyone within the limits of what is safe for all when that can be determined—a process that is never easy. To preserve the web of life, we must resist all deliberate infliction of abuse and violence and encourage the expression of anger at or resistance to oppression and injustice, especially in those victimized by misused power. We must create communities that minimize deception, unauthentic feeling, manipulation, resentment, guilt, shame, and hopelessness and that encourage the ethical, nonviolent, respectful treatment of all, including its least powerful members. In the midst of our fragility and the ambiguity of our lives, the courage to resist evil while at the same time loving fearlessly comes with self-respect and the practice of willful loving. To find the power of God to create and maintain the web of life—for the greening of our souls—we must look at our often frail, invisible, and ambiguous actions as we seek to minimize pain, empower others, and enable loving. In our acts of loving we find the divine spirit at work.

Theologically, examining the responsibilities of mothering shifts our relationship to God away from obedience and punishment and toward engagement and commitment. At issue here is not the conflict between love and power as opposites, but the assertion that those with greater power in loving relationships have greater responsibilities to protect life and nurture friendship at the same time that we keep in mind that love is not control and is not omnipotent to prevent pain and destruction. Perhaps, if we begin to reconceive our human relationships in these terms, as a reflection of our relationships to God, our images of father may also change and the phrase "fathering a child" will take on a new meaning of lifelong, engaged, intimate caring. Then God the Father will become an image of life-giving, nurturing power. And mothering will expand to include roles such as providing for families materially and teaching morals, physical prowess, and ideas to children. Our fully human responsibility to covenant is to be as caring as we know how, to take responsibility to nurture courageous loving in those over whom we have power and responsibility, and to expect those with greater power to be responsible.

Jewish traditions have understood this mutuality far better than Christian ones, even when their theology affirmed God's role as powerful judge. Judaism has long upheld the right of human beings to argue with God, as Abraham, Job, the psalmists, and the prophets do, a principle used to address profound human suffering in David Blumenthal's work *Facing the Abusing God*, in which he confronts the Holocaust and child sexual molestation through the lens of the psalms of protest and the voices of survivors—and there are many psalms of protest. If we understand right relationship to God as mutual and loving, then our willfulness and willingness to challenge what happens in our lives is part of loving. To hold God accountable to the demands of loving is part of our commitment to covenant, to engagement in relationship and to our confidence that God is loving, even when we do not experience that love. Our willfulness is part of loving and part of our responsibility to be discerning and faithful. We must trust our own experiences as a necessary part of the integrity of our relationship to God and to trust our right to speak to God when we do not understand Her silence.

Conclusion

Those who understand their covenant relationship to God as one of discernment, commitment, responsibility, and loving, will find comforting Marti Steussy's suggestion in Section I of friendship as our connection to the Bible and as a quality of relationship Jesus proposes to his disciples in John's Gospel (chapter 15) and the theologian Mary Hunt develops in her book on feminist friendship. Confidence in friendship comes not from blind obedience, but from lifelong engagement and interaction, from self-revelation and growing knowledge of each other, from honest confrontation when things seem to be awry, from caring passionately, and from profound listening. The life-giving promises of God come from a lifelong relationship that nurtures in us the capacity to take responsibility for our lives, the grace and generosity to love fearlessly, and the courage to challenge misuses of power wherever we encounter them. In embracing the web of creating, we find the graciousness to receive life and beauty around us.

The community of appreciative engagement and gracious commitment to justice—of covenant—is found in the church as it has been given to us by God and as we create community together. The body of the risen Christ, re-membered whenever we gather around the table together, is the gift of church. In that Body, we draw meaning from those who have gone before and from those who reweave with us our web of life anchored in our covenant with each other. In that web of verdant life, fragile and strong, we rest in the sacred mystery of God, a mystery that lifts and holds the nurturing love that we willfully, joyfully, and hopefully celebrate, and there we find the greening of our souls.

Works Consulted

Blumenthal, David. 1993. *Facing the Abusing God*. Philadelphia: Westminster Press.

Brock, Rita Nakashima. 1988. *Journeys by Heart: A Christology of Erotic Power*. New York: Crossroad Press.

Doyle, Brendan. 1983. *Meditations with Julian of Norwich*. Sante Fe: Bear & Company.

Greven, Philip. 1991. *Spare the Child: The Religious Roots of Punishment and the Psychological Impact of Child Abuse*. New York: Alfred A. Knopf.

Herman, Judith. 1992. *Trauma and Recovery*. New York: Basic Books.

Hunt, Mary. 1989. *Fierce Tenderness: A Feminist Theology of Friendship*. New York: Crossroad Press.

Isasi-Diaz, Ada Maria. 1993. *En La Lucha: Sisters in the Struggle*. Minneapolis: Fortress Press.

Johnson, Elizabeth. 1992. *She Who Is: The Mystery of God in Feminist Theological Discourse*. New York: Crossroad Press.

"Las Madres, The Mothers of the Plaza Del Mayo." 1986. Documentary film available from Women Make Movies, 225 Lafayette St., New York, NY 10012. 212/925-0606.

Noddings, Nel. 1989. *Women and Evil*. Berkeley: University of California Press.

Poling, James. 1991. *The Abuse of Power: A Theological Problem*. Nashville: Abingdon Press.

Ruddick, Sara. 1989. *Maternal Thinking: Toward a Politics of Peace*. Boston: Beacon Press.

Ruether, Rosemary Radford. 1983. *Sexism and God-Talk: Toward a Feminist Theology*. Boston: Beacon Press.

Uhlen, Gabriele. 1983. *Meditations with Hildegard of Bingen*. Sante Fe: Bear & Company.

Walker, Alice. 1981. *The Color Purple*. New York: Harcourt, Brace, Jovanovich.

Williams, Delores. 1993. *Sisters in the Wilderness: The Challenge of Womanist God-Talk*. Maryknoll, NY: Orbis Press.

8

 The Nature of
Christian Community

Kristine A. Culp

What are the possibilities for Christian community in our world? What are the possibilities for communities of faith that will ground and direct us in a world of both violence and compassion, of both profound isolation and deep interdependence? How can we begin to think about a community that draws us toward each other and the divine in a world divided by pain and abundance?

In this chapter, I invite you to explore these questions with me— to think along with me about the nature of Christian community. As a theologian, my task is not to describe actual congregations and denominations, but to offer ways of explaining and exploring what the nature and purpose of Christian community—of the church—is and ought to be. If Christian community is to enhance rather than to thwart life, what must it be like? This is an imaginative and a critical task. It is also necessarily an abstract task. And yet, our powers of imagination, critique, and abstraction must begin with the concrete experiences and stories of Christian communities that we have. Moreover, our imaginative and critical efforts must finally return to strengthen the actual communities in which we dwell and work and worship. And so, I would like to begin with some images and brief narratives of communities of faith and their practices. Next, I will sketch some ways that theologians, especially feminist theologians, have thought about the nature of Christian community. Finally, I will explore two models of and for Christian community: body of Life and testimony of survival and resistance. Along the way, I will address the demands of daily life in the U.S. to suggest how these two models can help us to live together justly and to dwell in the merciful abundance of God.

Images and Experiences of Christian Community

We have stories, images, and reflections about communities of faith from the Bible, from history, from books and stories, from our own experiences of such communities. We also have hints of what a sustaining and directing community of faith might be from a range of other experiences—from experiences of profound relation, from experiences of support and of tenderness, and from experiences of providing aid and advocacy for others—to list a few. We have knowledge of the limits and possibilities of communities because, whether or not each of us has "grown up in the church," our lives have been shaped in families and in a variety of communities of teachers and classmates, friends, colleagues, coworkers, neighbors, citizens. We have "grown up" in these communities and in their differing organizations, patterns of relationship, stories, languages, and interpretations of reality.

Body-related images

Let me begin with a narrative from fiction. In a remarkable passage in her novel *Beloved*, Toni Morrison portrays a "church" called together by a preacher named Baby Suggs. The story takes place just before the Civil War, in southern Ohio just across the river from slaveholding territory. In the fall and winter, Baby Suggs preached in AME, Baptist, Holiness, and Sanctified churches. But when warm weather came, she preached in a clearing deep in the woods and called her congregation to her from among the trees.

> She did not tell them to clean up their lives or to go and sin no more. She did not tell them they were the blessed of the earth, its inheriting meek or its glorybound pure.
>
> She told them that the only grace they could have was the grace they could imagine. That if they could not see it, they would not have it.
>
> "Here," she said, "in this here place, we flesh; flesh that weeps, laughs; flesh that dances on bare feet in grass. Love it. Love it

hard. Yonder they do not love your flesh. They despise it….*You* got to love it, *you!* …This is flesh I'm talking about here. Flesh that needs to be loved. Feet that need to rest and to dance; backs that need support; shoulders that need arms, strong arms I'm telling you. And O my people, out yonder, hear me, they do not love your neck unnoosed and straight. So love your neck; put a hand on it, grace it, stroke it and hold it up. And all your inside parts that they'd just as soon slop for hogs, you got to love them. The dark, dark liver—love it, love it, and the beat and beating heart, love that too. More than eyes or feet. More than lungs that have yet to draw free air. More than your life-holding womb and your life-giving private parts, hear me now, love your heart. For this is the prize." Saying no more, she stood up then and danced with her twisted hip the rest of what her heart had to say while the others opened their mouths and gave her the music. Long notes held until the four-part harmony was perfect enough for their deeply loved flesh. (88f.)

Baby Suggs enables her congregation to imagine grace and healing for each of their abused body parts and thus the grace of a laughing, weeping, dancing, whole, and beloved body. Compare a familiar passage from the Christian New Testament that also uses images of the human body. In a letter to the church at Corinth, Paul writes of the unity and diversity of the body and its parts. The image explains their relations to each other and in Christ. In the following excerpts from 1 Corinthians 12, Paul counsels that individual body parts are not to be despised but understood as mutually interdependent, each knit together into a dynamic whole.

For just as the body is one and has many members, and all the members of the body, though many, are one body, so it is with Christ. For in the one Spirit we were all baptized into one body— Jews or Greeks, slaves or free—and we were all made to drink of one Spirit.

Indeed, the body does not consist of one member but of many. If the foot would say, "Because I am not a hand, I do not belong to the body," that would not make it any less a part of the body. And if the ear would say, "Because I am not an eye, I do not belong to the body," that would not make it any less a part of the body. If the whole body were an eye, where would the hearing be? If the whole body were hearing, where would the sense of smell be?…But God has so arranged the body, giving the greater honor to the inferior member, that there may be no dissension within the body, but the members may have the same care for one another. If one member suffers, all suffer together with it; if one member is honored, all rejoice together with it.

Now you are the body of Christ and individually members of it. (1 Corinthians 12:12–17, 24b–27)

At this point I will not attempt to synthesize Baby Suggs's preaching about the community's body with Paul's imagination of squabbling body parts and their actual integrity. Instead, I want to continue my brief exploration of stories about and experiences of Christian community. In addition to these two organic or "body-related" images, I want to look at a second set of pictures of Christian community. They relate to the church's service to the world: they are three accounts of women and the work of the church that come from diverse times and places.

The work of women and the work of the church

1. The Beguines. In the thirteenth and fourteenth centuries, the Beguine movement flourished among women in urban centers across Europe. The Beguines were laywomen who shared not only common religious convictions but also housing and living expenses. By renting and bequeathing their houses to each other, they cared for and provided economic security for each other. In addition, they supplied a variety of services to the community such as nursing, wool processing, sewing, baking, spinning, and running hospitals and schools. Unlike nuns, the Beguines took no formal religious vows that consecrated them in obedience to the church hierarchy. Moreover, they sought no authorization for their movement and their work from Rome nor did they receive patronage from the church and its wealthy members. Whereas convents attracted unmarried daughters of the nobility and the resources to support them, beguinages attracted women from poorer classes who might otherwise have existed on the religious and economic margins of medieval societies. By pooling their resources and by providing services to the community, the Beguine movement flourished even without patronage. (One study of the medieval city of Strasbourg estimated that at least 10 percent of its population was involved in and around the Beguine movement.) With their success, however, both the church and the guilds began to view them as threats. That the Beguines could survive and even thrive autonomously elicited resentment. In 1311, the church's General Council of Vienne condemned the Beguine way of life.

2. "Middle-American" church women. The condemnation of the Beguines did not end women's expression of religious commitments through service to others. Christian women through the ages often have understood the support and enrichment of human life as integral to their religious vocations. Countless tales of service are told in the histories of Roman Catholic women's religious orders, of Protestant women's missionary societies, and of women's church auxiliaries. For example, over the years organizations of women in "middle-American" churches have studied and sewn, joined in mission around the world, visited the sick, built buildings, and founded schools. In cities and towns across the midwestern United States, women have offered sustaining meals in times of mourning and joyous feasts in times of celebration. They have prepared the dinners around which many church gatherings center. In their compassionate attention and gracious hospitality, God's own has been met. To be sure, what could be practices of extending hospitality to the stranger sometimes devolve into ways of being hostesses for the familiar. Nevertheless, the place of such women's groups in U.S. mainline Protestantism seldom has been addressed in theological, historical, or sociological studies. For example, dogmatic and historical treatises have focused on the eucharist to the neglect of actual meals and the women who usually prepared them.

Women have been artisans of communal survival in many places and times. They have practiced the domestic arts necessary for human life, such as cooking, nursing, and making a home. They have played a crucial role in transmitting the cultural foundations necessary for human community, for example, language. Across the centuries, women have sustained Christian community through teaching, advocacy for the vulnerable, patronage, care for the sick, and other ways. However, their work often has been understood as service rather than as vocation, thereby effectively rendering invisible countless hours of labor in contrast to the visibility of "men's work" as clergy, elders, and church board members. Yet assuredly, the economies of churches have depended upon the largely invisible work (*qua* work) of women just as the economies of families have been built upon the largely invisible work—albeit much less invisible and more often shared since the contemporary feminist movement—of keeping the young and vulnerable safe, clothed, and fed.[1]

---

[1] See, for example, Cheryl Townsend Gilkes' treatment of the dual-sex political economy within several black Pentecostal and Holiness traditions: "The Roles of Church and Community Mothers: Ambivalent American Sexism or Fragmented African Familyhood?," *Journal of Feminist Studies in Religion* 2, no. 1 (Spring 1986): 41–59. On household labor, see for example Barbara Hilkert Andolsen, "A Woman's Work Is Never Done: Unpaid Household Labor as a Social Justice Issue," in *Women's Consciousness, Women's Conscience: A Reader in Feminist Ethics*, ed. Barbara Hilkert Andolsen, Christine E. Gudorf, and Mary D. Pellauer (Minneapolis: Winston Press, 1985): 3–18.

3. The Salvadoran Christian mothers. In 1983 in El Salvador small groups of women began to meet to "reflect on the word of God and to see what it was saying to us and what we could do in our communities" (Venancia [pseudonym], a Salvadoran mother and catechist, as translated in Golden: 90–99). From these groups were born what are now called Congregations of Mothers for Peace and Life. The women began to organize to do what they could to help their poor communities struggle against the decimation of war. They started schools and literacy programs, collectives for food and health care, and sewing workshops; they engaged in Bible study and catechesis. They even confronted the army to demand their rights and, in doing so, empowered entire communities to work against political repression and economic oppression. Through such activities, groups like the Congregation of Mothers for Peace and Life have become what Renny Golden calls "crucibles of communal survival." The context of war and oppression in El Salvador highlights the commitments to justice and to community that must be made in countless daily ways. Golden explains, "If the war determines that many will die, the lives of Salvadoran women insist on deciding, until their last breath, how to live....When death lives so close to the bone and flesh, fatalism or organized ingenuity are the only choices" (193).

A Theology of Common Life Before God

The stories of the Salvadoran Christian mothers, of "middle-American" church women, and of the Beguines remind us of the role of communities in ensuring human survival and flourishing. The early church theologian Cyprian taught that "there is no salvation outside the church." He meant that the institutional church was the sole guardian and location of the means of salvation. For us this must mean not that institutional Christianity has a singular purchase on salvation, but rather that we cannot make our way in the world without communities of faith. Without such communities of memory and interpretation, of action and hope, we cannot live meaningfully and justly. To frame this in terms of the task of the theologian who turns her or his powers of imagination and critique to ecclesiology: what is required is not a theology of a particular church and its confessions and practices, but a theology of common life before God.[2]

Our time is a time when we strive to make our way meaningfully and justly in a world divided by pain and abundance. The images of organic community and stories of communal survival do not

---

[2] In other words, ecclesiology, or the theology of church, is reconstrued as a theology of sociality.

chart our path, but they will provide some resources. We can draw on them in combination with other experiences, metaphors, stories, and practices in order to explore what Christian community is and what it might be. The organic images and survival stories serve to enrich our imaginations and to sharpen our critical powers. For example, how are the communities of faith that we know like or unlike a body of many parts that sometimes hurts and sometimes rejoices? What is the grace that we can imagine? Is it possible to imagine an integrity formed from the fragmentation of our lives and our world— that is, to imagine that the Divine dwells with us and in us? Do the communities we know support human survival and flourishing or do they thwart it? How shall we together resist evil and survive amid the strain of daily living? Can communities of faith bear witness to the one who, in giving us our daily bread, exceeds our usual convictions of what is good and just?

Models of Church

Keeping these images and stories in mind, I now turn to more explicitly theological consideration of the nature of Christian community. From their earliest times, Christians have used images to describe and prescribe their assemblies together. As we have noted, Paul often used images of the body and of dwelling in Christ. Others have referred to communities of Christians as disciples, the faithful, servants of God, the family of God, the city of God, an ark of salvation, a covenant community, an assembly (*ekklesia*), the people of God. In his now classic 1974 book, *Models of the Church*, Avery Dulles identified five models that especially have shaped Protestant and Roman Catholic thought about the nature of the church: institution, mystical communion, sacrament, herald, and servant. An important and more recent model, the church of the poor, has emerged from locally based and popularly rooted Christian communities in Latin America. Such models of church gather together and elaborate related ideas and images of Christian community. Somewhat as a calendar, with its sequence of days and months, organizes human experiences of the changing seasons and knowledge of the planets and stars, so these theological models of church organize and direct our knowledge and experiences of Christian community. They provide synthetic pictures through which and against which to interpret, imagine, and enact Christian community.

In the last twenty-five years, feminist theologians have also written about the nature and purpose of Christian community. For example, Rosemary Radford Ruether writes about Christian feminist liberation communities (or women-church) as feminist base communities. She describes these communities as existing within and on the edges of existing church institutions. In them, women gather for the purpose of "reflecting upon, celebrating, and acting in the understanding of liberation from sexism." Feminist base communities search for "a meaningful union of inward spiritual growth and social praxis," thereby contributing to the broader goal of the liberation of all life. These North American autonomous communities of protest are located in women's struggles against patriarchy much as the church of the poor is located in the midst of struggles against economic oppression and political repression. Like many African-American and Latin American liberation theologians, Ruether interprets contemporary experiences of oppression and the determination for liberation in relation to the Hebrews' story of exodus and exile. She explains that "we are not in exile, but the Church is in exile with us," having fled together from the "idol of patriarchy." She finds that existing churches often operate as "counter-signs" to women's hopes for wholeness and God's reign of justice:

> Women in contemporary churches are suffering from linguistic deprivation and eucharistic famine. They can no longer nurture their souls in alienating words that ignore or systematically deny their existence. They are starved for words of life, for symbolic forms that fully and wholeheartedly affirm their personhood and speak truth about the evils of sexism and the possibilities of a future beyond patriarchy (4–5).

In general, feminist ecclesiologies agree on certain matters: 1) Like Ruether, they critique theologies, practices, and church structures that perpetuate and/or fail to counter sexism, the domination of women, and other often interrelated forms of oppression. 2) They assume that women have always been in the midst of, rather than on the margins of, the life of the church and the practice of Christianity. For example, New Testament scholar Elisabeth Schüssler Fiorenza has written about the long history of women's leadership and subordination within even the earliest forms of Christianity. 3) They critique hierarchical structures and theologies and suggest nonhierarchical alternatives. For example, Letty Russell has written widely on partnership as an alternative to domination and has suggested the "church in the round" as one way of understanding that God welcomes all persons without hierarchy. 4) They emphasize "embodiment" as well as proclamation of the gospel in their interpretations of church and ministry. Rebecca Chopp contends that the Christian message of emancipatory transformation is proclaimed and evoked "in the embodied relations of Word and words in the church." She writes, "there must be no illusion that the Word somehow founds community apart from the richness of the body of human existence" (96, 85).

5) Feminist interpretations insist on the church's transformative role in society. Throughout the history of Christianity, the institutional church and Christian movements have functioned both to sacralize the established political-cultural order and to critique it. Rather than critiquing and transforming the isolating, shallow, consumptive, and often violent society in which we live, many contemporary churches unwittingly have bolstered it. Fashioning themselves after corporate America, clergy become credentialed professionals who address laity as individual clients and appeal to them as private consumers of meaning, intimacy, and religious emotion. By contrast, feminist theologians, like many other contemporary theologians and Christians, believe that the church must challenge as well as comfort.

Four other areas of convergence relate to how feminist theologians proceed when thinking about the nature of Christian community. 6) Feminist theologians tend to take a broad view of Christian community. That is, they tend to assume that an understanding of Christian community should be developed in relation to ecclesial movements and local communities and not be limited to institutional Christianity. 7) Their processes of thinking about Christian community usually begin by considering and evaluating the practices and ethos of actual communities rather than with applying previous theologies. 8) They are practically minded about the truth of any image or model of the church. For example, whether a model or image encourages righteousness and sustains life is relevant in judging whether it is true. 9) They find images and models to be crucial for imagining and living as Christian community.

Two New Models

Images and models of Christian community offer vivid pictures to try on, live in, and move through as women and men of faith struggle to shape vital religious institutions, communities, and lives. Much as Jesus used everyday events—like a poor woman losing a coin—as parables to point to the reign of God, so models of Christian community use images and experiences from everyday life while also pointing beyond actual communities and daily existence. Images and models help us to consider, for example, how Christian community is in some ways like a body and in other ways like a powerful testimony. Just as Jesus' use of two or three parables at once could help his listeners have many points of connection with their lives and multiple ways of understanding the reign of God, so we can use more than one model for thinking about Christian community. Perhaps by thinking and living through multiple models we will be better able to live and think in relation to diverse—and possibly even conflicting—experiences, heritages, practices, and expectations.

I will explore two new models of Christian community. The first model, "body of Life," draws on organic or body-related metaphors. The second model, "testimony of survival and resistance," emphasizes protest and communal survival as central to the work of the church.

Body of Life

Among the most familiar and most powerful New Testament images of common life before God are images of "members of the body," "body of Christ," and "the resurrection body." The biblical image of the body of Christ expresses both participation in Christ and a necessary interdependence among the community of believers. In conjunction with the image of the body of Christ, Paul's letters sound themes of mutual aid, forgiveness, and concern. In 1 Corinthians 11, Paul admonishes "anyone who eats and drinks without discerning the body." He was probably scolding members who consumed most of what was to be a shared meal without giving consideration to other members who might arrive late and hungry due to no fault of their own. He also evokes another theme, that of participating in Christ by sharing a common meal and of eventual participation in the resurrected body of Christ. Romans and 1 Corinthians imply that we can neither understand nor partake of life in and with Christ apart from our life in and with each other.

Human bodily existence as a means of grace. In addition to wanting to stand in continuity with rich New Testament images, there are other reasons for reclaiming the body as a central image for Christian community. As Baby Suggs proclaims, providing care and safety for human bodily existence may offer the means by which persons experience grace profoundly. In general, theological reflection on the nature of Christian community has tended to ignore ways in which grace has been and might be mediated by addressing basic human needs. Basic human needs include food and shelter, as well as the need to mark and make sense of life's transitions and the need to belong and be valued. Moreover, the plights of homelessness and poverty bid Christians to change old habits of neglecting physical survival and bodily well-being as crucial dimensions of being human. In our time, truly to imagine and live among all embodied earthly creatures as an embodied community of God requires that we view the means of human survival and flourishing as crucial means of divine redemption and grace.

An embodiment of God. Thinking about the church as a body also causes us to attend anew to the way the church exists in the world and with God. Christian community does not merely *have* a socio-historical "form" or "body"; it *lives in* its actions and relations in society and history. Contrary to many prevalent assumptions, what is most "Christian" about Christian life is *not* what is most disengaged from history, culture, and society. Christian community, like all human life, is embodied; it has economic, social, political, temporal, and linguistic dimensions. These dimensions of common life provide the means by which faithfulness, integrity, righteousness, and love are cultivated in and expressed to—albeit most often ambiguously—persons, the world, and God. In other words, Christian community embodies and dwells in the Divine Life in and through its human, bodily, social, and historical actions.

When early Christian communities thought of themselves as "the body of Christ" and as "the resurrection body," they were daring to imagine and live as if God in Christ continued to be present in and through their life together. They came to believe that their intentional, enacted common life was inextricably wed to the Divine Life; they were the body and the bride of Christ. Such an audacious claim can express the profound and humbling realization that the merciful, powerful, integrating abundance that we name God is necessarily mediated (and limited or distorted) by our often faltering communities and institutions. Or, such an audacious claim can eventually result in truimphalism; an institution may come to believe that it and its duly appointed officers alone control sure and true access to the divine. Both have happened in the history of Christianity. If we are to fashion an acceptable continuity with New Testament body images for our time, we will have to take soberly and humbly the audacious claim that, in our life together before God, we are somehow a continuation of Christ and an embodiment of God. God dwells in the world and we dwell in God in and through our communities, language, and actions—frail and feeble as they may be. Nevertheless it is possible that in and through community and actions characterized by righteousness and love and seasoned with grace, persons may come rightly to experience the divine as the animator, power, sustainer of mercifully abundant life. By contrast, hierarchical, authoritarian, or abusive relations may lead persons to encounter the divine falsely as an unrelated and unfeeling, although all-knowing, tyrant.

*A body of **Life**.* Besides conveying the church's integral relation with the Divine Life, body images enable us to grasp how deeply Christian life partakes of human interrelatedness. And more, Christian communities participate in a changing, pulsing ecosphere as well as in human interdependencies. The space in which we dwell together with God is not only far wider than the space defined by church walls, it is also far wider than the places of human habitation. What, then, if we were to imagine and live as though the church were an embodiment of the interdependence and integration of all life, not only of human life, in God? What if we were to imagine and live Christian community as a "body of Life"?

To interpret and live Christian life together as the "body of Life" widens sacred space profoundly. Informed by a sense that Christian life and communities are embedded in a changing, pulsing ecosphere and by a sense of the profound interdependence of human life, the image of the body of Life affirms that God dwells or is incarnate in Christian community and the whole world. Thus the "Life" in "body of Life" includes human spirit-body life inseparably connected with animate and inanimate forms of life and with the teeming, pulsing universe of molecules and atoms from which living things spring and to which they return. "Life" includes the totality of earthly existence with its intricacies and lushness, its raw pain and barrenness, its solitude and interrelatedness, its movement and multiplicity, its resoluteness, its violence and terror, its harshness, its surprises. "Life" with a capital "L" also signals Christian sensibilities that our lives, fragmented and rimmed by mystery as they are, have ultimate integrity. It expresses this faith as the conviction that our lives and communities of faith are encompassed by the power of the divine, immanent in and empowering earthly life. It emphasizes that God lives near to us; God can be known as "Life Dwelling in the Many."

A finite and mortal body. If our common life as Christians is lived in trust about the mystery of the whence and whither of life, it is also lived under a sense of the precarious and constantly changing nature of daily existence. Those who have given and tended birth, who have nurtured and educated the young, nursed the ill, and cared for the dying; those who live under the threat of violence or who eke out an existence for themselves and their families on societal margins, certainly have experienced life's finite, particular span as a fact of their everyday existence. We can find similar convictions about life's ultimate integrity of life and yet its resolute concreteness when we read Paul's letters to churches. He writes about squabbling body parts of the body of Christ, about deep conflicts within us as sin, and about the resurrection of the *body* (not just the soul).

Nevertheless, much of our Christian heritage has fostered escape from bodiliness and finitude to an eternal, other-world. By the time Christianity was several centuries old, most Christians had come to hold the notion that the church was eternal and the individual soul was immortal. During periods of history when social life seemed chaotic and death especially near, these notions served as a shield from what was perceived to be the ravages of time, the burden of bodiliness, and the threat of interdependency with the rest of existence. But this part of our heritage hindered an understanding of how our fragile and yet tenacious *bodily existence* ultimately and mysteriously connects us to the Divine Life. Moreover, in the face of our ever-changing and even precarious contemporary existence on the planet earth, Christians can ill afford to dissociate "Life" from biological life in order to offer it in perfect and permanent supply after the death of the "flesh."

For Christian communities as for individuals acceptance of finitude and mortality implies facing hard choices, change, and death as part of existence. Recognition that there are limits to what persons and communities can do and be does not necessarily mean lessened responsibility for human doing and being. Surrendering pretensions of being able to be everywhere and to do everything, the church as the finite and mortal body of Life (vs. as the earthly but eternal body of Christ) is better able to accept responsibility for the limited power that Christian communities do have. Thus to imagine and live Christian community as the body of Life requires accepting responsibility for human abilities and recognizing human inabilities in the context of an encompassing universe of agents and existence.

The work of the church. What, then, is the work of the church, the body of Life? It is to embody and midwife the integrity of Life in the midst of the world. The task set before Christians and their communities is to uphold and fashion a holy wholeness of life before God from the fragmentation of our lives. This is not an entirely new understanding of the work of the church. Indeed, the more familiar metaphors of "conversion," "healing," "redemption" sometimes conveyed similar convictions. "Conversion," "healing," and "redemption" have suggested that, as persons are drawn together in life before God, warped and broken dimensions of human life are reoriented, the wounded are made whole, and what is presently ambiguous will be taken up into what is ultimately good. However, too often the work of the church—and interpretations of conversion, salvation, and redemption—have focused on producing Christians while neglecting the rest of life. In our time and place especially, we are called to midwife the integrity of all life and to embody its dignity. We are summoned beyond a limited focus on human or Christian propagation by a sense of reverence for the good gifts of creation, on the one hand, and, on the other, by a sense of foreboding about the cumulated powers of greed, cynicism, violence, and elitism.

The continuing incarnation of God in the world. Finally, in interpreting Christian community as the body of Life and in proclaiming Jesus as the Christ, we identify this community and this person as exemplary, but not exhaustive or preemptive incarnations of the Divine Life. Through the years, many persons have interpreted the church as the body of Christ as a way of emphasizing that Christ is the center of Christian life. Sometimes this emphasis has been to the neglect of the nature of the community itself. The model of the body of Life helps us to imagine and enact the reality of the continuing incarnation of God in Christian community and the world—not just in one individual, not only in human life.[3] We are enabled to imagine and live as community in relation with all of life and as an embodiment of the Divine Life. Our lives are drawn together with all of life and empowered by the One who is Life Dwelling in the Many. It is not only that we live and move and have our being in the Divine Life but also that the One who is the utter abundance of Life lives and dwells in, through, and with earthly life as companion and encourager.

Testimony of Survival and Resistance
A searing word and protesting faith. The body of Life model directs the full participation of all in God and embraces earthly existence as the place of God's dwelling. But common life before God sometimes requires separation rather than participation, and protest rather than embrace. The second model, testimony of survival and resistance, emphasizes communal survival and protest as central to the life and work of the church.

In 1964, concerned about the present state of Protestant churches in the United States, the theologian Langdon Gilkey called for the churches to revitalize their relation to the holy. Specifically, he proposed that they retrieve a distinctive Protestant sense of the holy by cultivating a sense of the "transcendent Word" of judgment and of grace in worship services. Gilkey believed that if the church failed to mediate the holy through its distinctive word, it would become captive to culture. He was not optimistic about the situation. According to Gilkey, "the word that is heard there [in Protestant churches] is

---

[3]Technically put, the model follows the incarnational sensibilities of sacramental interpretations of church, e.g., Karl Rahner's ecclesiology, while extending these sensibilities beyond human life and Christian communities. In other words, it assumes a theocentric rather than christocentric, biocentric rather than anthropocentric, and communal rather than individualistic interpretation of incarnation.

often either an irrelevant, unrelated 'gospel' that heals no one because it sears no one, or merely the accepted wisdom of the world, untransformed by any transcendent judging and healing elements, and therefore also ultimately sterile" (81).

Closer to the end of the twentieth century, the word that is heard in most U.S. mainline Protestant churches is no more "searing" than the one Gilkey observed. And yet at the same time, there are those within Christianity—including many feminist, womanist, mujerista, African-American, and other liberation movements—who are raising protesting voices. Within these movements, "protestant" faith is being revitalized by those whose daily survival requires resisting the powers of oppression and death. Fresh readings of the Bible have compelled new witnesses to faith and new practices of Christian life; emerging faith communities have given searing testimonies about God's justice and compassion in the world.

Lived testimony before God. The model of Christian community as a testimony of survival and resistance builds on these new and compelling ways of being a protesting church. It directs the church's life and practice in protest against exclusion and domination, that is, in protest against powers that controvert divine power. The testimony model addresses survival in and resistance to ecclesiastical institutions and societies that exclude and oppress. It emphasizes the tasks of resisting domination and exploitation and of building alliances among those who are resisting as integral to Christian vocation and community. It thematizes an interrelation among standing up for communal survival, standing against evil, and standing before God.

Because existing communities and institutions can function as countersigns to societal transformation, this model affirms the need for autonomous Christian protesting movements (feminist, African-American, etc.) that contend for survival and resistance. Communities of protest can be understood as standing in continuity with Jewish, Christian, and, to a lesser extent, legal traditions of testament, witness, proclamation, and martyrdom. These traditions have profoundly shaped Protestant communal life—with its touchpoints to the biblical "witness" and its worship services centered around the sermon—and Protestant theology, for example, neoorthodox theologies of the Word. However, unlike some of these earlier ways of thinking about church, the model of testimony of survival and resistance neither centers Christian community around proclamation nor proposes a new theology of the Word. It is less "the power *to speak*" than the disturbing contentions and unsettling advocacies—indeed, we might say the revelatory powers—of *particular testimonies* that must inform our life together before God.

For Christians, and especially those of Protestant varieties, the definitive instances of Christian testimony are arguably the *witness* of the life, teachings, practices, and death of Jesus as variously portrayed in the Gospels and the *witness* of Jesus' earliest followers to him. In these cases, as also for the Hebrew prophets, to give testimony or to bear witness exceeds speaking the truth and entails a total giving over of one's life to what is true. They "took sides" with what they knew and worshiped as truly divine in opposition to false idols. It is this sense of a total engagement of one's life that is conveyed by the image of "testimony of survival and resistance." More precisely, testimony refers to the total engagement of a life lived before God and especially to those words and actions that are spoken and enacted from within communities of faith in order to (1) document the afflictions and oppression of a people; (2) marshaling the community's heritage of language and action, transform people's pain and problems into a communal indictment of that which gave rise to their affliction and oppression, namely, a communal indictment of idolatry and injustice; and (3) transform people's suffering of afflictions and oppression into a covenant community's shared struggles against what gave rise to affliction and oppression. "Testimony" then becomes a metaphoric image for the entire shape, relations, actions, and commitments of Christian community.

The work of the church. Christian communities become testimonies of survival and resistance less by making single dramatic choices than through an accumulation of daily acts that resist resignation and build up communities. For the most part they give testimony in plain, small ways: in each choice and act that refuses to betray the trust of another, that refuses to cease from caring, that refuses to stop doing justice, that refuses to give up hope on this day. Daily acts to resist resignation and sustain communities can also be understood as basic acts of faith. When war, destruction, oppression, and neglect give good reasons for cynicism and resignation, to enable survival and community means to resist evil and to act in faith and hope of life and a future beyond death and destruction. These countless daily acts of resisting evil, doing justice, and living before God build up the reign of God. They are the work of the church. But whereas survival seems so evidently an act of faith and the work of the church in the war zone of El Salvador, it seems not necessarily so in other places where the everyday press of survival is seldom so immediate. And yet we have also seen the ways in which the work of the "middle-American" church has often been the work of communal survival.

What then is the work of the church, the testimony of survival and resistance? It is the work of communal survival: to care, to hope, and to do justice in daily ways. Arguably, much of this work always has been intrinsic to Christian community. But it has also been disregarded as "mere" service or as individual acts of devotion. However, these works are neither "mere" nor simply isolated, individual devotions. When we understand the church's work as the work of communal survival, we create continuities among our daily choices and more overtly political actions of resistance and transformation. Moreover, insofar as "doing one's job," caring for the vulnerable, sustaining committed relationships, and building community become heroic endeavors in increasingly violent and fragmented societies, the work of communal survival—as manifested in stewardship and vocation, attention to human need and earthly well-being, parenting, marriages and committed partnerships, friendships, and communal well-being—can be, like political protest and engagement, prophetic acts and acts of faith. These daily choices cumulate into a testimony of "sustained loyalty to humanity-yet-to-be," to use Daniel Day Williams' felicitous phrase. Christian life together bears witness not only to daily faithfulness and hope, but also to love as tenacious anticipation and as the impatient refusal to settle for inhumanity, fate, and injustice.

The risks of self-righteous separation, of "victimism," and of being shut out. Whereas the body of Life and other integrative models run the risk of embracing the world too uncritically, protesting movements run the opposite risk: they may tend to become narrow sects and to withdraw from the world.[4] To a large extent, any protest movement is defined by its act of negating: it protests *against* apartheid, *against* repressive political regimes, etc. Consequently, there is always the danger that protesting movements will fail to connect with and relate to others except in judgment. However, when uncompromising judgments serve not only to demarcate protesting movements but to place them above everyone else, knowledge and concern about the wider world can cease to inform their judgments. Nevertheless, these dangers of self-righteous separation should not be confused with the necessity of having the kind of critical distance required for astute cultural critique. To be a testimony of survival and resistance, Christian community must remain both dependent on and autonomous from the institutions and forms of human communal life that it attempts to transform.

---

[4] Cf. Janice Raymond's feminist philosophical treatment of dissociation from the world as an obstacle to female friendship, and especially Ernst Troeltsch's classic discussion of church, sect, and mystic types of Christianity.

The tendency toward sectarianism may arise in another way. Wearied from struggles that seem unending, protesting communities may be tempted to substitute confession of their powerlessness and victimization for the lived testimony of survival and resistance.

Perhaps the most prevalent danger of separation comes from without. Protesting movements face the possibility of being cut off from existing churches through the initiative of the latter.[5] This phenomenon occurred with nineteenth-century U.S. feminists who understood protest against injustice as integral to Christian faithfulness. According to one scholar, in their case, "responsibility for the disillusion of such women [in Christian churches] can more plausibly be laid to the insensitivity of the clergy to the claims . . . for justice for women than to . . . individual women" (Harrison, 202). Today, reaction to twentieth-century Christian feminists and other social visionaries threatens the same. When organized Christianity shuts out voices of protest, many of which first arise from within, it may actually be cutting itself off from meaningful engagement with the world and from a gospel capable of healing because it sears.

Tensive models

The two models of the body of Life and of the testimony of survival and resistance, remain in tensive correlation with each other. That is, they are interdependent but the contrasts between them are never resolved. The body of Life model is integrative and more universal in scope; it helps the Christian community to view itself as part of all life and in relation to the Divine Life. The testimony model is a protesting model; it helps us to understand how protest against injustice is basic to the nature of Christian community. One model uses mostly organic and relational images; the other uses mostly socio-political images. The body model highlights experiences of mystery when met by the immanent God dwelling in and empowering earthly life, of "Life Dwelling in the Many." The testimony model accents experiences of awe when confronted by the God who relativizes and judges human efforts and institutions, of "the One Who Dwells in Glory."[6] The body of Life model affirms life because God is the creator, redeemer, and inspirer of Life; it moves to em-

---

[5] At one point in his argument Troeltsch recognizes the polemical origin of "sect" and notes that the sect's position "outside the corporate life of the ecclesiastical tradition…was usually forced upon them" (*Social Teachings*, 333).

[6] On God as "Life Dwelling in the Many" and as "the One Who Dwells in Glory" see Mary Potter Engel, "Tambourines to the Glory of God: From the Monarchy of God the Father to the Monotheism of God the Great Mysterious," *Word & World* 7, no. 2 (1987): 164.

brace the world that God orders and sustains. The model of testimony of survival and resistance rejects all that is limited because God will not be limited; it moves away from that which constrains God. One model guides the enactment of God's promised mercy and abundance in the world; the other model compels transformative resistance to a world where God is effaced by violence and destruction.

If we imagine and live out Christian community as the body of Life, we can also understand the work of the church as embodying and midwifing integrity from fragmentation. We might also interpret the task of theology as discernment and poetic synthesis toward wisdom and righteousness, which in turn are ultimately grounded in mystery. If we imagine and live out Christian community as a testimony of survival and resistance, we can understand the work of the church as the work of communal survival and of struggling against evil toward justice. We might view the task of theology as testimony, as prophetic outcry, and as the proclamation and interpretation of a distinct and timely word, all of which ultimately refer to the challenges of the Sovereign One. Common life before God is more comprehensively expressed in the dynamic tension between the two models.

Conclusion

The truth of any image or model of the church cannot be determined solely by its "realism"—there is neither an archetypal essence of church nor a definitive human experience of sustaining and directing community with which to compare. Nor can their truth be determined solely by how well they "fit" with theological sources—although the models I have proposed can and must be evaluated in relation to experiences, biblical resources, Christian traditions, and prophetic vision. The truthfulness of these models is also relative to their ability to explain, evoke, and explore ways of living and being Christian community. That is, truth is not contained in the models but in how they direct our relations with all life—human, earthly, the divine.

Living among multiple cultures as well as among the divides of pain and abundance, we are often compelled to find truth in more than one way talking about or looking at things at once. Therefore, in our time we must be persuaded anew of the truthfulness of any interpretations of Christian community by the fruits that they bear. What is good and true and just must also be judged in relation to a model's effects on the precarious daily existence of ordinary persons like those who were called together by Baby Suggs, the folks in Corinth, women in medieval cities, "middle-American" church women, and the Salvadoran mothers for life and peace. Are these models responsive to the experiences, pressures, and delights of our lives? Will they ground and direct us in a world filled with violence and compassion, in a world where there is both profound isolation and deep interdependence? Will these models draw us toward each other and the divine in a world divided by pain and abundance? Will they open up possibilities for the merciful abundance of God?

Works Consulted

Chopp, Rebecca S. 1989. *The Power to Speak: Feminism, Language, God*. New York: Crossroad.

Dulles, Avery. 1974. *Models of the Church*. Garden City, NY: Doubleday.

Gilkey, Langdon. 1964. *How the Church Can Minister to the World Without Losing Itself*. New York: Harper & Row.

Golden, Renny. 1991. *The Hour of the Poor, The Hour of Women: Salvadoran Women Speak*. New York: Crossroad.

Gustafson, James M. 1961. *Treasure in Earthen Vessels: The Church as a Human Community*. New York: Harper & Brothers. [Chicago: University of Chicago Press, Midway Reprints, 1976.]

Harrison, Beverly Wildung. 1984. *Making the Connections: Essays in Feminist Social Ethics*. Ed. Carol Robb. Boston: Beacon Press.

McFague, Sallie. 1987. *Models of God: Theology for an Ecological, Nuclear Age*. Philadelphia: Fortress Press.

Minear, Paul S. 1960. *Images of the Church in the New Testament*. Philadelphia: Westminster Press.

Morrison, Toni. 1987. *Beloved*. New York: Alfred Knopf.

Niebuhr, H. Richard, in collaboration with Daniel Day Williams and James M. Gustafson. 1956. *The Purpose of the Church and Its Ministry*. New York: Harper & Brothers.

Phillips, Dayton. 1941. *Beguines in Medieval Strasbourg: A Study of the Social Aspect of Beguine Life*. Stanford: Stanford University Press.

Raymond, Janice. 1986. *A Passion for Friends: Toward a Philosophy of Female Affection*. Boston: Beacon Press.

Ruether, Rosemary Radford. 1985. *Women-Church: Theology and Practice of Feminist Liturgical Communities*. San Francisco: Harper & Row.

Russell, Letty M. 1993. *Church in the Round: Feminist Interpretation of the Church*. Louisville: Westminster/John Knox.

Schüssler Fiorenza, Elisabeth.1983. *In Memory of Her: A Feminist Reconstruction of Early Christian Origins*. New York: Crossroad.

—. 1993. *Discipleship of Equals: A Critical Feminist Ekklesia-logy of Liberation*. New York: Crossroad.

Southern, R.W. 1970. *Western Society and the Church in the Middle Ages*. Baltimore: Penguin.

Troeltsch, Ernst. (1981 ed.) *The Social Teaching of the Christian Churches*. 2 vol. Chicago: University of Chicago Press.

Welch, Sharon D. 1985. *Communities of Resistance and Solidarity*. Maryknoll, NY: Orbis Books.

Christian Life

Section III

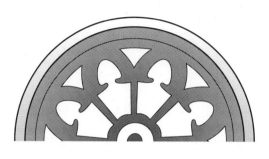

Introduction

to Section III

Rita Nakashima Brock

T o be alive, faith requires flesh, blood, and bone. The greatest Christian witness to the life-giving power of the gospel is its evidence in our lives, lived moment by moment. We manifest our faith daily in ordinary acts and in our participation in the life of the church. Christian faith that is a confession, but that does not inform and guide our lives, is a hollow shadow of the promise of life lived in God's grace. This section of our introduction to women in theological conversations explores how ideas of Christian life are being informed by women's lives and by the thoughts of women who have consciously reflected on their own and other women's experiences.

Traditional theology has called this study of Christian human life anthropology: *anthros*=human, *ology*=study of. Through theological anthropology we examine the nature of human existence as lived in life with God, how we are created and live *imago dei*, in God's image, and how we may fall short of our call to live in that image, a failing called sin. Topics such as ethics, pastoral counseling, Christian education, preaching, spiritual life, and ministry are used to study anthropological questions. From reading traditional theological anthropologies, one might conclude that women should be regarded "just like men," at best, and, at worst, inferior beings incapable of religious authority or the highest spiritual development because of our flawed nature. "Man" has been the theological subject of discussion, and the solutions to human dilemmas often ignore the complex realities of women's lives or use them to make us subordinate.

The particularly female aspects and responsibilities of human life have been used to show why women are supposedly inferior to men—ways in which our lives are trivial and we are less than men, who were supposedly less trapped by the demands of domestic life and the flesh and, therefore, freer to live in the flesh-denying spirit. In the face of such sexism, feminists have raised questions about theological anthropology. Where in theological discussions of human life does one find specific reflections on love and power as women might experience them: of hope in the shape of a young woman's aspirations as she reaches the crossroads of late adolescence, of brokenness experienced as the bearing of sexual violation and physical beating, of female perceptions of intimate love, sexuality, and menstruation, or the complexities of mothering—birthing, breast-feeding, or teaching language and conscience to the next generation? Are these unimportant or peripheral to life?

One of the first second-wave feminist theologians to raise the question of how women's experience differed from men's was Valerie C. Saiving in 1960, who is discussed more extensively by Bonnie Miller McLemore in her essay in this section. Saiving explored what women's different experiences might contribute to theology's ability to address the whole human situation, and she challenged the usefulness of the traditional idea of sin as pride. Saiving thought pride too lopsided an idea for women socialized to subordinate their lives, aspirations, and desires to those of families. For example, she noted that women who raise children with any success learn how to subsume their own perspectives to those of another. Traditional, stereotyped ideals of femininity emphasize passivity, acquiescence, self-sacrifice, and receptivity. The sin of pride assumes an assertiveness and quest for power typical of masculine stereotypes, contained neither in ideals of "true womanhood" nor in the nuanced psychological skills necessary for raising families and nurturing other human beings.

Yet, Saiving did not assume that lack of pride made women sinless. Instead, she challenged the basic androcentric definition of sin, which is based in the socialization of men to be competitive, aggressive, and dominating (and women who aspire to be "just like a man"). Saiving's goal was to create a fuller, more inclusive understanding of sin that affirmed a healthy, loving sense of self for all human beings.

To understand the importance of Saiving's question about sin, we need to keep in mind that the story of Adam and Eve's sin in

Genesis 3 has been interpreted by many theologians as the key to women's inferiority. We were assigned the responsibility for bringing sin into the world, "the gateway of the Devil," to use Tertullian's phrase, and this interpretation of the story was used to argue that women had an inferior moral capacity, that we were inherently more sinful than men. From feminist perspectives, the androcentrism of discussions of sin can be quite horrifying. For example, Augustine in sections 17–30 of *The City of God* tries to dissuade the raped women of Rome from suicide by telling them that they were adding the sin of homicide to the sin of adultery. And when the women asked why God allowed this horror to happen to good Christian women, he suggested that they may have an "unconscious pride," from which God humbled them through rape, thereby preventing them from committing the sin of pride in the future (Pellauer: 176–177). When placed in the life circumstances of African-American slave women, of children molested by parents, or of any of us who has been raped, such theological pronouncements seem to defend a particular view of God and humans at the expense of the suffering of real people. Is this good theological anthropology?

Saiving's work spawned a number of feminist studies of sin and salvation and was a harbinger of feminist work to follow. Mary Potter Engel, who worked extensively with survivors of rape and domestic violence, constructed a fourfold definition for sin. She proposed that sin be seen as: 1) the distortion of feeling, such as the denial of anger at violation by substituting self-blame, or moral callousness, the hardening of heart; 2) betrayal of trust, such as abuse and the using of another's dependency on us for our own gain, which shifts away from a focus on obedience; 3) lack of care, such as self-loathing or the inability to maintain appropriate personal boundaries; and 4) lack of consent to vulnerability, such as our inability to acknowledge our connections to and healthy emotional needs for love or our contempt for those who are weak and need our help (Engel: 156–163). As Engel's work shows, when we take the experiences of women seriously, theological anthropology can take on new life for us.

The life cycle and domestic responsibilities of women as a resource for theology were explored in second-wave feminist theology by Penelope Washbourne in her 1977 book *Becoming Woman*. She examines each stage of growing up female, becoming a woman, and having and raising children. In her "woman-centered" theological anthropology, Washbourne challenges the split between mind and body so common in Western Christian culture, a split antithetical to the idea of incarnation, in which spirit and flesh dwell together. Washbourne argues that women's bodily experiences, as well as our family responsibilities, reveal the sacred truths of love. Love means that we, male and female, are social beings who live organically connected to other beings in interdependent relationships through which we cocreate each other. She notes:

> As a participant in a physical process called conception, pregnancy, labor, expulsion, lactation, and a continuing participant in a process called menstruation and coitus, I have continually to ask myself, "What does going through all these events have to do with my perceptions about reality?...How does that relate to *my* theology...and to the meaning of my own human experience? How can I integrate my physical experiences with the religious tradition in which I was raised? How do they relate to non-procreative females or those in different cultural situations? Are they spiritual events of a new quality?" (Washbourne, 1981: 93)

Washbourne concludes that women's bodily and social experiences help us understand that personal independence is a self-deceptive fiction. She argues that the body has a wisdom that should be heeded rather than needlessly overridden by scientific control. She also points out that learning to adapt ourselves to the cycles of organic time teaches us patience, a deeper capacity to observe and listen to the seasons of life and the body, and the joys of bodily pleasure—all of which enhance our spiritual life. Finally, women's bodies are social bodies that continually connect us with larger temporal rhythms, with roles and responsibilities, with the tragic limits of our individual lives, and with the physical dimensions of spirituality. In other words, women's bodies present us with the reality of how connected we are to others and the organic world of creation, rather than separated as isolated individuals.

As three theological angles on women's lives Saiving, Engel, and Washbourne raise feminist questions about both the pitfalls and the possibilities of creating theologies more adequate to address the whole human situation, not an androcentric view of that situation. In listening deeply to their own experiences as women and in reflecting on those experiences in theological terms, they acknowledge the constant ambiguities of life, not only for women, but for all Christians who struggle to live faithfully, attuned to the lives God has given us. Their cautions and hopes point to how women's experiences reveal the pains and pleasures, the losses and rewards of our human covenants, of our connectedness. They show how relationships, for better or worse, are essential to our lives. In doing so, they herald the extensive work done on feminist ideas of love, ideas that explore our intimate, day-to-day experiences of empathy, passion, friendship, and compassion as forms of divine loving.

Taking the lives and loves of women and children seriously in reflecting on the responsibilities and promises of Christian life is central to feminist work in theology and continues to grow as more women become theologians. In 1968 Nelle Morton taught the first seminary class on feminist theology at Drew University Theological School and seeded a movement driven largely by the demands of the rapid increase of women in seminaries studying for the ministry. For the first time now in Christian theology and seminary education, feminist questions are being asked about the many dimensions of women's lives. How are we to understand forgiveness and sin in the face of abuse, violence, and incest? What does love mean when one has carried another human being inside one's own body, cared passionately about this new life, fed the infant from one's own flesh, and endured sheer exhaustion caring for her/him? What survival skills and faith are necessary to keep families together under slavery, grinding poverty, racism, and political oppression? What is the shape of hope that helps us through the struggles and joys that come from nurturing a child until it grows up to become a friend, and what is the nature of such friendship? How are we to teach conscience and truth in ways that enhance self-respect and self-knowledge in those for whom we have responsibility? What can we learn about the love of God from our complex, highly charged experiences of intimacy, friendship, and sexuality?

In addition to the social and personal issues that impact women's lives, Christian feminist thinkers have examined the life of the church. There are studies of the structure of authority for women pastors and leaders in the church. Feminists seek liberating, inclusive music and language for worship and examine the theology and the structure of liturgy. The right to ordination and the ways women preach have been discussed. The intuitive and aesthetic aspects of religious life emerge not only in inclusive hymns, but also in the creating of new visual images in our sanctuaries and the studying of the inner spiritual life of contemplation. Feminists have also addressed the special needs and the psychology of women as they reveal some of the inadequacies of traditional pastoral counseling. And the suffering of church members has been exposed through studies of the abuse of power and clergy sexual abuse. In addition, the ministry of the church in the larger society has been scrutinized from perspectives that examine ethics, social justice, peace work, ecological responsibility, and economics.

This section addresses a small segment of issues related to Christian life as understood from the experiences of the Protestant women who authored these essays. The authors discuss how each of us gives shape and focus to our personal lives and how we contribute to the life of our churches. Many women nurture and feed children, care for people who are sick or elderly, balance the demands of work and family, lead worship, maintain friendships, struggle to find words for our experiences, seek the authority to speak, and teach language and values to the next generation. Given such tasks, the essays in this section discuss how Christian life can be given flesh, blood, and bone: in mothering, caught in the tensions between nurturing and self-fulfillment; in prayer, lived out moment by moment in the routine of our lives; in preaching, torn between the silences imposed by tradition and those born of our own uncertainties; and in the embodiment of the Spirit in our own flesh, manifest in our relationships to food, body image, and breast-feeding. Mothering, counseling, prayer, preaching, and our bodies are issues for us all in the various shapes and forms they take in our own lives.

How we live our faith daily is not an easy question for women, for many reasons. We have felt conflicting demands between the "just like a man" and "woman-centered strategies." Our desires to nurture children and our sense of fulfillment from paid work do not coexist easily, a tension McLemore discusses in "What's a Feminist Mother to Do?" She notes that many feminist mothers grew up with unrealistic media and cultural images of mothering. For other mothers this tension is created by the economic necessity of undertaking paid work to support their families. McLemore explores new ways to consider how we can integrate our responsibilities for nurturing families with our needs for self-fulfillment. She also discusses the impact that feminist research on women's lives has had on pastoral counseling. Since the majority of parishioners who seek help are women and the majority of pastors and pastoral counselors are men, McLemore notes that the lack of scholarly attention to women's particular needs must be addressed by more feminist work if seminaries are to train pastors and counselors adequately.

Whatever the complex demands on our lives and our needs for healing, Kay Bessler Northcutt reminds us in "August in Her Breast" that we find our spiritual strength in prayer, in our attention to life as we live it moment by moment, step by step. In sidestepping conventional understandings of prayer as public words in worship or petitions to God, Northcutt opens paths for women's spiritual rejuvenation. She indicates that the status of our work and the attention the world pays to our labors are not what matter in prayer. Rather, Northcutt invites us to be touched in the depths of our souls and renewed in the energy of our spirits by the attention we give to our relationships to God, to each other, to the works of our lives, and to the limits of human finitude.

In the renewal of our spirits and reflection on our faith, many women have felt called to preach, but the church has not made this easy, as Mary Donovan Turner notes in her essay, "The Word, Words, and Women." Women have often been trapped behind the expectation that we "keep silent" and do the invisible, domestic background work for the church, and "real women" do not choose another calling above silent servanthood. The call that women have felt to serve the church in more visible leadership ways, like men have been allowed to do, has been at odds with traditional ideas of where women belong and what women should do. The preachers Donovan discusses, including her own students, give us hope for how, despite the struggle, women find our own, distinctive voices in the pulpit.

How women's faith and spirituality undergird our relationships to our bodies and food is explored by Nadia Lahutsky's essay on the fasting of medieval mystics, who saw fasting as an extension of their spiritual power. In seeking to understand the spiritual reasons for their refusals to eat, Lahutsky, in "Food and Feminism and Historical Interpretations: The Case of Medieval Holy Women," holds up a powerful mirror to contemporary questions about women and eating disorders, dieting, and our secular preoccupations with thinness in a world in which many struggle to find enough to eat. While cautioning us not to transpose our contemporary obsessions onto medieval women's fasting, Lahutsky nonetheless asks us to consider if our squeamishness about public breast-feeding and our preoccupations with dieting and fitness indicate that we have a healthier attitude toward our own flesh; for we live in a secularized culture in which flesh no longer has a spiritual dimension. She asks us how we can reclaim the love of our bodies as part of our spiritual life. And she gives us hope by reminding us that a people called to the table to eat and drink, as a central liturgical act, ought to be able to reflect on the meaning of nourishment and life in the flesh.

It is to that communion table that we turn in the final essay of this book. In a conversation among the authors, we discuss images of being fed, of presiding at the table, of changing the ritual and the role of ritual in change, the inclusivity of the table, the theology behind the table, and its symbolic functions. A defining feature of this conversation, and of feminist theological anthropology in general, is the search for the illuminating glow of the Spirit in the ordinary, in the daily moments of our lives, everywhere, in the often messy middle of life. By providing a roundtable discussion of the Eucharist, we sought to embody our work both as an everyday act and as a gathering of the faithful, equals at the table. May it be so.

Works Consulted

Andolsen, Barbara H., Christian E. Gudorf, and Mary Pellauer. 1987. *Women's Consciousness, Women's Conscience: A Reader in Feminist Ethics*. New York: Harper & Row.

Campbell, Joan, and David Polk. 1991. *Bread Afresh, Wine Anew: Sermons by Disciples Women*. St. Louis: Chalice Press.

Caron, Charlotte. 1993. *To Make and Make Again: Feminist Ritual Theology*. New York: Crossroad Press.

Case-Winters, Anna. 1990. *God's Power: Traditional Understandings and Contemporary Challenges*. Louisville: Westminster Press.

Christ, Carol, and Judith Plaskow. 1979. *Womanspirit Rising: A Feminist Reader in Religion*. New York: Harper & Row.

Engel, Mary Potter. 1990. "Evil, Sin, and Violation of the Vulnerable." In *Lift Every Voice: Constructing Theologies from the Underside*, ed. by Susan Brooks Thistlethwaite and Mary Potter Engel. New York: Harper & Row.

Golden, Renny. 1991. *The Hour of the Poor, The Hour of Women: Salvadoran Women Speak*. New York: Crossroad Press.

Harrison, Beverly. 1985. *Making the Connections: Essays in Feminist Social Ethics*, ed. by Carol S. Robb. Boston: Beacon Press.

Heyward, Carter. 1989. *Touching Our Strength: The Erotic as Power and the Love of God*. New York: Harper & Row.

Miles, Margaret. 1989. *Carnal Knowing: Female Nakedness and Religious Meaning in the Christian West*. Boston: Beacon Press.

Morton, Nelle. 1985. *The Journey Is Home*. Boston: Beacon Press.

Pellauer, Mary, and Susan Brooks Thistlethwaite. 1990. "Conversation on Grace and Healing: Perspectives from the Movement to End Violence Against Women." In *Lift Every Voice: Constructing Theologies from the Underside*, ed. by Susan Brooks Thistlethwaite and Mary Potter Engel. New York: Harper & Row.

Plaskow, Judith, and Carol Christ. 1989. *Weaving the Visions: New Patterns in Feminist Spirituality*. New York: Harper & Row.

Proctor-Smith, Marjorie. 1990. *In Her Own Rite: Constructing Feminist Liturgical Tradition*. Nashville: Abingdon Press.

Saiving, Valerie C. 1979. "The Human Situation: A Feminine View." In *Womanspirit Rising*, ed. by Christ and Plaskow. New York: Harper & Row. [First published in April 1960 in *The Journal of Religion*.]

Sewell, Marilyn. 1991. *Cries of the Spirit: A Celebration of Women's Spirituality*. Boston: Beacon Press.

Washbourne, Penelope. 1977. *Becoming Woman*. New York: Harper & Row.

—. 1981. "The Dynamics of Female Experience: Process Models and Human Values." In *Feminism and Process Thought*, ed. by Sheila Greeve Davaney. Lewiston, NY: Edwin Mellon Press.

Wren, Brian. 1989. *What Language Shall I Borrow?* New York: Crossroad Press.

9

What's a Feminist Mother to Do?

*Dedicated to
my great-grandmother,
Myrtle Alice Lee McAdow* *Bonnie J. Miller-McLemore*

F or those less influenced than I by commercial television of the 1960s, the question of "What's a Feminist Mother to Do?" is a play on words of an advertisement ditty for laundry detergent forever imprinted on my preadolescent brain some thirty years ago. Holding up a sad-looking pair of grass- and dirt-stained jeans, the TV mother laments, "What's a mother to do?" Or, at least, that's how I remember it.

Although I have forgotten whether it was Cheer or Tide that best solved this mother's problem, I have not forgotten another, more insinuating message: it is mothers who are essentially responsible for family stains and the task of keeping the household clean. Like it or not, the duty of preserving family purity in both its literal and symbolic forms permeated my earliest visions of motherhood. It probably did so for a multitude of white, middle-class, television-raised children. Yet who can blame the media and the market for capitaliz-

---

The writing of this chapter is partially supported by a Lilly Endowment, Inc. grant with which I am involved with several other scholars on The Family, Religion, and Culture. The chapter builds on my more extensive exploration of motherhood, *Also a Mother: Work and Family as Theological Dilemma* (Nashville: Abingdon, 1994).

ing on what were widely held cultural beliefs about mothers and family laundry?

Fortunately, popular culture was not the only influence on my dreams. On the corner of a table in my dining room sits an antique, leather-bound college album from the class of 1894 of Disciples-affiliated Eureka College. Within its hard cover, my great-grandmother, Myrtle Alice Lee, a member of an independent Christian Church, is pictured. She is one of the five women graduating in a class of seventeen, in many ways a position of privilege at a time when few women went to college. Although the point of her education may have been as much to enrich the life of the home as to equip her for a public vocation, her education was part of a broader movement that continued to expand the horizons of women at the turn of and into this century. A 1960 pamphlet of news of the graduates, inserted into the album later by my grandmother, her daughter, Lois Lee McAdow, tells us that Myrtle was class secretary and became a "fine educator," teaching in Eureka and Webster City, Iowa. She was also a mother.

My grandmother, likewise a college graduate, used to write me letters in French to help me practice a second language and exercise her own knowledge. She prized the activity of knowing. When she married my grandfather, a Baptist, they joined the Christian Church (Disciples of Christ) as a sort of compromise between their two church traditions. Although I cannot say that either my grandmother or my great-grandmother were feminists (and might even be bothered by such a label), they both participated in social, economic, and technological changes in this century that made the first and second waves of the feminist movement almost inevitable in response. From them, transposed across a few generations, I gained the value of learning, the import of Christian faith, and the strength of women's self-worth.

Rita Nakashima Brock's introduction to this volume suggests that understanding women's lives in the Christian church means "understanding how the feminist movement has touched women in churches, in seminaries, and in pulpits." Understanding our lives also means understanding how feminism has touched women in families, as mothers with children. This has never been an easy matter. Reigning stereotypes cast feminists as anti-men, and also anti-children. While these labels may capture a bit of the flavor of feminist struggles to claim a place for women, they sorely miss the substance of the struggle. Although feminists certainly challenged institutional views of motherhood and family that constrained and harmed women, and challenged the men who depended upon these views, few feminists are actually either anti-men or anti-children. These labels falsify history. They also deter us from accurate understandings of the difficult problems mothers face and the kinds of solutions feminists have tried to offer.

In this chapter, my intent is simply to broaden impressions and provoke curiosity about what Christian feminism may mean for women, mothers, families, and children. When feminism is defined as the repudiation of any ranking of people as inferior or superior according to various traits of human nature—a definition to which many feminists adhere—there are more women who qualify as Christian feminist mothers than most people might initially imagine. Yet, if cultural stereotypes continue to make "feminist motherhood" seem like a contradiction in terms, what's a feminist mother or, more precisely, a Christian feminist mother to do? Suffice it to say, the problems for women have always been far more complex than commercial lyrics would have us believe. Moreover, contrary to popular opinion, neither dirty laundry nor conflicts between work and family should ever be the sole responsibility of mothers and feminists. I would like to begin to correct some of the myths about feminism and motherhood by covering three vast areas in broad strokes: motherhood and North American feminism; motherhood and Christian feminist theology; and finally, feminism, mothers, and pastoral care. Obviously, this introductory chapter will not do justice to the historical and social complexity of any one of these matters, nor will it begin to cover the diversity of perspectives on motherhood, families, pastoral care, and so forth. However, it will attempt to initiate discussion of a subject often sorely overlooked in both church circles and theology, by first tracing shifting strategies in regard to motherhood in feminism in general before turning to some questions raised specifically for Christians. In both secular and Christian feminism, we will see a significant shift in feminist strategies from a rejection to a qualified restoration of motherhood, but the questions of motherhood and family are far from resolved.

Motherhood and North American Feminism

Motherhood presents feminism with a catch-22. In order to achieve equality in a male-dominated world, some have felt that motherhood must be completely rejected, or at least downplayed. But to downplay motherhood is to cast aside a basic biological, emotional, and social enterprise that stands at the center of the lives of many women and communities. Yet, how can women reclaim motherhood without giving in to the cultural tendency of defining women simply in sexual terms as wives and mothers? All too often, reproductive difference has been exaggerated and manipulated and the love of mothers for their children has been romanticized and idealized as innate and unconditional precisely in order to deny equality to women.

Hence, from the beginning of the first feminist wave to today, a tension has existed between feminists who claim the centrality of motherhood and those impatient with domestic distractions. It is fair to say that the conflict between women's claims as mothers and their claims for equality as individuals in the public sphere has been an ongoing, almost inherent, problem in the history of women and human rights. Indeed, the debate about motherhood is a critical ingredient behind the changes in strategies of the dominant, middle-class North American feminist movement that Brock described in the introduction. In this section, using Peggy Mackintosh's schema of five phases of feminist consciousness as recast by Brock, I want to look at some changes in feminist consciousness and tactics as they relate to mothers.

I am told that both my grandmother and my great-grandmother suffered mild depressions for which they received rather primitive treatment by today's standards. While it would be unwarranted for me blindly to rule out emotional problems as a cause, I am convinced that personal quirks were not the sole root of their anguish. The social limitations for women were at least equally responsible. For women with needs, talents, and desires for satisfying work of our own, the plight of determining the right laundry detergent—my metaphor for the social pressure to make domestic chores one's highest calling—could not help but lead to an inhumane deterrence from fully participating in life. When an early twentieth-century psychoanalyst, Karen Horney, attempted to understand the problems of women of this era, she described the contradictions of the "feminine type" in the 1920s caught between desires to pursue their own ambitions and desires to please fathers and husbands:

> Women were permitted to pursue education but expected to become mothers. They were encouraged to be sexually emancipated but supposed to limit sexual desire to monogamous marriage combined with asexual motherhood. They were told that they could have careers but were expected to defer to men at work and at home. They were enticed by ambition but taught to find salvation in love (Westkott, 1986: 50–51).

It is no small wonder that many women, my heritage included, suffered arrested energy and lost hope. What is surprising is that people like Horney were so quickly dismissed by both their contemporaries and, even recently, by clinic, academy, and church (she never made it onto any list of classic figures in either my academic or my clinical training, for example). As needed as it was at the time,

Horney's work did little to alter the bias against women at the heart of culture.

On the other hand, given the anxieties surrounding gender and change, maybe this is not so surprising after all. If we have managed to forget Mary Wollstonecraft's 1792 *Vindication of the Rights of Women* (another critical tract that never made it onto any list of significant Enlightenment readings or into any family table conversations), maybe it is just a matter of course that Horney, as *woman*, has also been disregarded. Yet, despite the slights of history, their prescribed goal—a "female hero" who assumes responsibility for claiming that she herself is worthy of care and that the world is her domain as well—has permeated consciousness more than we can ever know.

In the first phases of consciousness-raising—what Brock has described as "Just Like a Man" and "Add Women and Stir"—feminists contested powerful demons: a post-World War II North American mindset that idealized the breadwinner husband, his homemaker wife, and the increasingly isolated suburban, nuclear household with its fascinating gadgets and fast foods. Behind this stood the nineteenth-century Victorian ideal of motherly domesticity, now firmly entrenched in the modern psyche. These images of motherhood were bolstered by religious ideals of moral piety, sexual purity, and wifely submission. And they assumed a white middle-class whose ability to create such a unique home environment partially depended on immense sacrifices by the working class and other ethnic groups who often could not do so. By the mid-twentieth century, for the white middle-class, motherhood had became a profession in its own right, bolstered by home economic classes and majors in interior decorating.

Although people acted as if everyone had always lived in breadwinner-homemaker families from time immemorial, this image of motherhood was quite relative to twentieth-century Western society and remained beyond the pale for most working-class and minority families. When those in the women's movement in the 1960s challenged the 1950s image of happiness, they demanded something few women had ever had before—parity with men in the marketplace and in the household. However, in seeking equal pay and a shared family life, they neither anticipated the immense emotional and social roadblocks nor understood the ways in which their challenge to sexism was blind to racist and classist superstructures that also preserved structures of inequality.

Feminist strategies of "Just Like a Man" and "Add Women and Stir" urged women to enter the work force and seek the same rights as men, shattering the "cult of true womanhood" that defined the home as woman's sphere. However, these early feminist strategies tended to ignore an entire substrata of North American society. In contrast to feminist protests about the traps of home and the right to work, many women from the working class and different ethnic backgrounds had had no choice but to manage mothering and employed work side by side in order to survive. For many, dedicated motherhood was a key to the endurance of the family and community. Moreover, it is partially slave and working-class labor that made it possible for the middle class to restrict mothers to homemaking. Repeatedly, from slave to current times, white claims on black mothering have taken many women out of their own homes to care for the homes and children of whites. Without understanding this, women's "liberation" only perpetuated the pattern. Upper-strata mothers who desired creative, professional work often simply bought from those in lower economic brackets the home services needed to sustain family life—housekeepers, live-in nannies, gardeners, caterers, decorators, contractors. Women's "liberation" in this vein simply shifts the weight of domestic chores "from one group of exploited women—mothers—to another group—the babysitter, housekeeper, cleaning woman, day-care staff, teacher" (Miller-McLemore, 1991a: 12).

Here, in the tension between equality and family, we see an initial factor behind a shift in feminist consciousness and strategy. Growing awareness of the different ways women in diverse economic and ethnic groups experienced motherhood helped initiate a change in second-wave feminist strategies from the "Just Like a Man" and the "Add Women and Stir Strategies" to the "Women-Centered" and the "Include Everyone Strategies." Feminist protests about the entrapments of the housewife do not make much sense to those robbed of chances to establish safe, strong homes, or to those fighting to prepare their children for survival in a hostile, racist, discriminatory environment. Motherhood, rather than being derided as an exploitive, oppressive, or sexist institution, must be cherished to persist at all, for the sake of the endurance of the larger group. It is not motherhood that is the obstacle to freedom, but racism, lack of jobs, skills, education, and a number of other issues.

In the introduction of this book, Brock points to a second critical ingredient in a shift in feminist strategies: motherhood itself. Early feminist strategies also tended to ignore the real pleasures of motherhood, despite the multiple hardships. Sara Ruddick (1989) is not alone in her experience of motherhood as a pivotal turning point in her life, work, and feminist ideals. Autobiographical notes in the prefaces of books and casual remarks of other women reiterate the theme: "Until my children were born, I went along quite nicely" (Rossiter, 1988: 11). Simply put, woman cannot bear children "Just Like a Man."

Moreover, the capacity to bear children tends to change a woman's view of the world and what's important.

In *Maternal Thinking*, Ruddick dares to suggest that through the very act of securing children's survival mothers themselves engage in seldom recognized complex philosophical and ethical thought processes. A few other feminists began to use their embodied pregnant and maternal experiences as ground for new reflections (Kristeva, 1986; Suleiman, 1985; Young, 1984). In a kind of cultural gestalt, across a variety of disciplines, from law to literature, women began to notice the ways in which psychological analysis, literary critique, legal practice, moral theory, public policy, and so forth have ignored the mother as a subject. Many began to assert the role of the mother as thinker and participant in her own right. Feminists in psychology, for example, began to analyze not just the needs of the child in human development, but the needs of the mother's development in relationship to the child. As literary critic Pauline Bart remarks, time had come to consider "'Portnoy's *mother's* complaint'" (quoted by Luepnitz, 1988: 167).

Feminists still wanted equality with men, but now recognized that equality must recognize differences, including those differences created by motherhood. Law professor Mary Becker, for example, authored an essay in which she claims that in granting men and women the same right to child custody, divorce proceedings have failed to acknowledge the greater intensity of maternal involvement with children. Although not without its dangers as a position, she is right to underscore that failing to recognize "how difficult it is to equalize the emotional attachment of mothers and fathers to their children will inevitably cause continuing inequality" (Becker, 1992: 167). Only a recognition of certain differences between mothers and fathers will promote justice.

A third significant factor related to motherhood, women's immense workload as a result of the notorious "second shift," also influenced a change in feminist strategies. Middle-strata mothers who began to work "Just Like a Man" glimpsed problems that working-strata women and single mothers have always known and endured to some extent: what Arlie Hochschild popularized as the "second shift." Based on time use studies done in the 1960s and 1970s, Hochschild estimates that over a year women worked an *"extra month of twenty-four-hour days a year.* Over a dozen years, it was an extra year of twenty-four-hour days" (Hochschild, 1989: 3–4). When the framework is stretched beyond the United States, the distortions grow only more apparent. A 1980 United Nations report indicates that women worldwide perform two-thirds of the world's labor, receive 10 percent of the pay, and own 1 percent of the property.

In short, feminists realized the import of maternal and domestic labor. As long as the workplace still expects the worker to have a wife or a servant, as long as men are no more willing to pick up the broom than their fathers, as long as an underclass of women take care of the homes and children of those in the upper stratas, certain feminist strategies for change will simply be ineffective. And we must contend with what Hochschild calls a "stalled revolution" (Hochschild, 1989: 12). Intimate connections to children and desires to preserve the delicate, domestic fabric of home and community create problems that extend far beyond obtaining good, affordable child care or parental leave policies.

Resurrecting the stalled revolution involves challenging an economic and social system that views children, home, and community life as "nonwork" and that views market labor as almost completely independent of the labors of family and community. It means recognizing motherhood and domestic matters for their critical place in human survival and for the real hours of labor that they entail. It even means finding feminist values in motherhood in its many diverse shapes and forms without thereby returning women to motherhood and marriage as singular, viable, exclusive careers.

Motherhood and Christian Feminism

In a 1980 article on politics and the family, Roman Catholic feminist theologian Rosemary Radford Ruether states the "*imperative need* vigorously to contest the claims of the New Right to represent the interests of the 'family'" (Ruether, 1980: 264, emphasis added). Feminists and other progressives would do well to keep the issue of the family in our own camp, she argues, and not allow conservatives to accuse us of being against the values of families and children. She concludes, "The home is too important a place for all of us to give it away to the right" (266).

Among Christian feminist theologians, the discussion on the family has advanced beyond what Ruether proposes. In fact, feminist theologians have been talking about family values of a different sort for longer than many people might like to suppose. At the same time, it hardly seems that anyone has heard or listened. In too many cases, extremely helpful theological reconstructions of families and work based on just, shared responsibility have simply not reached ministers and congregations, much less families and the workplace.

Why is this? Broadly speaking, white, middle-class feminist Christian theologians have worked harder to promote the feminist view that the patriarchal family no longer has a place than actually to identify alternative Christian family models. The conversation is even more sparse when it comes to the role of motherhood. Many theologians are mothers, and advocate maternal God imagery and language, but few have investigated in any depth what is learned about Christianity from this pivotal life experience. Few have made the complex intersection of work and family a primary topic of theological research. A careful study of the complex relationship between Christian feminists and mothers is in order. This section will trace a process in feminist theology that closely resembles the general shift in feminist strategies that we explored in the last section from a rejection to a qualified restoration of motherhood.

I recall vividly one of my own experiences of a "woman-less church" of predominantly male leadership. At some point in the 1960s, my home congregation in the Christian Church (Disciples of Christ) voted to allow women as deacons. To young eyes adapted to all men marching down the aisles in dark suits and enamored by our own male minister, I felt strong cognitive dissonance: these women looked starkly out of place. But why? From almost everything I had been explicitly taught about the priesthood of all believers, the unity of all Christians, creation in the image of God, the love of Christ, and the justice of the kingdom, women belonged around the communion table as much as men. The best explanation that my youthful, naive reasoning could muster was based simply on clothing: it must be their colorful dresses, I thought, that convinced me that their participation was somehow "wrong." Now this memory simply serves to remind me of the extent to which antipathy toward women and resistance to inclusivity is deeply embedded in our human psyches and social systems, including (or especially?) religious traditions and practices.

Western theology and society have yet to recover from the likes of the author of 1 Timothy and the damage perpetuated in Paul's name. As Marti Steussy mentions in her chapter, in a few brief passages in the second chapter of 1 Timothy, women are indicted to "learn in silence with full submission." Women, Timothy declares, shall neither teach nor have "authority over a man." The very order of human creation dictates that women follow men, and in the fall, Eve, not Adam, was deceived. If there is salvation to be had, it is "through childbearing" (1 Timothy 2:11–15a). These ideas about female silence, sinfulness, and the sanctity of childbearing have done their share of damage. The model of male headship and female submission triumphed perhaps above all when it became the family model so enthusiastically affirmed by many (although not all) of our sixteenth-century ancestors in the Protestant Reformation. Most recently, the evangelical right has claimed these "traditional values" as *the* biblical stance on the family despite the fact that several other significant scriptures contradict this position. No wonder some feminists have done away with Christian notions of family values and with the value of motherhood altogether.

To make any progress at all in such a world, a first obvious step was to acquire what men already assume—the vote, a place in worship rituals, a position on the church board, fresh liturgical language that includes women, jobs held traditionally by men, equal education. The list goes on. In these and many other ways, women were added and institutions of work, church, family, school were stirred. In this feminist struggle for a place alongside men, the place of motherhood simply did not figure in as an important factor. Indeed, for many white, middle-class women, devoted motherhood and the family were seen as instruments of control, limitation, and violence.

While second-wave feminist theologians followed the consciousness-raising model of the women's movement that made female experience a primary source of knowledge, few initially chose the commonly shared experiences of mothering as a central text for study. Motherhood came too close to women's negative experiences of traditional biologically defined roles that feminist theology wanted to challenge. When the second wave of feminism condemned Christianity for lending religious sanction to male superiority and female submission, for the most part feminist theologians in the 1960s and early 1970s agreed with this critique. Religious reinforcement of sexism was contested on at least three fronts: male God language and ideology; the exclusion of women from religious vocation and reflection; and the religious sanction of subordination of women and mothers in the home. Initially, feminist theologians used the tactics of "Just Like a Man," "Add Women and Stir," and "Women as Victims" to challenge exclusive language, to secure ministerial positions, and to dispute male headship in the family.

By the late 1970s and 1980s, however, the feminist project in theology shifted significantly from a critique of a male-dominated Christianity to a reconstruction of its positive meanings based on a women-centered perspective. As Steussy, McAvoy, and others have shown in earlier chapters, this entailed the recovery of traditions at variance with male hierarchy within Christian scriptures, traditions, and communities, and the retrieval of alternative Christian symbols, myths, and rituals. Similarly, alternative Christian family values and norms for motherhood also surfaced. For the most part, however, the quiet stream of thought on mothers and families has seldom been lifted up and appreciated. While I cannot begin to tell half the story in just a few pages here, I will try to give a flavor of the discussion.

As Elizabeth Lee Thomsen's chapter on biblical interpretation illustrates, first-wave feminists themselves relied on, rather than rejected, church structures and religious tenets to further the cause of women's rights. Although the elite group of nineteenth-century women's rights activists such as Elizabeth Cady Stanton and Frances Willard had little sense of the problems so familiar to us today of female poverty, racial oppression, child care, parental leave, and so forth, they were among the first to make a strong case for gender-equal partnerships of shared responsibility in the home and for active, devoted fatherhood. A chief source for their position was belief in Christian principles of love and justice. In the secular histories of feminism, the important role of Christian values is all too often ignored. But, contrary to the impression given by the religious right, Christianity has not just endorsed male dominance and the patriarchal family as a religious norm; it has also acted to liberate women and has itself created precedent for gender justice and women's equal worth.

Significantly, a classic essay, written in 1958 at the very beginning of second-wave feminism, represents a powerful exception to the general antipathy toward biological mothering and cuts across several of our categories of feminist strategies. Valerie Saiving begins her article, "The Human Situation: A Feminine View," by plainly stating, "I am a student of theology; I am also a woman" (Saiving, 1960: 100). She has seen, she implies, some problems that men have traditionally overlooked. Her redefinition of sin as involving self-loss as much as pride and of love as requiring self-affirmation as much as self-giving should be recognized and remembered for priming the pump of a thirty-year period of revision and reconstruction in theology. And it is, I believe, her own maternal experience that furnishes the ground for a revelatory breakthrough in the nature of self-love and agape. Although she never claims so directly and few other feminist theologians tend to notice, implicit in her essay is a third qualifying phrase, "I am also a mother."

Writing under the guise of the third-person singular, Saiving struggles to understand the many implications of the "central fact about sexual differences": "In every society it is women—and only women—who bear children" and who remain "closest to the infant and young child" because of "the physiology of lactation" (103). While men must strive to achieve what mothers already have—a role in the powers of creation and the existential confirmation of childbearing—women face an entirely different set of temptations that male theologians have seldom understood. Rather than prideful, self-assertion that disregards the needs of others, mothers become so immersed in attending to external needs that they commit not the sin of self-centered will-to-power, but the sin of self-loss. Women's sin is better understood "as triviality, distractibility, and diffuseness; lack of an organizing center for focus; dependence on others for one's own self-definition...in short, underdevelopment or negation of the self." Then, she suggests something scarcely put forward as a religious ideal of salvation for mothers thus far: the moments, hours, and days of self-giving must be balanced by moments, hours, and days of "withdrawal into, and enrichment of, her individual selfhood if she is to remain a whole person" (108–9).

In a more recent interview about her essay, Saiving tells us about the personal context out of which she made her more abstract generalizations about female experience. Divorced, with a child, she had returned to graduate school after a thirteen-year hiatus to finish a degree in religion begun during World War II. At that time, she was the only woman accepted because "they were having trouble finding enough students [men] even for a ministerial degree." The paper itself was written for a class, while she was, in her words,

> trying to take care of my daughter Emily who was very small then. She was three, or four, maybe. I was trying to be a responsible student and also a good mother, and sometimes it just seemed impossible, especially since I was living in the city, and I didn't have any relatives or anybody like that to call on. I don't know what else to say....(Saiving, 1988: 108–9).

While Saiving draws implicitly upon her experience as a mother in her original essay, she did not or could not make the source of her inspiration explicit until more recently. Others, including myself, are freer to do so partly because women like Saiving opened the doors of Christian theological inquiry and vocational opportunity.

A recent essay by Sally Purvis, "Mothers, Neighbors, and Strangers: Another Look at Agape," suggests another reason why it has not been easy for many religious scholars, primarily men, to admit that children and parenting could be an important source of ethical theological reflection. Traditionally, male theologians have distrusted "special relations" between family members as too subjective, too arbitrary, too instinctual, too biased to inform objective, universal statements about the human good (Purvis, 1991: 19). Only recently have theologians begun to challenge this norm.

In defiance, a few feminist theologians, such as Purvis, Christine Gudorf, and myself, use maternal experience as a powerful tool to better understand theological categories of love, justice, redemption, human nature, sacrifice, and so forth. Contrary to everyone's instant assumption concerning Gudorf's decision to adopt a two-year-old who could not walk, talk, or eat, and a five-year-old who could barely walk, dress, or wash himself, selfless love, she realizes, was not a primary or sufficient factor. Her essay, "Parenting: Mutual Love and

Sacrifice," argues against Christian interpretations of *agape* as unconditional, self-disregarding self-sacrifice. Rather, Christian love must involve a measure of necessary self-love that actually enhances our capacity to give. As she discovers through her own investment in mothering, all love involves sacrifice, but ultimately aims at the give-and-take of mutuality. Moments of sacrifice, including Christ's sacrifice on the cross, are "just that—moments in a process designed to end in mutual love" (Gudorf, 1985: 186).

Just as in the feminist movement at large, women in other ethnic, religious traditions, both within and outside Christianity, have valued motherhood and respected maternal creativity and strength. As Paula Gunn Allen points out, the Lagun Pueblo/Sioux believe that at the "center of all is Woman." The ability inherent in mothering to transform something from one state to another is an ability "sought and treasured" among Native Americans (Gunn Allen, 1989: 22, 27). According to Delores Williams, African-American "womanist reality begins with mothers relating to their children" (Williams, 1989: 183). Mothers are honored for their wisdom about making "a way out of no way." In *Sisters in the Wilderness*, Williams lifts up the slave-girl Hagar—mother of Ishmael, Abram's first son—as a powerful figure in African-American women's religious experience. Hagar's example of willful survival with God's blessing has inspired mothers to support one another and to perceive the nurturing of children as a task of the entire community.

Other books signify a change in the times. In 1989, Anne Carr and Elisabeth Schüssler Fiorenza edited an issue of *Concilium* titled "Motherhood: Experience, Institution, Theology." It is suggested that greater explorations of motherhood have the capacity "not only for overcoming the split between the worlds of women and men but also splits among different cultures, nations, races, classes, and religions" (3–4). While this is perhaps far too optimistic a hope, essays in *Inheriting Our Mother's Gardens*, authored in 1988 by women from across the globe, seems to indicate that this is at least partially true (Russell, Pui-lan, Isasi-Díaz, Cannon, 1988). As Kris Culp asserts in her chapter, from the Beguines to the Salvadoran Christian Mothers for Peace and Life to middle-American church women, "women have been artisans of communal survival in many places and times," even though such public and domestic labors are seldom recognized as absolutely essential to the endurance of human society and human existence.

Feminism, Mothers, and Pastoral Care

Apart from a very important body of literature on domestic violence, abuse, and pastoral care (Clarke, 1986; Fortune, 1983; Pellauer, Chester, and Boyajian, 1987), little has been done on mothers and pastoral care per se. Although I have only begun to consider the implications of feminism and motherhood for the field of pastoral theology, I can say that one important development in pastoral care and theology today is a recasting of the field based on a better appreciation for the diversity of human experience, including that of women of diverse backgrounds (Miller-McLemore, 1993). In light of the discussion about feminism and motherhood, we would do well to review, even if only roughly, some changes afoot in pastoral care that reflect feminism's significant influence.

Pastoral care will never be the same. Pastoral theologian Emma Justes states that if clergy "are unable to travel the route of hearing women's anger, of exploring with women the painful depths of experiences of incest and rape, or enabling women to break free from cultural stereotypes that define their existence," they should not be doing pastoral counseling with women (Justes, 1985: 298). When those involved in pastoral care do not know how to recognize the realities of violence toward women, they foster further damage and violence. Particularly in situations of sexual abuse, for example, the problem in pastoral response is not too little empathy, but too much indiscriminate empathy by an uninformed pastoral caregiver that surfaces long-repressed feelings that overwhelm rather than help the person in need (Glaz, 1991). All pastoral caregivers must sharpen their sensitivity to the stress of women's experiences as wage-earners and homemakers (Miller-McLemore, 1991b), the economic devaluation of women in the workplace and women's poverty (Couture, 1991), health issues of concern to women ("Focus on Women," 1991), the implications of female images of God for self-esteem (Saussy, 1991), and so forth.

With a few significant exceptions, women in the field of pastoral care and theology have come up through the ranks of higher education approximately one generation behind women in religion and theology, such as Ruether and Fiorenza. One possible reason for the lag in the more active participation by women is the proximity of pastoral theology to the church and the conservative nature of congregational life. Despite the pastoral nature of much feminist theology and careful treatments of specific issues in pastoral care such as abuse or spirituality, there have been no books by a single author on pastoral theology from a woman's or a feminist perspective until quite recently (cf. Demarinis, 1994). And until the recent publication of *Womanist Care* (1993), which is not explicitly presented as a book on pastoral theology, the participation of African-American women has been almost entirely missing from the discussion. Meanwhile, more general books on theology such as Emily Town's *A Troubling in My Soul* (1993) and Williams' *Sisters in the Wilderness* (1993) are helpful resources and hopeful signs on the horizon of what it will mean to understand care from a womanist perspective.

What will it mean for the practice of pastoral care to bring new voices into play? *Women in Travail and Transition: A New Pastoral Care* offers an initial indication (1991). Edited by Glaz and Jeanne Stevenson Moessner, the book includes the work of five authors in ministerial settings and four in the academy. Chapters on new pastoral understandings of women in the first section and new pastoral paradigms in the final section frame other chapters in the middle on conflicts of work and family, alternative family forms, gynecologic processes and problems, sexual abuse, domestic violence, and depression. Almost every man who has read this text in my introductory pastoral care course testifies that it powerfully illumines women's lives. Women students want to send multiple copies to their ministerial colleagues, men and women alike. These students have heard a "cry," as one student expressed it, that they had never heard or understood before; they begin to hear in a different way that understands a woman's concerns from the inside rather than from the outside. Instead of blaming the woman, for example, for causing physical abuse and encouraging her to stay with her husband, a caregiver seeks to empower the woman to change the situation. Instead of assuming that women are equal now that they can seek jobs outside the home, hearing in a new way opens us up to the complex problems that continue to plague women and gender relations. Instead of presuming that they understand women—women who have suffered miscarriage or chosen abortion, women who are depressed, women who are sole parents, and so forth—many readers realize that they have only begun to sit down and genuinely listen.

Traditionally, those in pastoral theology have used Anton Boisen's powerful metaphor to define the proper subject of pastoral theology—the *"study of living human documents rather than books"* (1950, cited by Gerkin, 1984: 37). By lifting up the importance of the "human document" in theology, Boisen and others sought to revitalize theological reflection by turning away from doctrines and treatises to lived human experience and suffering as a deeper source of reflection. However, today, the "living human *web*" rather than document suggests itself as a better term for the appropriate subject for investigation, interpretation, and transformation in pastoral theology (Miller-McLemore, 1993). We can no longer focus on the "human document" as if it stands separate and alone from social and cultural forces. The focus on care narrowly defined as individual counseling must shift to a focus on care understood as part of a wider cultural, social, and religious context. Reflective listening in pastoral care, while a valuable tool in many respects, is insufficient to understanding the diversity of human experience within a variety of ethnic, economic, social, and cultural settings.

In other words, when an individual woman enters the pastor's office for counsel, her personal problem can no longer be understood or resolved without also understanding and addressing, even if only to a limited extent, social, cultural, congregational factors of oppression, alienation, exploitation, diversity, and justice. For example, a woman's struggle with her body image and sexuality or her fears about her work and her children after a divorce can no longer be seen simply as personal emotional issues; they are intricately related to a social system that fails to support working mothers and to a socialization process that forbids validation of female desire. Indeed, to think about pastoral care from a feminist perspective requires prophetic, transformative challenge to systems of power, authority, and domination that continue to violate, terrorize, and systematically destroy individuals and communities. This shift in commitment is evident in a variety of recent publications, such as James Poling's *The Abuse of Power* (1991), Pamela Couture's *Blessed Are the Poor* (1991), Larry Graham's *Care of Persons, Care of World* (1992), and my own *Also a Mother* (1994).

What can women and men in congregations do? Congregations need sensitive, informed, open public discussion of some problems that have been heretofore taboo for many congregations. Congregations and their leaders often have a close connection with the most intimate moments in people's lives over the human life cycle. For better or for worse, they stand in a critical place to influence people over intimate questions about work and family. When it comes to conflicts of families and work, time has come to disturb the "conspiracy of silence," in Janet Fishburn's words (1991: 141), that enshrouds what happens in the family lives and to break the unwritten rules about what can and cannot be discussed during "Joys and Concerns" in many typical small church worship services. If it is primarily or partly within the family that children first come to have a sense of themselves and a sense of human and human-divine relationships that is foundational to moral and spiritual development, then it makes all the difference in the world whether this experience is one of unequal altruism and one-sided self-sacrifice on the part of women and mothers or of justice, mutuality, and reciprocity. If Christian feminists and congregations do not get clearer about alternative egalitarian family and work values, then people will not have a good defense against the nostalgia for the "way we never were," as Stephanie Coontz's book title puts it.

Many people are hungry for stories by which to live. They want to know how to share domestic and economic labors, particularly in a society that typically forbids such equal sharing. Several kinds of questions are ripe for discussion. How can people change the division of labor inherent to conventional gender role definitions? Can we talk in greater detail about what democratic relationships between men and women might actually look like in real life, especially when such relationships involve children? What have people tried? What works and what doesn't? How can people change the division of domestic labors in the congregation itself, which continues to presume that women will run the Sunday school, coffee hour, nursery, funeral meals, and assume positions of leadership both in the congregation and in the work world? (I vividly recall a conversation in the church nursery a year ago in which a woman in her mid-fifties, who worked full-time as a legal secretary and was the mother of four children, lamented her inability to help with the church school program because she was also acting chair of the elders!) What will it take to teach men to tend to the chores of relationships, domesticity, and children? As important, what will it take to reclaim the values of caring labor in society at large for both men and women? At the very least, young boys and girls must begin to understand that a woman must not be expected to work full-time, mother full-time, chair the elders, and teach Sunday school, and that a man might not only be able to take up more domestic tasks in the home and in the church, but might even benefit and learn from them.

One of the more complex challenges facing feminist Christian discipleship is determining the place and role of motherhood and the family. The subject of motherhood has created both barriers to and, more recently, avenues for renewal for women and feminists. Not all women can, want, or need to become mothers. Women have paid and continue to pay dearly for nurturing children, costs that many men have not known, at least not in the same way. For mothers and children, the family has often been a violent, abusive institution. On the other hand, since more than 90 percent of all women eventually become mothers, for feminists to ignore motherhood in female experience is to bracket an immensely important factor. Moreover, many women have attested to becoming a mother as a "catalyst" that launches new worlds, possibly new schools of thought (Guerrera Congo, 1988:76). Maternal knowledge inspires new ways of thinking about God, obedience, freedom, love, justice, and so forth.

As I conclude in *Also a Mother*, in a society driven by the marketplace that devalues the taking care of children, elevates material productivity, places in jeopardy those in significant caretaking roles, and forbids men serious concern over friends, children, family, and domicile, we should not be surprised that mothers and children have neither been factored in nor fared well. Nor should we be surprised that when women sought liberation, the first order of business was not to secure the needs of mothers and children. Feminists have had good reason to feel reluctant about speaking up for the values of rearing children and motherhood.

Yet to disavow children is not, I believe, what truly thoughtful feminists ultimately had in mind in their struggle for equality. The dismissal of motherhood was more a matter of emphasis, priority, and self-protection than hostility and rejection. Now, because of those who have gone before us and those who have sustained each feminist wave through its almost inevitable backwash, Christian feminist mothers and theologians can ask, What is the value of reproductive labor? How does it belong to the Christian story?

Works Consulted

Becker, Mary. 1992. "Maternal Feelings: Myth, Taboo, and Child Custody." *Review of Law and Women's Studies* 1: 133–222.

Carr, Anne and Elizabeth Schussler Fiorenza, eds. 1989. *Concilium: Motherhood: Experience, Institution, Theology.* Edinburgh, Scotland: T & T Clark.

Clarke, Rita-Lou. 1986. *Pastoral Care of Battered Women.* Philadelphia: Westminster.

Coontz, Stephanie. 1992. *The Way We Never Were: American Families and the Nostalgia Trap.* New York, Basic.

Couture, Pamela D. 1991. *Blessed Are the Poor? Women's Poverty, Family Policy, and Practical Theology.* Nashville: Abingdon.

DeMarinis, Valerie M.. 1993. *Critical Caring: A Feminist Model for Pastoral Psychology.* Louisville: Westminster/John Knox.

"Focus on Women." 1991. *Second Opinion* 17/2.

Fortune, Marie Marshall. 1983. *Sexual Violence.* New York: Pilgrim.

Gerkin, Charles V. 1973. *The Living Human Document: Revisioning Pastoral Counseling in a Hermeneutical Mode.* Nashville: Abingdon.

Glaz, Maxine. 1991. "Reconstructing the Pastoral Care of Women." *Second Opinion* 17/2: 94–107.

Glaz, Maxine, and Jeanne Stevenson Moessner, eds. 1991. *Women in Travail and Transition: A New Pastoral Care.* Minneapolis: Augsburg Fortress.

Graham, Larry Kent. 1992. *Care of Persons, Care of Worlds: A Psychosystems Approach to Pastoral Care and Counseling.* Nashville: Abingdon.

Gudorf, Christine E. 1985. "Parenting, Mutual Love, and Sacrifice." In *Women's Consciousness and Women's Conscience: A Reader in Feminist Ethics,* ed. by Barbara Hilkert Andolsen, Christine E. Gudorf, and Mary D. Pellauer. San Francisco: Harper & Row. 175–191.

Guerrera Congo, Mary. 1988. "The Truth Will Set You Free, But First It Will Make You Crazy." In *Sacred Dimensions of Women's Experience*, ed. by Elizabeth Dodson Gray. Wellesley, Mass.: Roundtable. 76–84.

Gunn Allen, Paula. 1989. "Grandmother of the Sun: The Power of Woman in Native America." In *Weaving the Visions: New Patterns in Feminist Spirituality*, ed. by Judith Plaskow and Carol P. Christ. New York: Harper & Row. 22–28.

Hochschild, Arlie, with Anne Machung. 1989. *The Second Shift: Working Parents and the Revolution at Home*. New York: Viking.

Hollies, Linda H., ed. 1991. *Womanist Care: How to Tend the Souls of Women*. Joliet, Ill.: Woman to Woman Ministries.

Justes, Emma J. 1985. "Women." In *Clinical Handbook of Pastoral Counseling*, ed. by Robert J. Wicks, Richard D. Parsons, and Donald E. Capps. New York: Paulist. 279–299.

Kristeva, Julia. 1986. "Stabat Mater." In *The Kristeva Reader*, ed. by Toril Moi. New York: Columbia University Press. 161–186.

Luepnitz, Debra Anna. 1988. *The Family Interpreted: Feminist Theory in Clinical Practice*. New York: Basic Books.

Miller-McLemore, Bonnie J. 1991a. "Let the Children Come." *Second Opinion* 17/1: 10–25.

—. 1991b. "Women Who Work and Love: Caught Between Cultures." In *Women in Travail and Transition: A New Pastoral Care*, ed. by Maxine Glaz and Jeanne Stevenson Moessner. Minneapolis: Augsburg Fortress. 63–85.

—. 1993. "The Human Web and the State of Pastoral Theology," *Christian Century*, April 7: 366–369.

—. 1994. *Also a Mother: Work and Family as Theological Dilemma*. Nashville: Abingdon.

Pellauer, Mary D., Barbara Chester, and Jane A. Boyajian, eds. 1987. *Sexual Assault and Abuse: A Handbook for Clergy and Religious Professionals*. San Francisco: Harper & Row.

Poling, James Newton. 1991. *The Abuse of Power: A Theological Problem*. Nashville: Abingdon.

Purvis, Sally. 1991. "Mothers, Neighbors and Strangers: Another Look At Agape." *Journal of Feminist Studies in Religion* 7/1: 19–34.

Rossiter, Amy. 1988. *From Private to Public: A Feminist Exploration of Early Mothering*. Toronto, Ontario: The Women's Press.

Ruddick, Sara. 1989. *Maternal Thinking: Toward a Politics of Peace*. Boston: Beacon.

Ruether, Rosemary. 1980. "Politics and the Family: Recapturing a Lost Issue." *Christianity and Crisis* 40, September 29: 261–266.

Russell, Letty M., Kwok Pui-lan, Ada María Isasi-Díaz, Katie Geneva Cannon, eds. 1988. *Inheriting Our Mother's Gardens: Feminist Theology in Third World Perspective*. Philadelphia: Westminster.

Saiving, Valerie. 1960. "The Human Situation: A Feminine View." *The Journal of Religion*, April 1960: 100–112. [Reprinted in *Womanspirit Rising: A Feminist Reader in Religion*, ed. by Carol Christ and Judith Plaskow. San Francisco: Harper & Row, 1979. 25–42.]

—. 1988. "A Conversation with Valerie Saiving." *Journal of Feminist Studies in Religion* 4/2: 99–115.

Saussy, Carroll. 1991. *God Images and Self-Esteem: Empowering Women in a Patriarchal Society.* Louisville: Westminster/John Knox.

Suleiman, Susan Rubin. 1985. "Writing and Motherhood." In *The (M)other Tongue: Essays in Feminist Psychoanalytic Interpretation,* ed. by C. Hanae, S. Garner, and M. Sprengnether. Ithaca, N.Y.: Cornell University Press. 352–377.

Towns, Emilie M. 1993. *A Troubling in My Soul: Womanist Perspectives on Evil and Suffering.* New York: Orbis.

Westkott, Marcia. 1986. *The Feminist Legacy of Karen Horney.* New Haven: Yale University Press.

Williams, Delores S. 1989. "Womanist Theology." In *Weaving the Visions: New Patterns in Feminist Spirituality,* ed. by Judith Plaskow and Carol P. Christ. New York: Harper & Row. 179–186.

—. 1993. *Sisters in the Wilderness: The Challenge of God-Talk.* Maryknoll, New York: Orbis.

Young, Iris Marion. 1984. "Pregnant Embodiment: Subjectivity and Alienation." *Journal of Medicine and Philosophy* 9/1: 45–62.

10

August in Her Breast

This essay is dedicated to the "Women of the Word" Christian Women's Fellowship of Harvard Avenue Christian Church (Disciples of Christ) in Tulsa, Oklahoma, in honor of their study and discipline of prayer, in recognition of their lives of deep commitment, and in gratitude for their nurture of me as their pastor and teacher.

Prayer as Embodiment

Kay Bessler Northcutt

Absolute Attention

As a woman nourishes her child
with her own body and milk,
so does Christ unceasingly nourish us.
—Saint John Chrysostom *(Christian Prayer)*

My mother, whose infants arrived "before the days of clothes dryers," tells of hanging my diapers out on the line to freeze-dry in the January bitter cold. (Evidently there were any number of American women who preceded NASA in pioneering this particular technology.)

She laughs now, telling it, of the diapers "stiff as a board" flapping in the blow of the January winds across the Oklahoma prairie.

Her mother, imploring her to be sensible, wrote letters trying to dissuade her from such practices, cautioning my mother that she might "catch cold in her breast" while standing in the wind. Apparently my grandmother meant a breast infection when she warned my mother against catching "cold in her breast." A nursing mother with a breast infection *today* experiences intense pain, but the infection can be controlled by antibiotics. Nevertheless, my grandmother

205

advised a safer course of action: that my mother dry the diapers over the floor furnace.

Reflecting on those days thirty-seven years ago now, my mother confesses to me the carelessness of her youth, and that really her mother was right to caution her. But in her youth and confidence, all my mother could feel in her breast was August. In the freeze of January her body sang the warmth and power of late summer.

"And," she said to me, "those frozen-dry diapers were as soft as you could imagine after the wind had whipped the ice out of them. You see—it was all in the fold; I spent many hours debating with your Aunt Shirley about how to fold a diaper the best way. You just couldn't get diapers to fold right after they dried over the furnace. They were stiff. And hard."

That is prayer. It is the devotion of absolute attention. It begins in us "where we are." As James Carroll writes, "Prayer begins with the lives we lead...I presume that, since the Spirit lives in me already, I am already prone to pray" (26).

For Simone Weil, twentieth-century mystic and activist, the classic example of such absolute attention was study and the pursuit of Sophia wisdom (44-52); for my mother as a young woman it was keeping a beloved infant dry through absolute attention to the fold.

Such rapt attention—such prayer in whatever form—is fueled by desire; it receives the breath of life from love. Teresa of Avila writes in her autobiography that true prayer consists simply "when the soul loves, in offering up its burden"[1] (1960: 102). And further: "the important thing is not to think much but to love much..." (1979: 70).

And so we pray. Offering up the burden of our love as we bathe our babies' bodies, smooth and slippery in bathwaters of everyday baptism, and as we keep them dry against the wet of what would damage them. And we pray as we grieve—those of us who with Sarai (Genesis 16:1 ff.) and Hannah (1 Samuel 1:2 ff.) know the anguish of a womb that does not conceive, the babe absent from our arms; we know the prayer of tears burning our faces.

We pray whenever we bring the full force of our attention: as we make love to our husbands and life-partners, as we work to save a family farm, as we cook, garden, or pursue graduate studies or finish a GED, as we persist in our recovery from alcohol and drug addictions, as we practice law or answer phones, when we work for our neighborhood to be free of violence, when we resist sexism in

---

[1] Throughout this paper the words quoted from Teresa's autobiography are somewhat different from the ones the reader will find in the modern translation of the autobiography listed in "Works Consulted." The words I quote are from an older translation that was read to me, and which I transcribed into my journal.

our homes and our churches and our institutional relationships—we pray.

Simone Weil's notion of prayer as absolute attention contrasts a more common understanding of prayer many of us hold: as a mental letter to God during a distinct time set apart from the rest of the day's activity.

In a conversation about prayer, a friend observed to me that "prayer—even only five minutes of prayer a day, 365 days a year—is difficult." This is especially true of the traditional petitionary and intercessory understanding of prayer in which one speaks words, silently from one's interior, to God.

But prayer as attention, that is, prayer embodied in attentive action—could reside in the five minutes of absolute listening one gives to one's child upon picking her up from school. The breath of life is sustained by such listening in love.

The "Holy in the Ordinary"

We pray whenever and wherever we give ourselves in complete and loving attention. A prayerful life then, is not the custody of an elite class of ordained or otherwise set-apart "holy" people, nor is a prayerful life comprised of extraordinary, set-apart, "holy" experience.

It is true that many times we feel God breaking through to us in the extraordinary: in magnificent panoramas of the Rocky Mountains, or the ocean's breathtaking power and its seeming infinitude, or the exquisite movement of the earth's seasons. The azaleas of Oklahoma's springtime awaken in me the joy of rapt attention for our creating God.

Clearly such heart-stopping beauty fuels prayer. But it comprises only one small aspect of prayer. There exists for each of us the danger of falling prey to a constricted sense of God's presence limited to the earth's vastly beautiful seasons, or mountain's peak or beach's landscape in much the same way there also exists the danger of falling prey to a constricted use of language for naming God, as Jane McAvoy describes in her essay.

Romantic love and extraordinary beauty can inspire, evoking the soul to prayer, giving the breath of life to our praying. We know from the Hebrew Scriptures' Song of Solomon (4:9 ff.) that romantic love, particularly its erotic power, can serve as kindling for our desire for God.

But romantic love must give way to the work of love in our lives and in our relationships: the way we feel toward God in the azalea blossoms' leaping watermelon pink must not eclipse the same attention given to winter's dark skeletal days.

Intentional prayer of attention then, requires that we acknowledge "the God who speaks to us in our experiences at every moment" (Wiederkehr: xii). Teresa concurs:

> Granting that we are always in the presence of God it seems to me those who pray are in God's presence in a very different sense, for they as it were see that God is looking upon them, while others may be for days together without once recollecting that God sees them (1960: 109).

Attentive prayer requires living consciously in the presence of God, where we begin to see the holy in the ordinary mess of our lives. Teresa advised that we should "walk with special care and attention" especially in the faithful "performance of ordinary tasks" (1979: 106).

Julian of Norwich, a giant in the world of prayer, reassures us that even in the most ordinary of bodily functions, God is present. Born in 1342, this wise anchorite and mystic writes,

> Food is shut in within our bodies as in a very beautiful purse. When necessity calls, the purse opens then shuts again, in the most fitting way. And it is God who does this. (186)

Julian's wisdom that nothing is outside the presence of God, suggests that a fitting response to this mysterious presence is to *pay attention*.

Intentional prayer requires that we pay attention to what in American culture is perhaps our rarest commodity: time. In our lives of express mail, fast food, and rootlessness, we must pry open windows of time for exercising our capacity for attention. The practice of prayer, as Augustine knew well, is an exercise of the heart *and* mind (39 ff.). To grow and grow strong in prayer requires that we exercise both heart and mind so as to stretch our capacity for attentiveness. We must practice mindfulness. Thich Nat Hanh notes that mindfulness can be practiced

> ...when you walk, stand, lie down, sit, and work, while washing your hands, washing the dishes, sweeping the floor, drinking tea, talking to friends, or whatever you are doing....Each act must be carried out in mindfulness. (23)

The American culture in which we are embedded works against such mindfulness in a myriad of ways. The television has provided us with an electronic medium of consummate distraction. Televisions are occupying our living rooms, bedrooms, and sometimes our kitchens, where we are in danger of "amusing ourselves to death" (Postman: vii ff.). Television's distraction and noise eclipse the possibility of attentive prayer, of praying the holy in the ordinary, of stewarding our time. While watching entertainment TV we "are required...to pay attention to no concept, no character, and no problem for more than a few seconds at a time" (Postman: 105).

Television and the absence of attention it cultivates is the direct opposite of the attentive work of prayer. Television asks nothing of our attention; it wastes our time. Our hearts, minds, and souls become saturated with inattentiveness. It is impossible then, to love God with one's whole heart, soul, mind, and strength, *or* our neighbors as ourselves (Mark 12:30–31).

The gift of seeing the holy in the ordinary calls us to resist such evaporation of attention. Spiritual directors and teachers of prayer have for centuries warned those who would pray against the dangers of distraction. The distractions available to us today are legion, pervasive and tempting, most of them made possible through new technologies. Anne Morrow Lindbergh noted that with each new technology and its gains, we have failed to notice what has been given up, lost, or left behind: "Mechanically we have gained in the last generation, but spiritually we have, I think, unwittingly lost" (52).

Prayer itself resists anything that trivializes the holy in the ordinary. Rather than a withdrawal from the world, prayer risks paying attention to the world. It insists that we take time to recognize the mystery of the world, and that we begin to change our lives. Meister Eckhart envisioned a kind of attention that would become as natural as breathing. To paraphrase Eckhart: we must "breathe in the love of God, and breathe out the love of neighbor."

Such breathing, such constancy of attention does not come easily. Teresa of Avila writes repeatedly in her autobiography of the frustration of the hours and sometimes years of prayer that one can offer up without any "spiritual favors" being bestowed. Saint Benedict in his Rule is clear that we will never be anything but beginners, particularly in matters of prayer. Trappist monk and great spiritual teacher Thomas Merton concurs, "We do not want to be beginners. But let us be convinced of the fact that we will never be anything else but beginners all our life!" (37) For those of us who would practice prayer, *beginners always* is a good tune to hum to ourselves!

In the discipline of prayer and the ambiguities of spiritual growth, Teresa admits that while some of us "soar like eagles move," others of us "move like hens with their feet tied" (1960: 303). This is true, I think, not only for different persons but within different times of one's own prayer life.

As I live with the knowledge of my mother's devotion and her attentive work of prayer, it becomes clear that the freeze-dried diapers from January of my birth were *not* inspiring one year later, and the Sophia wisdom pursued in the diligence of the scholar's attention is *not* always revealed!

Praying the holy in the ordinary requires the discipline of constancy, like refilling the ice cube trays, carrying out the trash, and cooking dinner for the one millionth time. The ordinary nature of such constancy (as prayer requires) is illustrated graphically everywhere in our homes, apartments, offices: in the ubiquitous and generous balls of dust, the pile of mail stacked up on one's desk, the stack of unpaid bills on the table, the overdue library books, the letter of recommendation one must write, the child testing one's resolve and resiliency, the immutable ring in the toilet bowl and the unfolded load of laundry, the high school senior in trouble and the principal's phone call to inform you. These are things that must be attended to—most of the time without joy or enrichment or inspiration.

Such tedious, repetitive and demanding work provides insight into the *discipline* required to bring the prayer of attention wherever we are. We must be vigilant in our discipline of attention and prayer.

However, the greatest challenge to prayer as loving attention lies in the complexity of chronicity (Peggy Way). Chronicity is the continuing presence of those things in our lives (and the lives of the ones we love) that resist change *and* hope, resist healing, and in some cases may never change. Chronicity threatens our resilience. It stretches our limits to the breaking point.

Chronicity includes prolonged illness and physical disability, poverty, tired marriages and frustrated relationships, the constancy of racism and its equally constant denial, single parenting or being primary parent to one's grandchildren and even to one's own parents, the weight of bills from even brief hospital stays, and the loneliness and loss experienced during aging. Chronicity pulls at our capacity for attention like dead weight, and threatens to overwhelm it in frozen cycles of despair and hopelessness. Chronicity, as I employ this term, never includes abuse. It is about finitude and limits.

How is it possible for attentive prayer to respond to chronicity's challenge? Through pursuing the sheltering threshold of friendship and its living response *and* the balanced integration in our lives of action/work with retreat/rest. In the midst of thresholds such as these chronicity bends to the nourishment of attentive prayer. New hope and courage enter into the midst of our living. We become able to attend to the holy in the ordinary again.

Friendship

The great means of progress for a soul is converse with friends of God.

—Teresa of Avila (1960: 221)

In the midst of both the disciplined constancy of repetitive work and prayer in our lives and the challenge of chronicity, Teresa proposes this:

> I would advise those who give themselves to prayer to (particularly at first) form friendships.... (1960: 106)

> One who is beginning to love and serve God in earnest is encouraged to confide joys and sorrows—for they who are given to prayer are thoroughly accustomed to both. (1960: 107)

As women, we are brought to birth over and over again in the mirror of friendships, particularly with other women. It should be no surprise that our prayer life is brought to birth by friendships as well. Carol Gilligan notes in her book, *In a Different Voice*, that even as little girls we prioritize relationship over childhood games. Gilligan documented hours of little girls' play in which she discovered that if relationship is threatened during the course of a game due to the enforcement of a rule of the game, little girls abandon the game or change the rule. Early we prioritize friendship and such friendship is the taproot of prayer.

We speak here *not* of the social intercourse of shopping or lunch dates or conversations snatched with acquaintances at PTA meetings or sewing circles or potluck dinners or gospel choir rehearsals or church committee meetings or even prayer meetings! but intentional, sought-out *"converse* with friends of God." A Sunday school class or Bible study that takes place in a church *is not necessarily* "converse with the friends of God" either.

In "converse with the friends of God" we discover that the prayer that was *implicit* in our absolute attention and listening becomes *explicit*. By sharing it with another we give voice to what we have been giving attention and come to know even better what we have found there. This notion, that attentive listening precedes the sharing of prayerful friendship, enacts a dynamic that Leonardo Boff writes about in his theory of church, where he argues that *discens* precedes *docens*, listening precedes talking or teaching (138 ff.).

Our experience and enjoyment of these spiritual listening-talking friendships brings home to us the inexpressible delight and comfort that we glimpse as we come to understand we can be friends also—of God.

...no one ever took God as a friend who was not amply rewarded...prayer is nothing else in my opinion but being on terms of friendship with God, frequently conversing with The One who, we know, loves us. (Teresa, 1960: 110)

While there are these delights to friendship, there is also struggle. Friendship, at its depth, is born of struggle that releases greater intimacy. A fundamentally damaging toxin against greater depth of friendship and of prayer is *manners*. That we must be polite in prayer is an utterly unhelpful premise of prayer. Equally unhelpful: that prayer must be well ordered, in a mellifluous voice, and consequently a pleasant experience for all of us, particularly the God whom we are trying to reach.

To be permanently rid of such ill-conceived preconceptions of prayer, turn to the prayer book in the Hebrew Scriptures, the psalms. Read all the psalms and you will find there not only glorious praise, but red-hot, searing anger against God, self-righteous indignation, holier-than-thou-isms, bitterness, name-calling, brokenheartedness, and down right mean-spiritedness.

This is where the friendship aspect of prayer is so vital. A friend, because of mutuality and fundamental trust and respect, can speak even the unpleasant, even the ugliness of the human heart to another friend. The writer of John's Gospel tells us that Jesus finally called the disciples no longer servants, but friends (John 15:12–15). This decisive move in his theology is of vast importance. Teresa uses this model of friendship for prayer when she notes: "If words do not fail you when you talk to people on earth, why should they do so when you talk to God?" (1991: 177)

Anger, as well as frustration and disappointment, is experienced in friendship *and in prayer*. These experiences must be given voice in both friendship and prayer. In fact, a true friend brings *judgment* as well as grace to us, reflecting to us what she sees—even when it is not lovely, or inspired or good.

In the protective custody of a friend we are able to confess the ways and means in which others have trespassed against us; after years of keeping silence, in a friend's care we find courage to speak the secrets we have kept silent—the secrets that can damage us, keeping us from life more abundant. Rape, abuse, damages against us that we have not uttered because they are so horrible we thought we would cease to exist the moment we spoke it. But when we speak the horrible wounds of our bodies and souls in the strength of our friend's presence, already the power of that trespass against us begins to diminish. So it is with prayer.

With a friend we lose our manners and our "editing," so it must also be with prayer. When we realize and give voice to our entire experience—then *finally* we begin to find our balance in prayer and in life.

Through the precious crucible of friendship in which the unspeakable may be spoken, we find the finest model of prayer. We no longer choose which words to speak, or even feel limited by words at all. Basking in our friend's presence, we simply *are*. It is OK merely to *be*. Prayer becomes the breath of life, constant, everywhere, even as the molecules in the paper you now hold in your hand are bound in constant motion.

Friendship's Living Response

The first word of the Benedictine Rule is *obsculta*. "Listen." Not in the flat, one-dimensional sense of "hearing" we associate with the word *listen* in our culture. Esther de Waal, in her rich book *Seeking God: The Way of St. Benedict*, interprets listening as involving the

> listening of the whole person, of body as well as of intellect, and it requires love as well as cerebral assent. And it involves mindfulness, an awareness which turns listening from a cerebral activity into a living response. (42)

We are embodied. Our lives of interior landscape are lived out through our bodies as mother, daughter, sister, friend, lover, domestic servant, secretary, teacher, preacher, doctor, homemaker, scholar, cook, cleaner of corners—our prayer is rooted and liberated in this embodiment. In the company of our friend our prayer becomes a physical solace.

As we attend to converse with the friends of God, as we are praying the holy in the ordinary, the lifeblood of friendship will move us to responsiveness. Paying attention leads us into seeing the world with new eyes and to feeling the world in new ways. We forget our polite manners as we leave our temerity behind, crying out against injustice. New virtues of courage and boldness become ours.

The interior landscape of my mother's heart offering up its burden of love is revealed in the illumination of "August in Her Breast." Yet—*every interior landscape is embodied*—my grandmother understood this, as she cautioned my mother to be attentive to the very real vulnerability of a postpartum woman's nursing body, of her daughter's physical well-being.

Prayer opens up in us a vulnerable heart—vulnerable and responsive to the ones we know and love and the ones we *do not yet know and love*. It moves us to stand with one another in the midst of suffering and to resist pain's isolation, be it physical or political. We find we must respond.

The Integration of Action/Work, Retreat/Rest

I have tried to unsettle the traditional understanding of prayer, in which one leaves one's life and practices prayer as it is contained in a discipline *outside* the daily, holy mess of living. I have argued that we can, as women, practice prayer in the embodiment of our lives. Yet to make such a radical claim without explicitly staking claim to its equal partner of silence and solitude, is irresponsible.

Prayer as the embodiment of our lives requires *not only* absolute attention to the holy in the ordinary. It requires also the solidarity of spiritual friends with the consequence of rich, honest outpouring of our soul prayers. It requires not only the discipline of constancy and a living response to one another. It must have also the sheltering friendships that provide relief from chronicity. And, it requires breathing space. Time. Silence. Retreat. Solitude.

Luke's story of Mary and Martha (Luke 10:38–41) provides a wonderful model for us here. Martha welcomes Jesus and begins the work of hospitality. While Martha is industriously serving, Mary sits as Jesus' feet, resting. Drinking him in. Learning from him. In frustration, Martha attacks Mary's choice, imploring Jesus to set Mary to work as well.

Traditionally Martha is reprimanded for having her focus on the wrong thing. Mary, though, is committing a first-century scandal! A female sitting at a male rabbi's feet and learning! Jesus praises her as having made a better choice than Martha.

Perhaps Jesus was supporting Mary for making a choice against the oppressive structures of the society that would bind her into a limited, constricted role reserved for women. Probably he meant for Martha to have that freedom as well. But for centuries this text has been traditionally preached assigning blame to Martha for being mindful of the wrong thing. Why must either Martha *or* Mary be "right"?

In direct opposition to this either-or reading of Mary and Martha, Teresa teaches this:

> Believe me! Martha and Mary must join together in order to show hospitality to the Lord….How would Mary, always seated at His feet, provide Him with food if her sister did not help her? (1979: 192)

The prayer of attention evidenced in Martha's protestation of her exclusively-work model of life must be heard! As well as Mary's sitting, drinking in the one she loved. Each must inform the other. Attention must be, can be, devoted to both: action/work, Martha, and retreat/rest, Mary.

We must retreat. Enter into the listening of silence. The feast of solitude. Following our return from silence and listening, we enter deeply again our active, embodied sojourn of prayer developing a *living response*. Mary gives us a beautiful image in Luke's story that we must not forget. Sitting. Listening. Drinking in the presence of God uninterruptedly.

We do pray through our intentional attention in the midst of action, through what I have called stillness in action. But once we become aware of the capacity for and quality of this attention in us, we experience the necessity of enjoying *stillness*. We discover the desire for stillness itself.

Most days, this means that to reawaken our attentiveness and center down into our prayer, we must leave our lives in tiny snatches during the day, as we watch the finch or the cardinal at the bird feeder, in the fifteen minutes of focused attention at bedtime reading, or during a lunch break sitting outside. But also we must leave our lives even more substantially, to retreats of centering, renewing silence and listening. Days. Or one day. A week.

As women, we must learn to breathe again. Deeply. Meditatively. This breath sustains the embodiment of our prayer, the love of neighbor as well as the love of God.

Absolute Attention of Dying

All wisdom is contemplation of death.

—Anixamander

Our retreat into silence restores fullness to our sense of time. We understand the psalmist's injunction that we number our days that we might get a heart full of wisdom (Psalm 90).

The late theologian Joseph Sittler spoke often on the wisdom of attending to death in the midst of our living. He was particularly vehement about America's "silencing" of aging, dying voices:

> Why is it that people doing research on aging are not looking at what the aging are saying about aging? On the matter of aging, my credentials are existentially magnificent: I am eighty-two years old. I am also a professor of theology. (Northcutt: 14)

I asked Mr. Sittler to tell me what he had to say about aging. I came to know only later that Mr. Sittler was in the process of meeting his own death. One time he recounted to me the frustration and insight he found in giving a speech to a group of "oldsters" like himself:

I didn't know what to say to them because they were in my state—many of them losing vision, losing hearing. Among the things I could talk about, I talked about this fact—and it is a fact: the usual social scientific analysis of how to deal with aging is in some ways insensitive. I call it shuffleboard-school geriatrics: keep 'em happy, keep 'em sort of sedated by entertainment; teach 'em how to play bridge, poker; take 'em on bus trips around the town—diversion, entertainment, digression.

The usual investigation of geriatrics by social scientists misreads certain aspects of the problem...their investigation does not allow for the interior aspects of aging.

In talking to these old people, I thought I would try an experiment. I would *remember* them back into identity...I talked about the days I was a kid in southern Ohio—about what a little kid does. These old people started to cry, but it was not from grief. They went out of the room talking to one another as they never had. It was a recovery....

I think I've got hold of something here very important, *for the interior aspects of aging are loss of identity...peril of loss of role.* (15)

What angered Mr. Sittler was the attempt by well-intentioned caregivers to distract aging people from their real work of inwardness. What he discovered, I have found, is not unique to the aging. *Diversion from attentiveness, through entertainment and digression:* these forms of avoidance, which are particularly painful for the aging, are typical strategies in our death-denying culture.

In contrast to such diversion, death is the proper limit and criterion of our attention as it sounds the clarion, calling our lives back into attention.

For what was to be my final conversation with Joseph Sittler before his death, I took him a handful of the brightest, reddest autumn leaves I could find. He picked up the leaves and smelled them deeply. He said he could "almost see the red" in the brightest leaf I had brought. We spent the hour talking of spirituality and spiritual disciplines. At the end of our time he said, "Kay Northcutt, go enjoy yourself and *don't regret it!*...And take the leaves back where you found them...they'll make good humus" (18).

The attention of prayer does not forget death, but keeps it close, thriving in its presence. Such attention discovers what is holy about things in their passing. Like leaves, our lives should make good humus. In prayer, in attention to the most ordinary of things, we apply ourselves to wisdom. And her voice calls back to us.

With wisdom's quickening, we number our days as we bring our absolute attention to the work of ice-diapers and babies' bottoms to the translucent skin of aged ones whose work is death. In absolute attention we pray... admiring in silent, anguished wonder the passing moment that each life is.

As wisdom calls out to us, we find ourselves threaded through scores of human beings to the one—the several ones over a lifetime—who are for us the bread of heaven, the cup of hope. We find a table has been set for us, a feast of converse with the friends of God. In the midst of our life's labor and its wearing constancy, in the midst of chronicity which threatens to undo us, such friends bend the refreshing winds of the spirit toward us. We pray.

We press forward into work, straining against what would keep us, any of us, from life more abundant and we retreat into silence, reclining into the stillness that flows as water in the desert.

Bringing the full force of our loving attention, we pray. Beginners always, always beginning again.

Works Consulted

Augustine of Hippo. 1989. *On Christian Doctrine*. Translated by D.W. Robertson, Jr. New York: Macmillan Publishing Company.

Bessler Northcutt, Kay. 1993. "Aging and *Innerlichkeit*: My Conversations with Joseph Sittler." *Second Opinion*.

Boff, Leonardo. 1986. *The Church: Charism and Power*. New York: Crossroad.

Carroll, James. 1972. *Contemplation*. New York: Paulist Press.

Christian Prayer: The Liturgy of the Hours. 1976. New York: Catholic Book Publishing Company.

De Waal, Esther. 1984. *Seeking God: The Way of Saint Benedict*. Collegeville, MN: Liturgical Press.

Eckhart, Meister. 1981. *Meister Eckhart: The Essential Sermons, Commentaries, Treatises, and Defense*. Translated by Edmund Colledge, O.S.A. and Bernard McGinn. New York: Paulist Press.

Gilligan, Carol. 1983. *In a Different Voice: Psychological Theory and Women's Development*. Boston: Harvard University Press.

Julian of Norwich. 1978. *Showings*. Translated by Edmund Colledge, O.S.A. and James Walsh, S.J. New York: Paulist Press.

Lindbergh, Anne Morrow. 1955. *Gift from the Sea: An Answer to the Conflicts in Our Lives*. New York: Pantheon.

Merton, Thomas. 1990. *Contemplative Prayer*. New York: Doubleday.

Nhat Hanh, Thich. 1987. *The Miracle of Mindfulness: A Manual on Meditation*. Boston: Beacon Press.

Postman, Neil. 1985. *Amusing Ourselves to Death: Public Discourse in the Age of Show Business*. New York: Penguin Books.

Teresa of Avila. 1960. *The Life of Teresa of Jesus: The Autobiography of Saint Teresa of Avila*. Trans. and ed. by E. Allison Peers. New York: Doubleday.

—. 1979. *The Interior Castle*. Trans. by Kieran Kavanaugh, O.C.D. and Otilio Rodriguez, O.C.D. New York: Paulist Press.

—. 1991. *The Way of Perfection*. Trans. and ed. by E. Allison Peers. New York: Doubleday.

Way, Peggy. 1994. Phillips Graduate Seminary Ministers' Week, January 1994.

Wiederkehr, Macrina. 1988. *A Tree Full of Angels: Seeing the Holy in the Ordinary*. San Francisco: HarperCollins.

Weil, Simone. 1977. "Reflections on the Right Use of School Studies with a View to the Love of God." In *Simone Weil Reader*, ed. by George A. Panichas. Wakefield, Rhode Island: Moyer Bell.

The Word, Words, and Women

Mary Donovan Turner

> I want to posit the possibility that there is a word, that there are
> many words, awaiting woman speech. And perhaps there is a
> word that has not yet come to sound—a word that once we be-
> gin to speak will round out and create deeper experiences for
> us and put us in touch with sources of power, energy of which
> we are just beginning to become aware.
>
> —*Nelle Morton* (Chopp: 1)

E leven women sat in the circle; their bodies were stiff and their
backs were pressed tightly against their chairs. There was some
nervous laughter and some quiet chatter. They knew each other;
many of them knew each other quite well. But this was the first time
that the ten of them had gathered for their introductory class in
preaching. All of them were second- or third-year seminary students,
and some of them had even preached a sermon before, maybe two.
But for most of the ten students who gathered there with the professor, standing behind the pulpit to speak a word to the gathered community was not yet a part of their own life experience, nor were they
sure they wanted it to be.

The first assignment in the class was for each woman to come
with a written statement entitled "Imagining Myself as a Preacher."
"What do you see," the professor asked them, "when you imagine

yourself standing there in front of the community of faith? What do you hear?"

The reflections of the women the next week were perhaps not surprising, but as each woman spoke the group was overwhelmed by the enormous amount of fear and excitement that the preaching task held. One student, as she imagined herself standing behind the pulpit, saw looming over her head the many male preachers in her childhood, their index fingers pointed at her and shaking. She then saw the face of the male preacher who welcomed her into the church as an adult and gave her an unprecedented understanding of love and grace. When she tried to imagine herself speaking, however, there was nothing. There was no word.

The next student described herself as small and dwarfed by a large wooden pulpit. She was wearing a heavy robe and stole, so heavy that they rendered her powerless. Her arms could not be lifted. Others, when trying to imagine themselves as preacher, could not see themselves there at all. The pulpit was vacant; the room was filled with a deafening silence.

The conversation sparked by these "imaginings" had several dominant themes. Some could not see themselves in the pulpit because they had rarely seen a woman there. Some wondered if they had anything of value to say. Others wondered, even if they became experienced preachers, would the church community accept them? Would they be discounted or excluded? Would they be reduced to silence? One, trusting the members of the group, spoke of her own conflicting feelings about women and preaching. Should a woman stand to speak the "word of the Lord"? All ten of them were filled with anticipation. Ten Protestant women were beginning to wrestle with the personal implications of the Word and words—their own.

In some sense, the questions and concerns raised by the women in the introductory preaching class are puzzling. Many women who gathered there were well grounded in the work of feminist theologians and biblical scholars. They were acquainted with the many feminist Christologies, and throughout their seminary training had become well versed in the feminist issues related to ethics, church history, and a wide range of practical disciplines. They had participated in the planning and preparation of feminist worship and liturgy; they used inclusive language for humanity and deity. One might assume, then, that these women were ready to take their places comfortably, stand confidently, and "claim their authority" as preachers in their Christian communities. As we sat in the circle, however, we found each woman struggling, asking a new question—what does feminism mean for *me*, a preacher, one woman standing in one pulpit facing a community of faith?

The questions these women were asking were questions about "internalization." How can we find strength and a sense of groundedness in feminist thought that will enable us *to do* those things to which we have been called? Likewise, I asked myself as their professor of homiletics, how do I help each woman seated in this circle find *her own* voice in the Protestant tradition that has placed the Word at the center of its worship and reflection?

The semester progressed, and the class discussed exegetical and hermeneutical methodologies, our theologies of preaching, and sermon form. Finally the day came when the first student was to preach her sermon. The preacher was pale; the sermon manuscript was clutched in trembling hands. Before she stood to speak, I read to the group several stories, one an excerpt from the memoirs of Rebecca Jackson, an A.M.E. preacher in the early nineteenth century.

> In 1835, I was in the west—I thought I would not mention this but I feel it a duty so to do—persecution was raging on every side. The Methodist ministers told the trustees not to let me speak in the church nor any of the houses. And nobody must go to hear me—if they did, they should be turned out of the church.

Rebecca continued by describing the persecution she experienced and the churches in which she was forbidden to speak. And then, she added:

> This great persecution throwed open doors before me. Even a wicked drunken man, when the members was afraid to let me speak in their houses and the people waiting to hear the word, he opened his house and said, "Let her come into my house and preach. I don't belong to meeting." So when the people heard, they came and told me. I went. The house was filled and all around the house and the road each way.

We were, as a community of female preachers, overwhelmed by the dedication of this woman who felt her call so strongly that the oppression of the church could not stop her, a woman who would preach both "in spite of" *and* "because of." Was there no fear within her? Was she never pale? Did her hands never tremble? I read on.

> And at this time I had as much upon me as my soul and body and spirit was able to bear. I was all alone, had nobody to tell my troubles to except the Lord. When I got up to speak to the people, and seeing [them] on the fence, on the road, in the grass, my heart seemed to melt within. I throwed myself on the Lord. I saw that night, for the first time, a Mother in the Deity. This was indeed a new scene, a new doctrine for me. (Humez: 152-154)

Did Rebecca Jackson's story wipe away the fears of our preacher that morning? No, but there was a sense in which all of us seated in the chapel were comforted *and* challenged by the words we heard.

There is something quite comforting about discovering women who have gone before us—a great cloud of witnesses—women who courageously carved their own niches in the world of ministry. There is something quite challenging about knowing that women have bravely gone before us and that the women behind us are depending on us to do the same. The discovery of these women of the past and the discovery of mentors in the present are necessary phases in our development as women preachers. Historians and preachers alike have delved into the history of varying traditions, scrutinizing them for names of proclaiming women, names that had been lost, intentionally or unintentionally, to future generations.

The Search for Our Roots

The recent bibliography entitled "Women and Preaching" compiled by Robert R. Howard (1993) and published in editions of the journal *Homiletic*, includes a unit called "Historical Recovery." The extensive collection of listed books and articles demonstrates that many eras of church history have now been examined for names of "preaching women" of the past. A perusal of the same list indicates that few traditions are immune to such probing. A very small sample demonstrates the breadth of the search: women in Mr. Wesley's Methodism, the "preaching ladies" of the Salvation Army, the African-American women of the nineteenth century, the women preachers in mid-Victorian Britain. In a recent work entitled *Christian Church Women: Shapers of a Movement*, Debra Hull recounts and celebrates the lives of pioneering women—preachers, pastors, evangelists, reformers, and educators who belong to the history of the Christian Church (Disciples of Christ). The list is replete with the names of many forgotten women—women like "the three Marys," early Disciples evangelists. Mary Graft, Mary Morrison, and Mary Ogle were three laywomen who, for forty years, evangelized their neighbors and led the church in Somerset, Pennsylvania, to a membership of more than five hundred (Hull: 22–23). Hull also mentions Sarah Lue Bostick, who courageously organized black women during the last half of the nineteenth century by becoming a noted preacher in Arkansas churches (34). Hull recounts the lives of Disciples women, ordained and lay, who in the early years of the Campbell/Stone movement sensed a call to preach and found their voices in a church and a society that neither approved nor endorsed their being "proclaimers" of the word. Many of these women had to claim the "world" as their parish because the pulpits in the churches were closed to them.

The authors of the various monographs, dissertations, theses and articles about preaching women articulate their intentions and hopes in diverse ways. For many, the search for these women of the past is simply a conscious step toward a more inclusive history and is grounded in the belief that a more richly "textured" picture of this history will be beneficial to all. From our foremothers, others say, contemporary women can learn strategies for coping with and changing prevailing attitudes toward women in the church. The recovery of these stories can establish precedents for the ministry of contemporary women and encourage hope that, in the midst of resistance, ministries can be productive and fruitful. These early stories can provide an "iconic function"—they can be lifted up as a visible sign to those who feel powerless and invisible (Noren: 33). The hunger of women to discover remarkable women of the past is, as Rita Nakashima Brock has pointed out in the introduction, a natural outgrowth of the loneliness and isolation women feel when they find themselves working and surviving in a world dominated by men; recovering the forgotten women is to recover a part of the church's story where women's visions and hopes can be anchored.

The histories remind us that during the nineteenth century many women felt God's call and found their way into this country's pulpits. Frances Willard indicates in her treatise on women and preaching published in 1888 that there were, at that time, approximately five hundred preaching women. Additionally, Georgia Harkness indicates that by 1920 there were three thousand female ministers and preachers in this country (129). Movements that emphasized the importance of the Spirit, such as the Holiness Movement, tended to give a greater role to women by recognizing the autonomy of the Spirit to call and use persons apart from the usual (Dayton and Dayton: 67).

So, why study these women? The most obvious reason for studying the preaching women is because *they are there* (Chilcote: 1). In great numbers they are there, and they exerted a strong practical and theological influence on the world in which they lived.

If women have been successful preachers even in our most recent pasts, the question that begs to be asked is—why, then, the continued resistance to women in the pulpits of Protestant Christianity? That there is such resistance is no secret, and the answer to the question is complex. At its root, however, the stubborn opposition to women preachers is cultivated in the social sex role conditioning of our culture—one that has not welcomed or acknowledged women in positions of authority. The patriarchal "bent" of the church, whether reflected *in* society or reflecting society, has continued to deny women access to the Word.

Justifying the Women's Place in the Pulpit

Martin Luther, the Protestant reformer of the 1500s, was not known for his support of women's rights. He spoke to the issue of women and preaching in his treatise on the "The Misuse of the Mass." Though he felt that men were more skilled at speaking—were more eloquent, had more suitable voices, and were more naturally gifted— in the end, he was unable to ignore the biblical witness. Acknowledging that there was a promise in the book of Joel that daughters will prophesy, that in the New Testament Philip had four daughters who prophesied, and that Miriam and Huldah were Old Testament prophetesses, he conceded that *if no man were available*, a woman should have the right to preach (Luther: 151f.). From the birth of the movement, Protestants have struggled with this sensitive and tenacious issue. The struggle was never more intense than on the American frontier.

In 1859 Catherine Booth summarized that century's most popular arguments against women preachers: when women indulge in the ambition or vanity associated with preaching they become unfeminine; biblical injunctions bid women to keep silent; women cannot convey the word as Christ did because he was a man; public speaking is not a natural gift; home and family will suffer; the credibility of the church will deteriorate; and finally, women lack the vocal power or stamina for public speaking (Zikmund: 12).

In light of these objections, the early American foremothers were called upon to justify their preaching. Most often this was accomplished through vivid recountings of their "call." Women told of visionary, dramatic encounters with the God who had chosen them. That call "legitimized" their presence, and although many of them did not pursue ordination, they enjoyed the audience of many as they traveled or found themselves serving the members of a local congregation.

There were other justifications as well; women's preaching should be recognized and encouraged, some advocated, simply because it was effective. John Wesley's views toward women and preaching were in part formed by his experience with his mother, Susanna, often called the Mother of Methodism. Deciding that she perhaps could do more for the spread of the gospel than teach the children in her own home, she turned her Sunday family worship into an evening service where as many as two hundred would attend. Her husband questioned the propriety of a female-led service, but was, in the end, unable and unwilling to deny her success. He capitulated. Later, her son, John Wesley, aware of the success of women such as Mary Fletcher, who preached to crowds of two or three thousand people, encouraged women to preach as much as possible. Mary's preaching, he stated, was as "fire, conveying both light and heat to all that heard her" (Dayton and Dayton: 68–69).

The preaching women of the 1800s also turned to scripture to support their claim to the pulpit. Mary Fletcher, in response to one who said it was immodest for a woman to preach, said:

> Now, I do not apprehend Mary could in the least be accused of immodesty when she carried the joyful news of her Lord's resurrection, and in that sense taught the teachers of mankind. Neither was the woman of Samaria to be accused of immodesty when she invited the whole city to come to Christ....Neither do I suppose Deborah did wrong publicly declaring the message of the Lord. (Palmer: 11)

The early preachers looked to scripture for positive role models—stories of women who actively and overtly spread the gospel. Moreover, they did not ignore the challenge of the very few New Testament texts that could be construed as prohibitions against women preaching. Frances Willard in *Woman in the Pulpit* gives lengthy treatises on those very texts, providing for the reader quite a sophisticated interpretation of the Pauline letters, and why, in her opinion, the admonition for "women to keep silent" is, in itself, no justification for barring women from speaking the Word. Willard calls for a "pinch of common sense" when interpreting scripture. She questions the male bias of biblical authors, translators, and interpreters. Additionally, she suggests that there are thirty or forty texts that would support women's ministry and only two that would deny it. Willard insists that the "stereoscopic" view of truth evident in the biblical text can be heard only when women and men together discern the "perspective of the Bible's full orbed revelation" (Willard: 21).

Contemporary arguments that support women and preaching are, in the main, vastly similar to those of a century ago. Because of the recovery of many historic role models, women now justify their preaching ministries on the realization that preaching has been a right long held for women.

Women today still speak of their "calls" (Sehested: 24; Kelly: 67–76). While some describe dramatic and abrupt experiences like their foremothers, many women speak of a slow and unfolding awareness of their calls to a preaching ministry. The justifications for such ministries, however, are, now as in the past, complex and comprehensive.

From the earliest days of the Disciples movement, women who studied scripture realized that there were laws, religious ideas, structures, policies and attitudes that discriminated against women. Brock describes this phase in the development of women's consciousness as the "women as victims" stage. Women have realized that the "system is unfair and sexist." As a result, women have turned to the biblical text and have addressed the church community's concerns particularly about Pauline and other epistolary texts that, on the surface, would seem to deny women pulpit access. Scholars, with increasing sophistication, have taken these texts seriously, trying to understand the cultural context in which they were written. In addition to the examination of the "problematic" texts, women have searched for the more positive texts that encourage both women and men to respond to the demands and calls of the gospel. They have searched the Old and New Testaments for texts with a "liberating word." They have read scripture with a discerning and "suspicious" eye in an effort to peel away the androcentric layers that have, throughout the centuries, hidden or distorted the liberating impulses of God.

Beyond appeals to scripture, arguments for women and preaching, as they did a century ago, take a pragmatic turn. Since women *are* preaching and *are* nurturing and challenging our church communities through the words they speak, then it seems logical to assume that the Spirit that uses them and inspires them, endorses them. Does gender matter, some ask, if the preaching task is being fulfilled well and with integrity?

As in other disciplines, the appeal for women as preachers is often based on the principle of "fairness." Women should be accorded the same rights and privileges as men. Some arguments are based on expediency; churches will be without preachers if women are not allowed in the pulpit.

It is important to ground the study of feminism and preaching in an understanding of the past. The awareness of the many women preachers in history, their struggles, and the intense passion of their calls invites us to realize that to be pro-women preaching is not simply an accommodation to the most recent secular feminist movement. The woman's struggle to find her way into the pulpit began in this country with women who fought against slavery, fought for temperance and a right to vote—women such as Sojourner Truth and Susan B. Anthony, who had a strong sense of God's calling for reform. Their longings were rooted in the gospel and in their sense of having been called to proclaim that gospel to a world that did not and would not understand.

The Gifts We Bring

While it may be difficult to isolate and define the difference, few would deny that when a woman stands in the pulpit to preach, there is a distinctive flavor to the experience. While an objective and empirical analysis of the differences between the preaching of men and women may not be possible, many have undergone helpful studies to determine the particularities of the preaching of women.

A New Understanding of Authority

The analysis of women's preaching cannot be divorced from the vast research done in the past decades that has examined the communication patterns of males and females. Generally, studies have found that women are more likely in their conversations to modify their directness, often making queries rather than statements. Women are more apt to make initial suggestions in a collaborative discussion rather than make final, conclusive arguments (Walansky: 9).

It is not difficult to see that these patterns could make a significant impact on the woman's preaching style. Some would say that these general tendencies to ask instead of state and to suggest rather than demand, undermine the preacher's authority and thus her effectiveness. Feminists suggest that what is at work is not a lack of authority, but a different understanding of authority, one that arises from connection and not autonomy.

A woman preacher finds herself in a curious and tenuous place. On the one hand, she receives criticism from the segment of the church that would question a woman's right to speak to the gathered assembly. On the other hand, she can receive criticism from feminists who view the history and function of preaching as authoritarian. Why would a woman choose to engage in an activity through which one person has wielded power, sometimes abusively, over another?

As a result of these conversations, women have been called to justify not only their right to preach but also their interests in doing so to those who see the pulpit as a place that oppresses and marginalizes others. Those interested in the study of homiletics have thus begun to question and reexamine traditional understandings of ministerial authority. Historically, *authority* has been defined as the quality of proclamation that pertains to special rights, power, knowledge, and the capacity to influence and transform. Feminists are redefining the term, recognizing that it has to do with the quality of the content of the sermon, the authenticity of the message, and the messenger. As the discussion of strategy four in the introduction to this book indicates, this woman-centered approach to women, authority, and preaching gives us new ways to understand the preaching role.

Preaching, then, becomes not an oppressive activity, but a mutual one, an intimate faith sharing. At the heart of the preaching task, then, would lie these questions—In the sermon moment, what are *we* trying to explore, create, or articulate? What can *we* see in these moments of proclamation? What do I illumine for you? What do you illumine for me? What truths can *we* bring to light together? A feminist understanding of preaching is one that strives for an ever-expanding inclusiveness—so that all feel that in the proclamation of the Word they have been given "voice" (Smith: 44–58).

The understanding of "ministerial authority" is, of necessity, contextual. That is, women will need to struggle and come to understand their own definitions of authority that grow from their own cultural and religious traditions and out of their own life experiences.

New Perspectives on the Biblical Text

Just as our understanding of women and preaching is related to the contemporary study of communication, so it is also dependent on research in the fields of sociology and psychology. Many in those fields contend that women understand and experience the world in gender-specific ways. Women preachers, first inclined to emulate successful styles of their male counterparts, have begun the search to find styles of preaching that are consistent with women's ways of knowing and being where relatedness and attachment are at the center of development (Smith: 27). Through the realities of the female experience and all its particularities, the sermon is borne. Women's preaching, as a consequence, is generally thought to be more intimate and personal than the preaching of their male counterparts.

The life of the church has been enriched by women's proclamation in ways not imagined by women preachers of the past. As women have gained access to biblical texts and have sought to interpret them out of their own life experiences, the Word has been opened in new and compelling ways. Diverse and pluralistic interpretation opens to the church community a new awareness of the dynamic nature of scripture. Women enter into a dialogue with the weekly lections and open the texts in a myriad of ways that have brought their communities new understandings and perceptions. Sermons have focused, for instance, on the devastation and abandonment of Hagar and have called the community to eliminate from our world the abuses withstood. Women have noticed the absence of Sarah in Genesis 22, the plight of the Levite's concubine in Judges, and the favored position of the women who first went to the resurrection site and became its first witnesses.

The Bible, our Old and New Testament texts, stands with us and, as feminists have so clearly articulated, against us. As women come to interpret the text from their positions of marginality within the church, they have searched for the biblical discourses that have spoken of emancipation and freedom for themselves—for all of God's creation (Chopp). Women have engaged in the dialogue with our scripture in openness and with a restless hunger for a life-giving word—a word that is sometimes openly available, sometimes deeply buried.

It is this restlessness that has stimulated the recovery of our biblical foremothers—those who withstood abuse and isolation and who valiantly made contributions to life. The need to recover the stories of our ancestors has led to significant change in the Revised Common Lectionary. As a result of this commitment to women, narratives about Sarah, Hagar, Rebekah, Leah, Miriam, Deborah, Lydia, the woman with the issue of blood, the Syrophoenician woman, the woman of Proverbs (Proverbs 31), and Hannah are only now part of the three-year cycle of texts used by many liturgical traditions.

To identify women's stories alone is not adequate. A feminist "hermeneutics of proclamation" acknowledges that: (1) there are texts in our Bible that demonstrate an androcentric worldview and texts that deliver a message of liberation; (2) the Bible contains texts that portray women's suffering and oppression and those that affirm women's power; (3) feminist interpretation uncovers lost traditions, corrects mistranslations, and peels away androcentric scholarship (Schüssler Fiorenza, 1984: 44).

A feminist preacher, then, carefully evaluates the nature of the biblical text, and insists that the texts that are proclaimed are those that articulate a liberating vision of human freedom and wholeness. Or, the preacher exposes the oppressive elements in the text, those that do not articulate a liberating vision of human freedom and wholeness. Preachers must carefully *anticipate and evaluate* the oppressive or liberating impact of the Word and their words in the specific cultural situations in which they preach.

It is imperative that the preacher ask herself fundamental questions about the Bible and its use in the community of faith. What is my understanding of the revelatory nature of scripture? What kind of authority do I accord it? Is the androcentric bias of the biblical text so extensive and the liberating impulse of the text so repressed that I must look elsewhere to find an emancipating word? What will undergird my preaching? How can I bring a "liberating" word to my community—in our own particular time and place? Can I give "uncritical assent" to a biblical text that puts women in a negative light and limits women's understandings of themselves as persons created in the image of God? As Marti Steussy challenges us to ask in her essay, "How is the Bible my friend?"

The Distinctive Woman-Word

Do you remember the first time you heard a woman preach? Was it in your childhood? Were you an adult? Were you surprised? Pleased? Confused? What was your experience? What did you think and feel? Did you hear new language, a new understanding of Jesus Christ, new imagery for God, a new perspective of a biblical story?

In 1888 Frances Willard cataloged the differences she witnessed between the preaching of men and women. Men, she said, preached a creed; women declared life. Men's preaching left hearts hard. Men reasoned in the abstract, women in the concrete. Generally she found that women used inclusive language and "women's language" more consistently (Willard: 46–47). While there are *no* gender-specific absolutes when describing the preaching of women and men, homileticians have continued the search for general patterns evident in the preaching of women. How do women preach?

Christine Smith's interviews with men and women who teach homiletics revealed that, generally speaking, professors thought their female students' preaching to be imaginative, relational, and intimate. The preaching of women tends to be more concrete, professors said, and it deals with life's everyday issues (Smith: 12). In studying the preaching of African-American women and men, Cheryl Sanders found little gender-based difference in the form or theme of the sermon, or in the choice of biblical texts used. She did discover, however, that women's sermons often offer more personal testimony than that of their male counterparts; women stress their own life experience. Moreover, women's sermons include topics related to survival and healing. Women and men preached the same Word, she concluded, but with "different accents." Women's preaching calls men to incorporate into their preaching issues such as survival and healing. Women's use of inclusive language challenges the male preacher to demonstrate through language his appreciation of the presence and participation of women in their church communities. Women's sermons can teach men to temper criticism with compassion. At the same time, she determined, women can learn how to sharpen their testimonies and calls for Christian commitment (Sanders: 22).

While there is no conclusive answer to the question about the role gender plays in preaching, it is clear that when women's preaching is evaluated: (1) it is most likely to be viewed positively when it is consistent with society's general understanding of the feminine—when it is nurturing and enabling (Troeger 108); (2) there is, when women preach, a heightened awareness of gender—deficiencies in a woman's preaching are likely to be correlated with her gender; and (3) a woman preacher is seen as a representative of *all* women who preach.

There is no doubt that women's preaching is making a significant impact on the life of the church. Ninety-seven percent of 635 women surveyed for *Women of the Cloth* evaluated themselves as very effective or quite effective in preaching and leading worship (Carroll, Hargrove, and Lummis: 238). As church communities, one by one, are experiencing the proclaimed word of individual women, the cry of the feminist preacher is changing. No longer is the appeal to simply "let us in." The appeal is *"share our vision"* (Chopp: 17)—recognize the common experiences that bind all women and men in the world. We are divided by culture, ideology, race, and religion; we can share experiences of struggle and hope and deepen our own understanding of the Word and how it liberates us.

Some Concluding Thoughts

The great historical pile of quotes against women's preaching is the best evidence that women have been preaching since Christianity's inception (Procter-Smith: 5). Though labeled as impostors and heretics, women through the ages have courageously stepped forward. Women continue to respond to God's call, and many in the church community continue to resist; some are afraid.

The women in the introductory preaching class stand in the pulpit—faces pale and manuscripts clutched in trembling hands. Yet, when they speak their first words, even if those words are tentative and spoken in whispers barely heard, the bonds of patriarchy are shattered. These women become a visual and unmistakable reminder that the work of clergywomen and laywomen in the church is neither peripheral nor superficial.

Do women preach? Yes, they always have.

Should women preach? Most certainly.

Why do women preach? They feel called and challenged to proclaim the Word to a world desperately in need of it.

There are many wonderful collections of sermons by women. You may want to read the following:

Bread Afresh, Wine Anew: Sermons by Disciples Women, ed. by Joan Campbell and David Polk. St. Louis: Chalice Press, 1991.

Those Preachin' Women: More Sermons by Black Women Preachers, ed. by Ella Pearson Mitchell. Valley Forge: Judson Press, 1988.

Women of the Word: Contemporary Sermons by Women Clergy. Atlanta: Susan Hunter Publishing, 1985.

And Blessed Is She: Sermons by Women, ed. by David Albert Farmer and Edwina Hunter. San Francisco: Harper & Row, 1990.

Sermons Seldom Heard: Women Proclaim Their Lives, ed. by Annie L. Milhaven. New York: Crossroad, 1991.

Works Consulted

Carroll, Jackson W., Barbara Hargrove, and Adair Lummis. 1983. *Women of the Cloth: A New Opportunity for Churches*. San Francisco: Harper & Row.

Chilcote, John Wesley. 1991. *John Wesley and the Women Preachers of Early Methodism*. Metuchen, NJ: Scarecrow Press.

Chopp, Rebecca S. 1991. *The Power to Speak*. New York: Crossroad.

Dayton, Lucille Sider, and Donald W. Dayton. 1975/6. "'Your Daughters Shall Prophesy': Feminism in the Holiness Movement." *Methodist History* 14: 67–92.

Harkness, Georgia. 1972. *Women in Church and Society*. Nashville: Abingdon.

Howard, Robert R. 1992/3. "Women and Preaching: A Bibliography." *Homiletic* 17/2, 18/1, 19/2, 20/1.

Hull, Debra. 1994. *Christian Church Women: Shapers of a Movement*. St. Louis: Chalice Press.

Humez, Jean McMahon. 1981. *Gifts of Power: The Writings of Rebecca Jackson, Black Visionary, Shaker Eldress*. Amherst: University of Massachusetts Press.

Kelly, Leontine T. C. 1985. "Preaching in the Black Tradition." In *Women Ministers*, ed. by Judith L. Weidman. San Francisco: Harper & Row. 67–76.

Luther, Martin. 1959. "The Misuse of the Mass." In *Luther's Works*, ed. by Abdel Ross Wentz. Philadelphia: Muhlenberg Press. 151–152.

Mitchell, Ella Pearson. 1991. *Women: To Preach or Not to Preach*. Valley Forge: Judson Press.

Norén, Carol M. 1991. *The Woman in the Pulpit*. Nashville: Abingdon.

Palmer, Phoebe. 1872. *The Promise of the Father*. New York: WC Palmer.

Procter-Smith, Marjorie. 1987. "Why Women Should Preach." *Homiletic* 12: 5–8.

Sanders, Cheryl J. 1988. "The Woman as Preacher." *Journal of Religious Thought* 43: 6–23.

Schüssler Fiorenza, Elisabeth. 1983. "Response." *In A New Look at Preaching*, ed. by John Burke, O.P. Dublin: Veritas Press. 43-55.

—, 1984. *Bread Not Stone*. Boston: Beacon Press.

Sehested, Nancy Hastings. 1988. "By What Authority Do I Preach?" *Sojourners* 24: 24.

Smith, Christine M. 1989. *Weaving the Sermon*. Louisville: Westminster/John Knox Press.

Troeger, Thomas. 1981. "We Had to Sacrifice the Woman." *Christian Century*, Feb 4–11: 108.

Walansky, Maxine. 1982. "Gender and Preaching." *Christian Ministry*, Jan.: 8–11.

Willard, Frances E. 1888. *Woman in the Pulpit*. Boston: D. Lothrop Co.

Zikmund, Barbara Brown. 1989. "Women as Preachers: Adding New Dimensions to Worship." *Journal of Women and Religion*: 12–16.

12

Food and Feminism and Historical Interpretations

The Case of Medieval Holy Women

Nadia M. Lahutsky

I n an ordinary mall in the U.S. recently, a mother was arrested and evicted for breast-feeding her infant in public. It appears that the charge was "indecent exposure."[1] Such is the symbolic meaning of a woman's breast today, even when she is feeding a child. By contrast, many medieval paintings of Mary portrayed her with one breast exposed and offering her milk to the infant Christ child or even to the viewer. The symbolic meaning there of breast as food, essential human nourishment, is equally obvious. How should we think about the differences in these meanings? In these two stories lay some profound differences between our culture and that of medieval Europe and, thus, differences in our understandings of the religious significance of food and of the female body. In these differences and the way we "read" them can also be seen the gains that can be produced when women with an awareness of themselves as women are looking at a topic or story from the past.

---

[1]The incident happened in December 1993. A subsequent "nurse-in" by the offended mother and fifty other breast-feeding women brought the issue to public notice. On May 19, 1994, then Governor Mario Cuomo signed a bill protecting a woman's right to nurse her babies in public and private. The *New York Times*, May 23, 1994, editorialized in support of the woman, the governor, and the legislation.

In the last few decades the problem of eating disorders has mul-
tiplied and is especially visible on college and university campuses
across this country. Interpretations of the causes of anorexia nervosa
vary greatly, but many theorists agree that the refusal to eat can be
seen as a reaction to cultural images and expectations of women.
Devout persons in the Middle Ages often admired those—many—
saintly women who claimed to be unable to eat ordinary food and
thus existed solely on the Eucharist. Catherine of Siena (d. 1380) lived
on bread, water, and raw vegetables from age sixteen through twenty-
three. At that time she gave up bread, surviving on consecrated eucharistic hosts, cold water and bits of food (bitter herbs that she sucked
on). For the last month of her life she refused even water, offering
her sufferings for the sake of the crises facing the church of her day.
She died when she was thirty-three years old. Her story was powerful to her contemporaries, but not especially unusual.

Catherine of Siena belongs to a large number of women saints
from the Middle Ages (roughly 1100–1500) who exhibited extraordinary kinds of ascetic practices. Asceticism usually refers to the practice of disciplining the body to attain some spiritual benefit. Ascetic
practices have almost always included fasting or abstaining from
particular foods and choosing to be celibate. More extreme forms of
asceticism would involve subjecting the body to excessively high or
low temperatures, self-inflicted forms of pain, and depriving the body
of sleep. Asceticism was by no means new to the medieval world.
But it did take on new dimensions, some of which will be revealed
here. The women under consideration in this essay were not merely
inclined to asceticism, they recoiled from anything that smacked of
moderation. Thus, celibacy, or avoiding marriage and sexual relations, was a minimum for them. They often pressed the limitations
of the body by depriving themselves of food or sleep or comfort,
subjecting themselves to the vilest humiliations. We are hard-pressed
to read today of their actions without experiencing a wave of revulsion. These women starved themselves and wore out their already
weakened bodies in serving the sick and the poor; they subjected
themselves to pain by such means as wearing a wreath of iron barbs
or putting stones inside their shoes, or self-flagellation. They kissed
the wounds of lepers or drank of the pus drained from the ill they
were tending. They pressed the tolerance of their families by their
frequent opposition to family values and plans. They often pressed
the patience of the parish priest with their occasional criticisms of
him and with their requests for daily communion, a very rare practice at that time. Furthermore, these women have troubled later historians in whom we find attempts to explain their bizarre and pain-

ful religious practices. How should we understand their behavior? What was the point of these experiences of humiliation?

Historical study has been ruined for many people by being presented as a dreary run of names (mostly men's names) and dates (often of men's events, such as battles). What a mistake! The work of history is most significantly an attempt to understand how people in an earlier time understood themselves and how they lived their lives and by so doing to understand ourselves better. To be human is to have a perspective or to be situated in history oneself; thus, historians, in the course of doing their work, tell us as much about themselves as they do about their topic. To say this about the writing of history doesn't mean: "Don't read history." It does mean: "Read history with an eye on the present, also." It may also mean that we must give ourselves permission to see our contemporary questions as important and maybe even valid to ask of the past, even if we don't much like the answers we hear.

In this best sense, history should help us understand why these medieval holy women did these things to themselves. It should help us understand what these actions meant to them and to others around them. To attain this best that history can be, we must try to put aside *our meanings* for these actions and our revulsion at those actions and listen to what the women themselves were saying. It's very tempting to see these women's lives only through the "women as victims" model. Perhaps they were also wonderfully creative agents of the religious life, as it was presented to them.

Historians from pre-feminist days did, indeed, notice that female medieval saints were more likely than male saints to be extreme fasters. They could hardly miss it; the male writer of a saint's life (often the only or main source for information about her) went on and on lamenting that he himself could not attain such heights in asceticism. Writers like this seemed to be both in awe of the holy women's strength and a bit frightened by it. They were giving the medieval equivalent of "Don't try this yourself at home." They may have exaggerated information to make a point important to them. Thus, their words must be read with a slightly jaundiced eye.

Historians have been aware of the fasting holy women, even if they did not bother to read their words themselves. Some historians have wondered if the clustering of extreme fasters among women rather than men is sufficient to be seen as a significant difference. Weinstein and Bell have recently analyzed the stories and characteristics of more than eight hundred saints and charted the results. The answer is: Yes, women who were subsequently canonized as saints were significantly more likely to exhibit extreme fasting and to show various food miracles as a part of their holiness than were men who were named as saints. Historians have also wondered what such a difference might mean. This is where matters get interesting.

The explanation of the meaning given to women's fasting often depends on one's view of asceticism, this practice of self-denial (usually a denial of the body) for some spiritual goal. Ascetic practices have a long history in Christianity. Recall Paul's discussion in 1 Corinthians 7 about remaining unmarried. Everyone in the ancient world would recognize that as an ascetic practice. Not everyone appreciated it as a valuable thing, then and now. Ascetic practices as a means of getting closer to God developed over the next thousand years, often in tandem with Christianity's adopting of dualistic patterns of thinking. Dualism shows up in attitudes that stress the value of the spirit over the body and suggest that the body does little more than drag down the spirit. These attitudes are rather foreign to the Hebrew roots of Christianity and owe much more to Greek ways of thinking. No matter what their origins, dualism and asceticism became part and parcel of Christianity, in Europe, at least. Some recent historians, often from the Catholic tradition and thus ones who value the medieval church, frequently note the depth of piety in these women and acknowledge their refusing to eat, sleep, or meet normal physical needs as special graces from God. Furthermore, they tend to stress the mystical experiences of these women, their close connection with God as sometimes exhibited in the appearance on their bodies of the wounds of Christ (a phenomenon called the *stigmata*), and often, their eventual canonization by the church (that is, their names being put on the list or canon of saints).

There have been other commentators, mostly Protestant, who, like their forebears in the sixteenth century, reject the claims of special spiritual value in the ascetic practices of anyone—male or female. Not eating a particular food doesn't make anyone a holy person, they say. Thus, the cases of fasting women are of no importance. Fair enough, one might respond. But doesn't anybody want to try explaining *why women* fasted more extensively than men? Some historians have been interested enough in this question to attempt an answer to it.

What can it possibly mean for a woman to engage in what are, to us, such clearly self-destructive activities? In our culture, we would identify this kind of behavior as a pathology and ask what could have caused the self-loathing that precipitated acts of self-destruction. Not surprisingly, most historians, when they have bothered to comment on women's extraordinary asceticism, have tended to see it this way, as exactly what could be expected given the circumstances. Women were viewed by theologians as the inferior sex, more inclined to sins of the flesh than men.[2] This was the logical (?) extension of the dualism that had captured early Christianity. Spirit/soul/mind are superior to flesh/body/matter. In the metaphorical way of thinking that people found congenial at that time, men were symbolically representative of spirit/soul/mind and women were symbolically representative of flesh/body/matter. Who decided this? Male philosophers and theologians, of course. They probably thought it made sense. Men were, after all, interested in philosophical questions and took the time to pursue them. Women, on the other hand, were closely associated with and even defined by their childbearing role. Of course, these early Christian dualists recognized and acknowledged that men have bodies and that women have minds, but these were not each gender's *defining* characteristics.

Some historians have acknowledged these issues. Their views can even have a kind of feminist ring to them, suggesting that inasmuch as women were devalued because of their body and thus victimized, their abuse of the body makes perfect sense. On this reading of things, medieval fasting women heard the message of their church and their culture and were, so to speak, casting off the right hand that caused so much offense.

Such a view seems to make sense on the surface. And, indeed, it may apply to certain situations in early medieval Christianity. For example, the twelfth-century abbess and visionary Hildegard of Bingen herself opposed extreme ascetic practices. Writing to a fellow mystic, Elisabeth of Schonau, Hildegard warns her against the life-threatening asceticism she has only heard about and even hints that the pursuit of such extremes might have been a suggestion of the devil! Don't fast to death, for such a practice seems to deny God's plan for the human creation as both body and mind (Wiethaus: 105). If it is a denial of one's own goodness to fast excessively, who is more to engage in the practice than those whose essential goodness is questioned by patriarchal ideology?

Hildegard wrote to her friend Elisabeth in the twelfth century. At that time the extremes of asceticism were rather rare. The domi-

---

[2] This view is not the exclusive property of Christianity. The identification of women with fleshly things apart from matters of the mind (or soul or spirit) was part and parcel of ancient Greek philosophy. It was, after all, Aristotle from whom Thomas Aquinas (d. 1274) got his notion that a girl child was a "misbegotten male." That is, something had gone wrong in the gestation process, for the male seed ideally produces its like. A female would be something of a mistake. Aristotle and subsequent Greek and Roman thinkers viewed women as naturally inferior to men, slaves as naturally inferior to free men, and barbarians as naturally inferior to Greeks. In the realm of theology, this "inferior" status has often translated into "more inclined to sin."

nant monastic order then, the Benedictines, always espoused a moderate asceticism, and Hildegard represented that style of moderation. Furthermore, Hildegard may have been fearful that Elisabeth's behavior too closely resembled that of the Cathars, a group of extreme dualists who explicitly condemned all of the physical world as evil. The Cathars prohibited marriage and procreation for "the perfect" among themselves and rejected the sacraments of the church. What good could it do a dualist to eat "the body of Christ?" The medieval Catholic church rejected their views and set the Inquisition and later a crusade against them. But nothing stays the same. The Cathar, or Albigensian, heresy was extirpated and the sources suggest a subsequent rise in the practice of extreme asceticism in European Christianity beginning with the thirteenth century, even among those who considered themselves most orthodox.

A closer look at the writings and lives of many such holy women from the later medieval period suggests the possibility of reading a different meaning from their actions. The historian Caroline Walker Bynum has proposed new interpretations of the lives and writings of medieval holy women, thus executing the historian's task of asking questions of the past while illuminating the landscape of the present. In *Jesus as Mother: Studies in the Spirituality of the High Middle Ages* (1982), she has brought forward for our remembering the profound feminine imagery used in medieval piety, imagery used even of Jesus Christ! (19) Whereas most Christians today would not likely think of themselves as nursing at the breast of Jesus, Bynum has shown that it was not at all uncommon among twelfth-century monks and nuns to do so, probably associating breast and Eucharist as food, apparently with none of the post-Freudian anxiety about gender roles that affects us. More recently, in *Holy Feast and Holy Fast: The Religious Significance of Food to Medieval Women* (1987), Bynum has explored in detail the lives and, where available, the words of the fasting saints and, in so doing, has turned upside down previous interpretations of their behavior. This particular issue thus becomes an example of what can happen to "the conventional wisdom" when new voices and insights are a part of the interpretive dialogue. One thing that can happen is that we can today do more than pity the poor medieval woman, victim of a hateful official theology. We can, perhaps, marvel at the ingenuity and creativity of so many of these women and witness to their profound theological insights and their ability to turn the hateful theology to their advantage. To witness to the creativity of these women is to adopt a more women-centered reading of their lives. Such an appreciation does not, however, mean that we should or could adopt their understandings for ourselves! It does mean that things are often more complicated than they may seem at first sight.

Food, eating, body image—all these issues come into play as we think about the stories of medieval holy women. Food preparation and serving has been, in nearly all cultures, a predominantly female concern. It is the one *thing* over which women in medieval Europe had control (Power: 96–119). Lacking power and property, they could hardly engage in the dramatic acts of renouncing them, the kind of action that set St. Francis of Assisi on his spiritual journey. To renounce something, you have to have it first. Medieval women had control over the family's cupboard, whether they managed the kitchen staff or prepared the family meals themselves. Their control showed up often when they used the precious and sometimes limited family food to feed others less well off. This control is seen in the popular fear expressed by men concerning *what* their wives are feeding them. And this control can be found in women who decided for themselves when and what to eat, in spite of urgings and even commands from family, friends, and spiritual advisers (Bynum, 1987: 189–193).

The giving to others and withholding from themselves of food was particularly appropriate for women for reasons that go beyond the specifics of the household economy. It represented part of what was involved in being a woman in a culture in which most people experienced hunger as a regular concern. Women's bodies not only brought forth new life; they also kept it going. The simple fact is that during that time, unless some woman nursed a child at her breast, that child did not live.[3] The function of the breast as essential to human nourishment was integral to everyone's understanding and experience of the world. That it would figure even—maybe especially—in Christian symbolism is understandable; hence, the many paintings or statues in which, for example, the Virgin Mary is offering her breast. She offers it to Jesus, of course. No doubt this was one reason for the popularity of devotion to Mary. She was the woman whose body fed the infant Savior. The infant Savior nursing at his mother's breast would grow up to become the crucified Savior on whose body

---

[3] Modern ears shudder at the statistics about children sent out to be wet-nursed who did not survive. Although most manuals describing the roles of a good woman insisted that she would breast-feed her own children, in fact, it seems that a wet nurse with good references had no trouble keeping busy. To be able to afford a wet nurse for your wife was a sign of a man's economic well-being. Use of a wet nurse also may have served, however unintentionally, to help limit family size. Some discussion of the high mortality rate for children sent off to a wet nurse can be found in Anderson and Zinsser 139–40; see also Vecchio.

all Christians feed when they receive the Eucharist. Mary's maternal feeding makes possible the sacramental feeding that brings salvation. Thus, the connection was made between the breast and the eucharistic host. This connection can help us understand the medieval view that Mary also offers her breast to all Christians. Most famous of all was the legend that Bernard of Clairvaux (a contemporary of Hildegard) had been nursed by the Virgin Mary. There are also other paintings, available in any book that surveys medieval art, in which Mary offers her breast to the devout viewer; in clearly parallel images, Christ offers his wound as a source of nourishment. This would have seemed perfectly appropriate to medieval people, as the theory then was that a mother's milk was made out of her blood. A woman nursing her child was, literally to them, giving of her lifeblood. Christ's blood was directly shed for persons; the mother's blood was transmuted (dare we say *transubstantiated?*) into something else lifegiving, that is, milk.

If, in an opinion poll, Americans were asked today to identify the "sins of the flesh," their list would be headed no doubt by sexual indiscretions of various sorts. We might joke about the lustful monk running hither and yon breaking his vow of chastity, for most of us remember *something* from having read *Canterbury Tales*. Medieval lore holds a great many more unflattering stories about the gluttonous monk and those other persons who hoarded food. For medieval people, to give up food was far more difficult than giving up sex.

Nevertheless, sex and food and women are related or, rather, interrelated. That is, women and sex were associated. Recall the long traditional association of women with the body and especially with childbearing, always preceded by the act of sexual relations. Women were most frequently the food managers in a household's economy.

"Where's dinner?" "Feed the baby." "You're the weaker sex." "You're not as 'spirit-minded' as men are." "Mary gave birth to Jesus, our Savior." "Jesus suffered and died on the cross." "Suffering has spiritual benefits." "Suffering means redemption."

These are the kinds of messages, direct and indirect, that medieval women heard in their lives, from their culture and from the church. Keeping in mind these various messages and the cultural roles of women in medieval Europe can help us understand and maybe even appreciate the decisions they made for their lives and the way they lived out their Christian faith. Look now at some of the details from a few of those lives. Some of these women's stories may be known; others are probably unfamiliar. All their lives reveal an extraordinary creativity in light of limited outlets for religious fervor.

Mary of Oignies (d. 1213) became famous for her piety, thanks especially to the writing of James of Vitry who admired her spiritual gifts. She was one of the first of the food-obsessed holy women and one of the first of a group called the Beguines. Prior to the thirteenth century, only women of wealthy families could enter the Benedictine monasteries that dominated monastic life, as a substantial dowry was required. The Beguine movement consisted of women of quasi-monastic status, often living together, supporting themselves, and practicing spiritual disciplines. Many of the early Beguines were among the first women in whose lives and spiritual writing food metaphors became prominent. Mary was determined to receive communion frequently. She often experienced the taste of honey in her mouth during mass, even when she was not receiving communion. She, like other such holy women, were said to be able to distinguish a consecrated from an unconsecrated host. The latter invariably caused her to vomit. Mary was famous for her ability to fast. She regularly ate only once a day, took no wine or meat, and when she did eat, it was often only coarse dark bread. On breaking a particular fast of thirty-five days, she simply could not eat earthly food. While this kind of behavior can be seen as a punishing of the body, that is not how James of Vitry describes Mary's own reflections on her experiences. Rather, she spoke of imitating Christ, a recently popular theme in piety. In her own effort at *imitatio Christi* she even mutilated herself in the form of Christ's wounds (Bynum, 1987: 113–119).

Two hundred years and many other holy women later, Lidwina of Schiedam (d. 1433) had many of the same experiences as Mary of Oignies, and then some. In fact, the prevalence of food as a metaphor for spiritual truths was even more central to Lidwina's life than to Mary's. Lidwina was said, even as a child, to be drawn to acts of piety, for example, slipping into church to pray to the Virgin Mary when she was supposed to be taking food to her brothers at school. She avoided marriage, threatening to pray for a physical deformity rather than be considered pretty. At age fifteen she fell while ice skating, an accident from which she never fully recovered. The fall left her paralyzed, except for her left hand, and subject to vomiting and fever. Writers on her life report, furthermore, that her body putrefied and pieces fell off, that she bled from the mouth, ears and nose, and that she stopped eating. The extensive food abstinence seems to have interested contemporary writers most. Her food consumption gradually diminished until she was taking only a bit of river water a day.

Some persons charged that Lidwina must have been possessed by the devil (a charge more likely to be heard in her time than two centuries earlier), but she was vindicated by an investigation conducted by the town fathers and also, ultimately, by church officials.

Lidwina neither ate nor excreted normally, but her body exuded extraordinary alternative substances. The body parts she dropped, the wash water from her hands, even milk from her virgin's breasts, all were said to have extraordinary healing powers. She gave alms that bought more food than they should have and when she shared the wine from her bedside jug with visitors, it resembled the widow's jar of oil in seeming inexhaustible. While Lidwina seemed to eat no normal food, she craved the Eucharist. Her frequent reception of communion required the cooperation of the parish priest. When he balked, even publicly proclaiming that her miracles were from the devil, Lidwina managed to outflank his efforts. She claimed a vision in which Christ appeared to her, first as a baby but then grown, bleeding and suffering. He gave her the *stigmata*, the marks of his passion, on her own body and a napkin containing a miraculous host. Lidwina was subsequently vindicated by the bishop, who may have ordered the parish priest to offer her frequent communion without further testing her or resisting her requests. She remained respectful of the clergy, but her visions allowed her to bypass or even to judge individual priests at times. Repeatedly, Lidwina's story emphasizes not a punishing of her body, but an increasingly close identification with the suffering body of Christ. She denied herself natural food but she fed others. Her own body produced food to feed others. She herself fed only on the body of Christ. As Bynum puts it, "Food is the basic theme in Lidwina's story—self as food and God as food. For Lidwina, as for the many Flemish holy women before her, eating and not eating were thus, finally, one theme. Both fasting and eating the broken body of Christ were acts of suffering. And to suffer was to save and be saved" (Bynum, 1987: 129).

Mary of Oignies and Lidwina of Schiedam both came from the Low Countries. Women's fasting and spiritual eating was not confined to the North, however. Italy, too, produced its virtuosi fasters. Many Italian holy women had reputations for extraordinary fasting and a great eucharistic devotion, but Catherine of Siena (d. 1380) is most compelling, perhaps because her mystical experiences led her to take on a public role in the ecclesiastical affairs of her day. Furthermore, Catherine of Siena also wrote (actually, dictated) quite a bit—letters, prayers and the *Dialogue*. Thus we can explore through her own words the meaning of her actions.

Food was, quite simply, central to Catherine of Siena's spirituality, as seen in her behavior and in her own writings. If the details traditionally given of her biography are accurate (or even merely an exaggeration of what did happen), 'tis no wonder that food played an important role in her view of eternal realities. Catherine's biographer, Raymond of Capua, wrote that she was the twenty-third child born to her mother, was one of a pair of twins, and was the only child that the mother nursed at her own breast. The twin sister, Giovanna, was sent to a wet nurse and died. The twenty-fifth child was also a daughter and also given the name Giovanna. To complicate food matters further, Catherine's older sister Bonaventura went on a hunger strike, starving herself until her dissolute husband should mend his ways. A happy end to this effort led Bonaventura, joined by Catherine, to venture into the gaiety and mild vanity of fancy dress. Not long after this bit of fun, the elder sister died in childbirth. The message was not lost on the fifteen-year-old Catherine. Fasting had brought successful results to a problem, whereas marriage and sexuality brought pregnancy and death.

Catherine's vocation was set early in her life. As a child she fasted and gave up meat; as an adolescent she turned conflicts with her family into occasions to increase her ascetic behavior. She refused to consider marriage; she scalded herself instead of lounging at the baths; she cut her hair; she was glad when a bout with the pox left her face scarred. Remaining at home, as she did all her life, she nevertheless withdrew from her family and inflicted herself with deprivation of both food and sleep (Raymond of Capua). They refused to allow her to be alone and gave her onerous household tasks to perform in an attempt to break her will. Such opposition seemed only to steel her in her convictions. Furthermore, she learned how to construct her own room, an interior, private space of psychological solitude; she made a cell in her mind.

Catherine's father eventually conceded to his daughter's personal choices, and ordered the rest of the household to refrain from interfering with her wishes. These included, eventually, beseeching entry for Catherine in the Sisters of Penance, a group of third-order Dominican women. It was an unusual move, because in Siena, third-order Dominican women were nearly all older widows who lived at home or, as they said, "in the world." The group was reluctant to admit a young virgin until, seeing her pockmarked face, they were assured that she would not be attractive to men and become cause for a scandal. They relented; her mother, Lapa, ceased her opposition to the proposal; and thus did Catherine become like a nun in her own house. From that place she devoted herself to the salvation of the souls of all her family, then to serving the sick of Siena, and finally to restoring the church of her day, by trying to persuade Pope Gregory XI to return to Rome from Avignon, France. She became convinced that these three tasks required increasing austerities from her coupled with ferocious activity. She would go for days without sleep, engaged in a frenetic level of activity in preparing food for others and nursing the sick.

Catherine's life was one great conflict with her mother. Indeed, commentators have had a field day explaining her choices in psychological categories. It's rather easy considering the obvious favoritism Lapa showed her. A hypersensitive person might try to compensate for this fact, as Bell suggests. Catherine's own words use other categories, of course. She said that she was willingly embracing physical suffering, some of it from not eating, and that her suffering was for a purpose. While the practice of offering up one's suffering for another purpose was not new by any means, the explanations given by Catherine of Siena add a particular focus to it.

She was a woman who abhorred her own flesh, subjecting it to various mortifications. But flesh could not be avoided in the process of salvation. Christ's flesh was, in Bynum's words, not "some sort of miraculous protection to save us from human vulnerability, but the 'way' or 'bridge' to lead us to salvation through suffering" (Bynum, 1987: 175). In her writings Catherine stresses the similarity between *to eat* and *to hunger*. To eat, for her, means to eat Christ in the Eucharist, and thus to join with Christ on the cross. To serve, as to hunger, is, like Christ, to suffer for the sins of the world.

Many previous writers, among them some of the Beguine mystics, had talked of fusion with Christ, using erotic imagery, largely borrowed from the Song of Songs. When Catherine of Siena talked of union with Christ, of her mystical marriage to him, the images are not erotic at all. Rather, it is Christ's bleeding flesh with which she sought and received mystical union. To be the bride of Christ is to take on his suffering, a suffering without which the salvation of the world was not. She knew the Western theological tradition well enough to realize that, in that worldview, the woman and her body especially, represent fleshliness and sensuality. Christ, through his body broken, brings salvation. Since Joseph played no role in this process, Mary's body provided the material stuff or the flesh for Christ's body. Christ bled for us/fed us. Catherine herself often said that in her visions she nursed at the wound of Christ—a perfect blending of metaphors, especially in light of the medieval theory that breast milk was the mother's blood in another form.

How *perfect* can this blending of metaphors have been when it led women to self-destruction? we might ask. It is a reasonable question. We may well experience a wave of disgust on hearing about these women and their practices. It's easy, very easy, to adopt the language of our day and bemoan their lack of self-esteem and wonder what program could have been initiated to relieve them of this co-dependency! But careful reading of these women's words and listening to their stories in light of the contemporary value of the symbols they used, can lead us to appreciate rather than merely to pity them.

All the women included or mentioned here believed themselves to be made in the image of God, in spite of the long scriptural and exegetical tradition to the contrary. They were all aware of the prevalence of the idea that woman is to man as flesh is to spirit. But whereas men writers used this dichotomy to castigate particular women and to differentiate male and female roles and characteristics, women whose own theological reflections we have, often used it very differently. *Female as flesh* became the basis for an argument that made women the very best representatives of the *imitatio Christi*. Thus, they could see themselves, and all women, as symbol for all humanity; no longer did the male/female dichotomy matter in light of the divine/ human dichotomy. This symbolic reversal worked, so to speak, also because of scientific theory at the time that described the mother as contributing the material stuff of which the child was made (as in Aristotle's material cause) and the father's sperm as contributing the form or human nature (as in the formal cause). Since Jesus Christ had no earthly father, Christ's flesh was female, even to a greater extent than that of other human beings. This could mean that female flesh, in fact, redeemed the world! Christ's flesh—perfect that it was— proceeded from the virgin's womb and was the virgin's flesh. In fact, Hildegard of Bingen had argued this point precisely in her *Scivias*.

Furthermore, this emphasis on the fleshly humanity of Jesus Christ was expressed using images of the infant child nursing at his mother's breast. Woman was not only the source of the body (even Christ's body), woman's body *was itself* food. A mother literally gave of her life-blood to her beloved child, as Christ gave of his blood to beloved humanity, as Mary had fed Christ at her breast. There was also a blending together of the imagery of breast as food with the wound of Christ, such as we saw earlier in Catherine of Siena. This created a powerful set of associations for people whose primary religious ritual was the eating of the flesh of Christ in the Eucharist.[4] It may be that this complex set of interwoven symbols made it easy for women "to identify with a deity whose flesh, like theirs, was food" (Bynum, 1987: 275).

With their Olympic-class asceticism these women were not fleeing the world or even attempting to escape their own bodies. They were, rather, employing all their resources to exploit all the possibilities inherent in their situation of being in the flesh, and the prime

---

[4] By this time, lay men and women were allowed to receive only the host (body) of Christ. The cup was withheld and taken only by clergy, perhaps to avoid spilling. The theological doctrine of concomitance, that the whole Christ is present in any part of the Eucharist, probably developed to explain and justify the practice.

metaphor for human fleshliness. They seemed less consumed by guilt over having a body than they were overwhelmed by the opportunities to use their bodies to the fullest to reach God. Caroline Bynum demonstrates that women and men chose different symbols from the reservoir of the Christian tradition. Men, who by their gender roles had the occasion to exercise domination over others, often chose renunciation of this power or of wealth. Women, lacking power or wealth, used food renunciation as the primary symbol to express their spirituality. But rather than reveling in reversals and oppositions,[5] women's spirituality seemed to take what was given (woman as flesh) and clarify deeper meanings and value in it.

Thus, at its heart, women's body asceticism was not a punishing of the inferior gender. It was intimately tied to our being human, both spirit and flesh. It was their elaboration and acting out of what it means to be made in the image of God, as flesh and spirit, and as capable of imitating Christ. "Thus they gloried in the pain, the exudings, the somatic distortions that made their bodies parallel to the consecrated wafer on the altar and the man on the cross. Religious women in the later Middle Ages saw in their own female bodies not only a symbol of the humanness of both genders but also a symbol of—and a means of approach to—the humanity of God" (Bynum, 1987: 296).

I join Bynum in encouraging a sympathetic reading of the religious food practices of medieval women in part because I am hard-pressed to see modern understandings of self and female body and food as particularly better. Late twentieth-century U.S. culture also seems to identify women with food, especially food problems, be they overeating or its opposite. We have a dozen different cultural interpretations of our modern epidemic of eating disorders, virtually all of them divorced from any spirituality. Americans spend billions of dollars each year on diet aids and plans and health club memberships. We have more good nutrition information available to us than any other group of people in history. Yet it seems that we are not any healthier, according to recent government reports.

You can hardly sit down to eat your lunch without someone commenting, probably negatively, on the contents of your brown bag. We exercise, obsessively, of course, turning even the simplest of activities, such as walking, into an occasion for buying or wanting the most expensive clothing and gadgets. We hear on the evening news about the "most recent study" that contradicts last year's study. We

---

[5] Religious practice is full of symbolic reversals. For example, in the medieval celebration of the Eucharist, a male is the food preparer and server, and he wears a skirt!

seem obsessed with nutrition and health, but not very much of it seems healthy.

"Be fit." "Just do it!" "Eat healthy." "Lose ten pounds (maybe more)." "You're too fat." "But nothin' says lovin' like something from the oven" (so be sure to cook lots of yummy treats for others). "Bring a covered dish to the church meeting." "Cook this, but don't eat it." "Feed your kids well."

Many women's magazines are shameless in the contradictory messages they give—a cover that announces both "Fifteen Recipes for Yummy Cheesecake" and "Best Ever Ten-Day Diet." Women in our culture are bombarded with many and conflicting messages about food and their body. It's frightening to think how our daughters are processing them. Not very well, in the case of Christy Henrich, a twenty-two-year-old almost-Olympic gymnast who died in July 1994 weighing 54 pounds. It seems that, among other things, she had been told by a judge in a competition a year earlier that she was overweight. The correction for this "problem" turned out to be fatal.

All of our discussions of food and body image are divorced from any deep spirituality. Our publicly received images are provided by the soulless media of our time. The privatization of religion keeps spiritual themes locked away from public images. Marketers of blue jeans decide how to fill that corner of the brain that contains our sense of body-self. Even in Christian communities, we hardly ever hear about maintaining good health as a mark of gratitude for the gift of embodiment. Good health is, like so many other things in our culture, a task to be pursued, often accompanied by regret at what we have to give up. We secretly or publicly chide those who do not measure up to particular standards of healthy behavior. Our efforts seem often directed at the issue of control, not surprising in a culture that self-consciously seeks to control climate, fertility, and pain, among other things. These are not bad things in themselves; I, for one, would not want to give up air-conditioning in a Texas August or have surgery without a painkiller. I do not want to return to a world before antibiotics. But, is *control* of food and one's body the issue for a Christian? for a feminist?

We can claim that we have moved beyond the dualism of an earlier Christianity, that we have a healthy view of sexuality and marriage, and that we see procreation as a good thing and no cause for shame. Medieval culture glorified virginity and tended to denigrate childbearing. But in that culture food and the body were intimately associated with generativity and suffering and, as we have seen, salvation. And the connections *were obvious* to everyone. In our culture, most frequently, body images tend to signify an eroticism that is based on exploitation, glorifying only one kind of female body—young, lithe, usually white, and usually unattainable. Any other female body—older, chubbier, or darker—is subject to being seen as indecent, not unlike the nursing mother evicted from the mall.

We might wonder, with Bynum, if our modern confusion with regard to food and the female body is related to a fear of admitting that our control is still limited, that the body born of a woman and nurtured by her own body will someday be claimed by death (Bynum, 1987: 297–302). All our high-tech efforts at control have been unable to conquer this last threat. Of course, we cannot simply repeat the words and images of the past; in our culture they would have different meanings. Nevertheless, a people who gather around a Table weekly to *eat* from a loaf and *drink* from a cup are, it seems to me, well equipped to begin to fashion from these elements and from the pieces of their culture, a healthy set of meanings for both food and those bodies, especially the female, that prepare and consume it. I hope the conversation continues.

Works Consulted

Anderson, Bonnie S. and Judith P. Zinsser. 1988. *A History of Their Own: Women in Europe from Prehistory to the Present*, Vol. 1. New York: Harper and Row.

Bell, Rudolph. 1985. *Holy Anorexia*. Chicago: University of Chicago Press.

Bynum, Caroline Walker. 1982. *Jesus as Mother: Studies in the Spirituality of the High Middle Ages*. Publications of the Center for Medieval and Renaissance Studies, UCLA. 16. Los Angeles: University of California Press.

—. 1987. *Holy Feast and Holy Fast: The Religious Significance of Food to Medieval Women*. Los Angeles: University of California Press.

Catherine of Siena. 1980. *The Dialogue of Divine Love*, trans. by Suzanne Noffke. New York: Paulist Press.

Hildegard of Bingen. 1990. *Scivias*, trans. by Mother Columba Hart and Jane Bishop. New York: Paulist Press.

New York Times. 1994a. Editorial. May 23, 1994.

—. 1994b. Christy Henrich, Obituary. July 28, 1994.

Raymond of Capua. 1960. *The Life of Catherine of Siena*, trans. by George Lamb. London: Harvill.

Vecchio, Silvana. 1992. "The Good Wife," trans. by Clarissa Botsford. In *A History of Women: Silences of the Middle Ages*, Vol. II, ed. by Christiane Klapisch-Zuber. Cambridge: Belknap Press of Harvard University Press.

Weinstein, Donald and Rudolph M. Bell. 1982. *Saints and Society: The Two Worlds of Western Christendom, 1000–1700*. Chicago: University of Chicago Press.

Wiethaus, Ulrike. 1993. "In Search of Medieval Women's Friendships: Hildegard of Bingen's Letters to Her Female Contemporaries." In *Maps of Flesh and Light: The Religious Experience of Medieval Women Mystics*, ed. by Ulrike Wiethaus. Syracuse: Syracuse University Press.

13

Setting the Table

Meanings of Communion

The conversation happened in a cramped hotel room; the authors sat cross-legged on the beds, perched in chairs, or huddled on a few available spots on the floor. We met in November 1994 at the annual meeting of the American Academy of Religion in Chicago. Most of the floor space was taken by a room-service cart on which sat half-eaten pizzas, soft drink cans, and pieces of chocolate dessert. Nine women, one nursing a baby, sat munching and sipping together as we talked about the holy meal that lies at the center of our communities of worship and faith.

The Christian Church (Disciples of Christ), the first Protestant denomination founded on U.S. soil, placed great importance on communion, a focus less typical of many Protestant denominations, some of which had communion services as infrequently as once a year. Disciples continue to have communion weekly and count the celebration of the Eucharist as one of only two rituals that identify our community of faith.[1] In following the biblical text that asked Christians to celebrate the holy meal as often as they met together, Disciples made communion central to worship.

---

[1] The other ritual is believer's baptism by immersion.

In addition, the principle of the priesthood of all believers led Disciples to welcome lay elder leadership at the communion table. Today, in some churches, an elder of the church, not the ordained pastor, presides at the Eucharist, reflecting on the meaning of the meal, saying the words of institution, and praying over the elements. This Disciples history of the centrality of communion and the openness to lay leadership are part of the spiritual legacy shared by the authors of this book.

Communion is an act of celebration and remembrance by the community. The relational nature of communion led the authors to decide that our meditation on it should represent all of us, rather than a single person. Hence, we offer the following conversation for reflection on the meaning of communion. Not everyone present below was in that crowded hotel room for the conversation. Some have added their reflections to the discussion as it was mailed to all the authors of this book. In the spirit of the way we wrote this whole project, we struggled to find ways to include those who could not be present with us physically at the Table, as well as enjoying the company of those who could be there.[2]

We have tried to convey the atmosphere of our conversation as well as its content. The baby gurgling and fussing, the sighs of agreement, the interruptions, and the offhand comments are here so readers will understand how this conversation about communion reflects the reality of our lives as women: as scholars at a conference, as friends piled on beds like a slumber party, as colleagues engaged in excited discussion, as mothers nursing children, and as Christian women sharing food and drink together.

Images of Communion

NADIA: For as long as I can remember, I thought of food, eating, as central to communion. I was raised in the Russian Orthodox church. To receive communion, I went forward and opened my mouth. A priest put into my mouth a spoon filled from the chalice, bread soaked in wine. When I think about the spoon, whatever the theological explanations may be, I experience communion as an oc-

---

[2] The total conversation, including those who added comments later, involved Kay Bessler Northcutt, Rita Nakashima Brock, Claudia Camp, Kris Culp, Serene Jones, Belva Brown Jordan, Nadia Lahutsky, Jane McAvoy, Bonnie Miller-McLemore, Nancy Claire Pittman, Sondra Stalcup, Marti Steussy, Elizabeth Thomsen, Mary Donovan Turner, and Karen-Marie Yust. Yust is not an author included in this volume, but is a member of the Forrest-Moss Institute, and she and her infant son, Michael, joined us for the conversation.

casion of eating: nurture, nourishment, wholeness, and all of those good things. This attunement to eating calls us to act and speak on issues relating to nourishment, and wholeness for all people. How can any of us eat at any time without the awareness of those who are hungry? I try to resist the temptation to spiritualize the hungry or the needy. There are other kinds of hunger, but physical hunger is a reality we should be aware of when we celebrate communion.

SONDRA: The image that came to my mind as Nadia shared was the movie *Babette's Feast*. As a living eucharist, Babette's lavish meal for an oddball group connects for me love and sharing that are motivated from joy, the joyous giving of oneself to others. I don't want, however, to go too far on the notion of self-giving. We are all aware that love can be self-giving, but we need to have a good sense of 'self' in order to be able to give of ourselves to others. The image of communion in *Babette's Feast* does that for me: a self-giving love that also respects self. Wholemaking self-giving comes from fullness, from depth, from joy, from wanting to, and from loving.

KRIS: There are two images that come to me from my youth and childhood in a Disciples church: first, the not albeit very sensuous experience of having communion trays passed through the pews, and second, images of church potluck dinners. In both I think of feeding and sharing and coming around different sorts of tables. Women often prepare both sets of meals, whether as deaconesses or as CWF women.[3] The other thing that comes to mind is the prayer Jesus taught his disciples, "Give us this day our daily bread," which reminds us to think of God as the one who gives us our daily bread and who continues to exceed our most vivid imagination of what that means, to be given and to share bread.

NANCY: My earliest memories of communion do not have as much to do with the worship service as they do with the cleanup afterward. My mother was a "deaconess," so many times after church we would help her wash the trays and the little cups (they were glass in those days). My sister and I got to pour the grape juice from the unused cups into one big glass and drink it. Finally, we got as much of the juice as we wanted! My mother always seemed to enjoy this task that she shared with the other women of the church. Their laughter and talk made the time together seem less like a chore and more like fun—something I learned to associate with "church work" and communion at a very early age.

---

[3] The Christian Women's Fellowship (CWF) of the Christian Church (Disciples of Christ) is an international organization of women in the church with local chapters in each congregation.

JANE: To me the passing of the tray was the sharing, and I really liked it. *("hmms" from the group)* I was taught somewhere that when I receive communion, I should serve the next person. To me that was Disciples communion, one layperson serving another layperson— sharing. I connect this book project with such sharing, the way we passed our papers and our ideas around. Now I worship in a UCC church where there is no passing around and I miss it. I appreciate the UCC tradition more and more each day, but it does not have that sharing part to it.

BELVA: My experience is similar to Jane's. Communion to me is an equalizing event that connects each of us with our diverse gifts. We go to the Table and serve each other. It is important to me to pass the trays. As a child before I was baptized and could take communion, my mother and father taught me that the way I participated was to serve the person next to me. I always felt I was a part of the event. Sharing was equalizing because we are welcome as we are and bring what we have as we partake of the holy meal.

NADIA: Yes, the passing of the tray can be a powerful sharing. But many people in our pews don't know, or didn't learn to serve the person next to them. (Belva, I'll have to try that approach on my assertive five-year-old. I will let you know if it works.) It is important to serve each other, even if your neighbor resists your offer of serving, to counter the tendency in American Protestantism toward individualism. *We* eat together, *we* are the body of Christ. Communion is not simply a private act of piety. While it has an important personal dimension, it is certainly not *just* "me and God." It's all of *us*, brought into being by God's gracious love.

BONNIE: That is a moving statement. It made me think of a time when I was young and went with good friends of ours to a Missouri Synod Lutheran worship. It was the first time I ever felt excluded. I was shocked—amazed—I could not partake in communion. I had faith in Christ, but I was not welcomed. I learned Disciples theology from this experience—the welcome to all of us. The inclusivity is also feminist in some ways. It affirms all of us.

I do not want to lose a point Nadia mentioned yesterday to us— women's hangups today with food and our inability to give to ourselves. Women are constantly dieting and depriving themselves of nourishment, of care, of pleasure. A theology of communion ought to affirm how we are valued as women who not only feed others from our own bodies, but who also feed ourselves and allow ourselves to be fed. One great thing about this group is that we have given to ourselves as we have given to each other. One of my strongest memories of how we began was in Kris's kitchen and her gar den. We went outside and picked fresh things we were to eat together that had just grown in Kris's backyard. That meal was a special one. I remember having to fly home to my children. I am aware of how much I enjoy the time to commune with you all. I think this project has been centered around communion in a Disciples way.

RITA: Your comments about Kris's garden remind me of what I often experience during communion—the sense of the host of invisible powers present in the celebration of the meal. The sun, rain, earth, and the labor of many hands we have not seen come to us in the bread and wine, seasoned by time—the wine especially. *(laughter)* Communion is an act of remembrance, of remembering what we cannot see. Power that comes to us in the physical, natural elements, the power of the cosmos, of light and water, and life-giving power. Also present are the host of witnesses who have gone before, the powerful legacy we inherit. The invisible power of presence and of memory are what strike me when I think about what is happening to me in the service. I am there with others sharing in that moment together. Communion coalesces so much about the whole Christian symbol system, a very powerful and rich experience.

MARTI: I, like Kris, thought of the fellowship dinner, the pitch-in supper and the tuna noodle casseroles. *(laughter)* Rita's imagery of the cycles of life and creation that have gone into making what is there on the table is great. Religion tends to spiritualization in the bad sense, but communion is such a powerful anchor to our belief that God's will is for us to have rich lives as embodied creatures.

The other thing that comes to mind is a troublesome image that I am not willing to do away with—the image of sacrificial love. In a positive sense, it is love that reaches out for community and the commonwealth of God, over and against the powers that want to control us through greed and fear for our own little selves. Brave love sacrifices, not because sacrifice is good but because there are wonderful things that are worth being brave for. In churches I go to, somewhere around that Table, we talk about forgiveness and acceptance. Part of what makes us able to forgive is knowing that our gifts will be accepted, even though we are not perfect.

ELIZABETH: The cup comes associated with blood language, but this need not conjure up blood sacrifice. For me, communion is a celebration of the life-giving properties of the blood that courses through our veins every minute. When we come together over the cup and the loaf, we do not just remember Jesus as a cognitive process; we re-member, put back together the body of Christ. Surely this should be a joyful celebration, although the painful parts of community life are *included*.

CLAUDIA: One thing difficult for me is the continuing language at the Table in terms of the broken body. One of the most important things about communion is the Pauline idea of the body of Christ that is the church. That body is created in communion and that creation is one of the most important things to me. That creation is not traditionally spoken of at the Table. We are left with damaging language to many, especially women. The image of the broken body can be useless and hurtful to those who know it all too well. One of my wishes for communion is more language at the Table that affirms that the body is created by communion. The body broken on one level is not bad. We have to be able to talk about death. We can talk about death in the cycles of life and in the sowing of seeds, but when we leave it simply as a sacrifice, it becomes difficult.

SERENE: When I come to the communion table, I sometimes think of death as well, and not just in terms of natural cycles. I think about Jesus' very unnatural death; how his body was brutally tortured, broken, and destroyed by the religious and political authorities of his day. And when I remember this, my feelings at communion are of deep grief for the ways our bodies continue to be broken by people with power. I think of the Last Supper and the cross that follows. The pain of the Table wakes me up to the pain of the world.

I also feel immense anger when the Table reminds me of this brutality, anger at the injustices that destroy our good and loving bodies every day. Often at the table with me are thoughts of battered and raped women, of children who will suffer from Proposition 187 in California, of unemployed workers in Flint, Michigan. But with these thoughts, there is hope as well. When I taste the bread and wine, it's as if I am being filled up with the sustenance needed to fight those injustices. Profound grief, anger at injustice, and hope for the struggle, that is a lot to get all at once from a simple meal, isn't it?

NANCY: For me, it is important to remember that brokenness is not the only claim made about Christ in communion, or even the most important claim. In Paul's recounting of what we know as the "words of institution," he concludes his remembrance with the words "until he comes again," a reminder that Christ's death is not the final act. Whether these words are an allusion to Christ's resurrection, to a future advent, or to the times in our life when we really know Christ's presence with us, they point beyond death to the resurrection. They remind us that whatever death, whatever pain, whatever suffering lay behind us, those things are not our future. Our future, tasted together around the communion table, is the joyful feast of new life at which no soul will go hungry and no pain unassuaged.

NADIA: Yes, that is why it is important to resist the individualism that infects our culture and our congregations. Indeed, I believe that it is in the act of sharing communion that the church comes fully into being, reconstituting itself anew each time we gather to eat what God has offered us.

ELIZABETH: This may sound strange, but the broken body image I find most helpful regarding communion is the broken body of a woman in childbirth. That is a healthy model, not a macabre one, and it emphasizes the *life*-giving nature of the brokenness. The body is "broken" to give life. Then it heals, and repeats the process. We women know a lot about blood and brokenness. Until our daily knowledge is factored in, we will maintain images that cause fear where there is no need for fear. The loaf too is clearly within the purview of women's knowledge. We know what daily bread is, in terms of bodily maintenance. We also know what "daily bread" is with regard to the spirit and the soul. The church needs our insight and our voices!

JANE: Yes, I agree that the image of creation and renewal are part of the experience of communion. On the other hand, the service includes, as Serene said, the remembrance of death. Maybe the need to speak of death is why in Disciples churches, communion is a time of confession and personal reflection, a time of forgiveness, as Marti said. Communion is the part of the service in which we admit to brokenness in the world and in our lives. Many Disciples services have no time of confession, so communion takes on that function. That time to confess and reflect is important to many people.

NADIA: Perhaps Disciples congregations need to revise the worship structure to include a time of confession. I would much rather see that than turn the Table into an occasion for breast-beating. Communion should, I think, be a time for joy.

Women Presiding at the Table

BONNIE: Claudia's qualifying of communion was helpful to me as I think about what bothers me about it. What I would qualify about communion is that it has often been celebrated not by a woman but by a man. One of the most moving experiences I have had was when a woman said the words of institution. Often in Disciples-style services, the celebrant includes a meditation about what the communion means. One time, Karen Martin, a Disciple in school with me years ago, was preaching at a service. Her meditation was moving to me because it touched on the labor of women over the generations. *(baby gurgling sounds)* She mentioned her mother and her mother's mother, and down the line all the women who had prepared the bread and glasses of juice. Behind the communion table stands women's work caring for others.

KAREN-MARIE: Bonnie's comments remind me of the first time I had the opportunity to preside at a communion service. I anguished before the service about whether I should take that role because I believed it was a layperson's role, not my clergy role. Yet, I had never done it or been allowed to do it. I was raised in a Southern Baptist tradition in which women never would have presided. Some of the women encouraged me to preside because of my longstanding sense of exclusion. As I said the words, broke the loaf, and lifted the cup, I felt for the very first time truly allowed to be present at the Table. I felt included and empowered. *(baby gurgling)* I experienced communion as a working force in my life as never before. *(more baby fussing sounds)*

SERENE: Karen-Marie, you just helped me remember the first time I presided at communion in my placement as a student ministerial intern in Midwest City, Oklahoma. I was so nervous I got tongue-tied and asked everyone to "eat the cup" and "drink the bread." Luckily, in the joyful spirit of communion, the congregation just chuckled and partook gladly. The fact that Disciples are so relaxed about liturgical "appropriateness" makes it easy for the spirit to flow through even the humor of mistakes.

NADIA: I find the tension among lay, clergy, and women presiding at the Table quite interesting. In the Disciples tradition, the local elders were ordained. They were not, therefore, "lay leaders," strictly speaking. They were lay as in nonspecialist, nonprofessional, nonacademic. Somewhere, the "permission" for such folks to serve the congregation and hence preside at the table seems to have become—in people's memories—a requirement. How odd to think that the ordained person should not preside. Are we clear on the distinction between preside and offer prayers? I should think the issue is: Who is appropriate for this occasion? It might be the preacher, might be the local elder, hardly ever would it be the guy from outside who doesn't know this community.

MARTI: I had a moving experience in Israel two summers ago when the group I was traveling with held an evening communion service by the Sea of Galilee. *(baby fussing noises)* I wasn't going to preside because being a minister and serving at the Table had to do with a relationship with the community, and I did not feel I had that relationship with this community. But they wanted someone ordained to do it. I said fine, not thinking much about it. However, afterward one of the women came to me in tears and said, "We've never seen a woman do this before." They were from other churches that don't have that kind of leadership. I was very moved.

The other thing I felt deeply on that trip was that a piece of my identity was tied up with being a minister, which I had been denying throughout the trip. Presiding broke that open, and I felt like I was whole again. It surprised me.

BONNIE: I think many Disciples churches have the ordained minister preside and ask the elders to pray over the elements. In churches that emphasize lay leadership, an elder presides, but an *elder*, elected by the congregation to that office, not just any member. The problem for women, of course, has been that until recently, most elected elders, as well as ordained ministers, were men, so women rarely presided at the Table.

JANE: That is one reason we are doing this book. There are all sorts of ideas about why women can't serve at the Table. A lot of those ideas need to be rethought and swept away. We need to be made whole again. If the result of our thinking together and people's reading it allows another woman at the Table, I would say we could have no greater result.

KRIS: We also, by our work, connect the women who preside at the Table with all those who have been preparing the meals for years and years and years, as well as the "deaconesses," such as Nancy's mother who clean up after the service. *(sounds of agreement)*

MARTI: The line about doing this as often as you break the bread makes me wish we would do the remembrance every time we eat, instead of splitting communion off as separate. If we would do that, it would be harder to hold to the sacred as different from real life and separate from what women do. We ought to be remembering at every table with every loaf.

SONDRA: I feel pride again at our Disciples concept of lay leadership and our sharing of Eucharist together. We do not require the presider to be ordained. The presider *can* be a minister, but ordination is not necessary. I often have mixed feelings about presiding since I am ordained, because I want us to protect what we have. We offer the value of lay presidency and leadership to other denominations. If we have anything to give, it is our being in the Eucharist together, a nonhierarchical, nonclerical notion of what it means to share in God's gift. Mixed in with that are some childhood images. Most Disciples congregations have deacons and elders serving communion, but when I was growing up, those elected officers were men.

It was powerful to me the first time I saw women elders and experienced communion with a woman presiding, and the first time I heard a woman preach.

There are women for whom it is still very difficult to preside or pray at the Table. Maybe this book will invite women who have hesitated to serve as an elder or do the meditation to do so. I want to say to them, "You belong." I think of my mother who, over the years, has done so much in church leadership and can speak in public easily. But she actually gets "weak-kneed" when she presides as an elder. She carries an early childhood message from church that she was lesser and did not belong. After all these years of presiding, she still trembles. If *she* is nervous about it, can you imagine how someone feels who is not as otherwise extroverted and active and experienced? I hope our book will touch other women and they will know, this is your Table too.

NADIA: Sondra, tell your mother that my knees still shake (just my knees) when I lead in worship, and I speak in front of groups of people each day!

BONNIE: When you mentioned women's presiding, I thought of women's voices and how uncomfortable many women are in hearing their own voices. Women often do not honor our speaking as part of the Table. One of the wonderful things about communion I would like to affirm for women is its concreteness. People reading this should know we are sitting around eating pizza, a baby is nursing, and my notes now have pizza sauce all over them. Communion affirms us as embodied people who need to eat, as messy and as wonderful as that is. It has not been part of the Christian tradition to affirm us in our bodies, in our wholeness, as living people. It needs to. Women can help bring that wisdom back in. Watching the baby nurse tonight has been part of this experience and conversation.

Changes in the Ritual

BELVA: I think about the times as a youth that we took crackers, Kool-Aid, and other nontraditional elements to take communion. *(chuckles and nods of agreement from group)* Those times were as significant as being in the sanctuary and taking traditional communion. Sometimes it is hard for adults, however, to understand that the youth way of taking communion is just as significant. Adults will sometimes say that such elements are not communion. For young people, the communion language of hope and affirmation easily transfers into other settings and elements. They can find the holy in the ordinary.

RITA: Yes! The use of nontraditional elements is also a cross-cultural issue. One function of the elements at the Table is to symbolize basic sustenance for a culture. I once did a communion service in an interfaith setting for Asian Americans. For the elements we used rice and green tea. I remember an elderly Japanese American Methodist man who came to the Table with tears in his eyes. He said "I have taken communion my whole life and never been served rice and green tea. They are so important to the culture I came from, yet it never occurred to me to do this. Today, communion made sense as it never had before. I am going home to tell my pastor, we have to use rice and green tea!"

The question of the use of nontraditional elements is also raised in many Asian countries that were colonized by the West. To them, bread is a symbol of colonization, not of life and sacred power. In India, China, and many other countries, the Lord's Prayer is translated to "our daily food," not "our daily bread," to convey the theological meaning of the prayer. The power of the elements lies in what they mean to us and how they feed us. In many cultures, the body is not fed by bread and wine, but by tortillas and water, or rice balls and tea.

SONDRA: As Belva talked about her childhood memories of crackers, I thought about what children notice being part of the service. I want to hang on to the "daily food" aspect, yet children do notice the actual elements of the ritual as part of the *worship* service in their community. We always used crackers in our service when I was a kid. And so, anytime we had crackers at home, my sisters and I played communion. Sometimes, on special occasions, we also got grape juice to use. I think we didn't have it often because it stains. *(laughter)* We *knew* we were reenacting something important, something holy and connected to God. Communion play was special, as was our practice of baptizing each other in the swimming pool.

What we communicate to children is very important. We ought not to take lightly what we *say* at the Table and what children see. I am terribly uncomfortable and dissatisfied with the image of blood sacrifice and the theories of atonement that I ruled out in writing my chapter. Feminists are not the first ones to say that these ideas are abhorrent. But we've continued the criticism that has gone on for centuries about the limitations and actual harm from these ideas. What kind of loving God requires the death of a child? What kind of God requires the execution of anyone in the name of love? As women we are asking the questions with new fervor perhaps because we have some direct experience with harm. Women suffer most from a theology that equates self-sacrifice with real love. We can say to the

Christian community that the blood sacrifice image is not ennobling or redemptive.

I explain to my children that, in the elements of bread and wine, imagine that God is saying to you *very directly*, this is for you, I love you; this is for you, accept it, share it and live it. I don't know how to simplify it much more than that. If we're not doing that for children at the Table, we are falling short of what communion is.

KAREN-MARIE: What saddens me is the assumption that there is a right way to do communion. We are told we have to follow a traditional method, much like we are told to fit into "right" roles in the church. Communion affirms both what we share in our love and commitment to God and the uniqueness and embodied individuality of each of us. The challenge is to celebrate our togetherness while still recognizing that we each bring something unique and special to that moment. *(baby gurgling)* Too often, I see communion celebrated blandly, as one unified reality. The celebration of uniqueness is missing. We need to find ways to affirm differentness. In one communion service I attended the worship bulletin asked us to hold our bread and eat it together as a sign of our common vision, yet to take the cup individually as a sign of our individual relationships with God and our unique presence in God's world.

KAY: I want to respond to things just said by Belva, Bonnie, and Karen-Marie—we *are* embodied—communion is also a visceral experience. As a Chi Rho'er at summer camp, I remember pushing some boundaries, as youth typically do.[4] We decided to have communion in the swimming pool. Our minister saw no problem with this, so we gathered that evening dressed in swimming suits, all sixty of us sitting in a row on the edge of the pool, our feet dangling in the water. Our minister—instead of sharing the elements of communion—swam to each person, and washed our feet, like Jesus had done for his disciples. It was so humbling. We were stunned. In fact, we were silent for a good several minutes—and dove into the pool together. It was so visceral, so embodied; and it remains important to my understanding of communion even today.

BONNIE: Kay's comments bring up the issue of the freedom by which we celebrate and the ways we think about communion. I am struck that a more "high church" view of the bread is that it is indeed the body, so it cannot be touched in certain ways or by just anyone. Protestants have mostly resisted that tradition. I keep thinking of

---

[4] Chi Rho is the Disciples designation for junior high youth organizations.

my sons who, during coffee hour, are ready to finish off the communion bread, which they do, or they feed it to the birds. This brings
it back to the ordinariness. Yet the ordinariness does not take away
the specialness of the way in which we regard the elements. To me
this freedom and reverence are a powerful Disciples theological statement.

Expanding the Welcome of the Table

RITA: For me another symbol of the welcome to the Table is that,
to come to this table, you don't have to belong to this church or any
faith community because God sets the table and welcomes everyone. Because everyone is here with us, anyone can take the communion because all are welcome. This inclusivity is powerful to me.

KRIS: There is a spiritual called the welcome table. The table is an
image of joining together in communion. However, it is also the image of the coming reign of God. For me, it is as much the Table itself
as the elements placed on it that invites us to gather around. Although
we don't always gather around in the most welcoming way, the Table
can still bring us together—sometimes despite the way it has been
set and despite the way someone presides over it.

I think of table when I think of our writing project. We sat around
a table in the Disciples Divinity House library. That seminar table
became a welcome table of ideas that nurture us on a daily basis and
feed our hopes, desires, and passions for what will be.

SERENE: And some of our most exciting conversations were around
the tables of our meals…not only the one in your house, Kris, but
around those old wooden tables in the Mexican restaurant run by
women, and around the long table where we ate enough Thai food
for a week, and also stuffed in a small booth at the local diner where
we ate pancakes and eggs every morning. These are tables where I
really got to know and love the hopes, desires and passions of you
all. Round tables, long tables, old tables, new tables, all the different
places community can happen.

RITA: At my church last Lenten season, we were asked the week
before to bring to the communion table symbols of what our life's
passions were. The Lenten theme was "Embracing Our Passions,"
affirming what gives us life. People brought old photos, gifts from
childhood, pictures of lovers and partners, favorite toys—I was fas-
cinated by what appeared on the Table. I thought of that collection
when I thought about how we worked together on this project. We
brought to the Table (or in some cases, sent through the mail) those
things that are the passions of our lives. I believe we have not done

this project as an intellectual exercise, but as part of our journey in faith together. We trusted each other to value each other's gifts, to nurture our ideas with gentle criticism and helpful suggestions, so that we could all share. Our ideas are not separated from our work and lives.

CLAUDIA: The other thing that has been happening as I listen to people talk about different symbols is that participating in communion in alternative ways expands our definition theologically of what it means to be Christian. Often, the commonsense view of the elements is that the bread and wine are rather literal symbols of the broken bread and spilled blood. Even if we are not Catholic transubstantialists, the broken bread is broken body and the wine or grape juice is important because it "looks like blood." With those elements, we are stuck very closely to the sacrifice model. But when you go to green tea and rice *(phone rings for Sondra, we take a break)*, it no longer has to be sacrificial broken body and blood. A different set of symbols breaks open to new meanings and evokes different feelings. The notion of the pool and foot washings that Kay mentioned is highly biblical. Yet, as Last Supper imagery, it is usually is excluded from the service. What would it do to the meaning of "Christian" to expand our communion imagery?

NADIA: These are powerful points, Claudia. There is symbolism lost when tea and rice are used instead of bread and wine. Rita's also right that the elements symbolize basic sustenance. In some cultures that is something other than bread and what grapes produce! Just goes to show us that this meal has many meanings. It is important to remember that to change part of it is to change some of its many meanings. But let's not assume we are the first ever to introduce changes!! When the early church made the shift from a series of small, house-church communities to being the imperial church (with large basilicas and images of Christ the Universal Ruler replacing Christ as Good Shepherd) the meanings of the meal changed. The only thing that can be said is that they must stay the same and they must change. Both are true; both are required to give symbols life in a community.

BELVA: Another symbol or image that comes to mind for me has to do with the table. I see a table that grows. *(baby sneezes)* It gets larger and larger and extends all the way to the back of the sanctuary and opens the door and says "welcome, welcome ...." The Table itself extends an invitation. For people who are part of the Christian community who feel marginalized, the Table stretches out to the margins and beyond. It is a table of invitation. Every time a person is born, the table gets a little larger—so that everybody can get around the table. The Table is a symbol of invitation and reaches out to those who come into the church. But we, who are a part of the church, sometimes don't make other people feel very welcome there.

MARY: Communion is a time for me also when I think about the table expanding. I long to see new faces around it—faces of those in the world who do not now feel welcomed at *any* table. But communion is also a moment when I travel back in time and stop to remember the people with whom I have shared the bread and wine in years gone by. It is a time of "connections"—I see the faces of family members, childhood friends, seminary classmates, and members of churches I have attended and served. It is a wonderful experience—this remembering. It makes me feel hopeful and loved; for some reason it empowers me.

NADIA: Does everyone remember the final scene in *Places in the Heart*? All those folks taking communion together—black and white, rich and poor, living and dead. What was happening then, in those pews, is a vision of what the church ought to be.

Changes in Theology and the Role of Ritual

RITA: I want to pick up on Sondra's mention of blood sacrifice because that also bothers me, especially given the positive images of inclusion in a widening table. An act of sacrificial violence becomes the center of salvation, an idea of salvation that troubles me. The martyr's question, as Delores Williams has said, is to ask what we die for, and if we ask that question, somebody will be quite willing to oblige us and kill us, especially if we belong to a marginalized or oppressed group. It's the wrong question. Our question should be, What are we willing to live for? For me, the symbol of the Table and the broken body points to what Jesus was willing to live for passionately. To live that way involves risks. What we are willing to live passionately for empowers our ability to take risks—to have courage for love. What I value about Jesus is his life, not his death. I ask: Why can't we, as Serene suggests, grieve the fact that he died? Why do we believe theological ideas that encourage us to be grateful that someone, even God, was tortured and murdered?

CLAUDIA: I think it is hard to change the theology because of the function communion plays for us *ritually*. Rituals enact world order and help us affirm that the world is ordered. Ritual is their affirmation of order in the face of all the ambiguity and change in their lives. I am not trying to justify it. It is simply understandable. The way we experience communion has an interesting dynamic or a dialectic. Without the special moments, we do not experience ordinary moments as special. There is and there is not a difference between the special moments and the ordinary moments. The dynamic is difficult to negotiate, but humans need the special and the routine. The special moments come into ordinary life, making the ordinary meaningful. We are in a real period of transition right now because as our sense of the real changes, ritual has to change. The changing of that reality-affirming ritual is the hardest. If you had asked me twenty years ago whether we would have a problem today with calling God "She" as well as "He," I would have said, "Of course not. Twenty years just to change the way we talk? No problem!" It took me twenty years to realize that language is, in fact, reality to people.

SONDRA: A pastoral issue is involved, and I appreciate your bringing it in. We must have a certain amount of understanding and acceptance of where people are, of what is touching them spiritually. The literal words are sometimes less important than the total experience, because of what ritual does. It can be uncomfortable to change at all. We all know that we are in a transition time, and it is hard to be patient. But we can offer much to the transition that affirms God's unconditional love for each person—which is the point of it all, isn't it? The words of institution may change slowly, but perhaps in the meditation on communion, we can offer new interpretations. It is hard, though. In some of our congregations, the most traditional language and theology comes up in the prayers, negating what was just explained.

CLAUDIA: The big question I ask: Is it possible to make sacred ritual out of ambiguity and change? In the human experience, the sacred has been identified with what is unchanging. It would be changing everything if we change that.

SERENE: Maybe we have the basis of that ritualizing of change and ambiguity already there for us in the Supper, Claudia. I think of Jesus as a very destabilizing figure, not only in his public ministry but in the intimate closeness of the Table. Jesus' disciples thought they had everything figured out, and his giving them these elements disrupted all their expectations about how the world should be. It could be seen as a destabilizing event, a rupture in the ordinary. And the elements, bread and grape juice, aren't very permanent: they mold, they decay, they are digested; they are impermanent, changing, and yet they give life.

NADIA: I have this conviction that as we change the way we live in families and in congregations and in church life, the words will change and those that do not will take on new meanings in the new context.

RITA: I agree, Nadia. I believe the change in the ritual comes after the change in the culture, even though, as Serene says, the ritual has symbols of change in it. Ritual usually follows rather than leads ambiguity and change. The enormous change happening today in women's lives—women's new sense of ourselves and our expanded places in society—leads to a hunger for different symbol systems that answer our spiritual needs. Change in ritual did not produce change in women. *(wind roars through a partly opened window)* Because ritual is order preserving, one of the last places where change appears is in communion. Hence, it is interesting to watch what is happening to Christian ritual right now.

BONNIE: I would qualify that. I think change goes both ways. A changed ritual can have power to change a person before she or he might be ready culturally or personally to change. I remember how I was changed when I first saw women deacons. As an eight-year-old, I first thought: this is wrong. I had no explanation for that thought. All I could figure was they were wearing the wrong clothes. That thought began the process of change and acceptance, of my coming to think of women looking right, adequate, and complete in serving others the elements.

MARTI: When I was in college I decided I wanted to go to seminary and be a minister. Somehow, with one thing and another, time went by and I did other things. Then four or five years later, just after I got married, I started attending a little country Methodist church that had a woman preacher. Three months later I decided to quit the graduate program and go to seminary. At the time I had no awareness of a connection between those events. And yet I cannot imagine that it was coincidence. She was the first woman I had ever seen being a minister. In college I thought, with my head, that there was no reason a woman cannot be a minister, but seeing a real one clicked for me in a way that had not happened before.

Communion as Symbol

KAREN-MARIE: Your experience, Marti, highlights why the church must pay attention to the many messages conveyed in our ritual celebrations. My children take communion on the first Sunday of the month. They can't understand why they get a tiny little piece of bread and a tiny amount of juice. It's not filling at all—and they don't get to drink more later during cleanup as Nancy did. So how are these little morsels and drops an image of God's fullness and love? *(applause and laughter)* They want to drink my juice too. They notice that few people in the congregation pull off a piece of bread from the large hunk. Most take the tiny symmetrical pieces that have been cut before the service and arranged neatly on the plate. I worry about what images are resonating in my children when they experience communion as a paltry bit of God's love, instead of the fullness of God's love.

RITA: In the earliest church, such meagerness was not the custom. Communion was part of a meal. It was really nourishing then.

MARTI: I thought about that when I was mulling over this upcoming conversation. I think the transition is in the New Testament where Paul says, "Don't eat all the food and leave nothing but an empty table for those who come last. If you need to eat before you come, do." People did, and so what was formerly served as the love meal, became less and less. In one way it makes me sad, but in another way, the commitment to defying greed and fear as the driving forces of our lives is important.

RITA: By the fifth century of the church, the newest initiates who were baptized and had their first communion, were given a cup of milk sweetened with honey to symbolize the life and promise of God. There is a compulsion to make the communion table a nourishing place—if not in the bread and wine, then in the milk and honey, to symbolize the richness of God.

BONNIE: Symbolizes. That word is powerful to me. I, too, watch my children process this odd little piece of bread, and I see them begin to understand that a church is a place where certain things point beyond what they are. They must take that difficult cognitive step of thinking of how things can point to more than what they appear. In our materialistic culture, to learn those kinds of lessons in the church is powerful. They learn that we have other kinds of hunger that cannot be nourished simply, that we must sometimes reach, desire, and wait, rather than always having our needs satiated and met. In contrast to the constant messages of our consumerist, market-oriented society, we have religious desires and needs that cannot be met in any other way than through communion. Children can begin to perceive this. *(baby noises)* I think of Belva's emphasis on invitation. I think about how best to include children. We have mixed traditions in the Disciples about whether children should partake of communion. There is an important question or problem in making this a wholly inclusive meal *and* one you choose. You ought to be able to think and choose it. Children can begin to choose it in their own way and their participation is important. This is different from many other traditions.

MARTI: I have heard language used at the communion table that this is the table for all God's children. If we throw around language like that, then everybody whom God loves needs to be able to come to the Table, which includes children and non-Christians. If we change the language and say that this Table is for people who are making their commitment to Jesus Christ, then you can do it differently. But if we say it is for everyone whom God loves, then there is no way I am going to tell my children that they cannot partake.

KAREN-MARIE: I agree that we need to teach children about symbolism, but I also sense that for a lot of adults the experience is not symbolic of God's fullness or love. Perhaps communion has become so manageable and so ritualized that there's not much risk going on in it. Do we want to experience the fullness of God's love, or are we more comfortable with the crumbs?

NADIA: Some of that specialness was aided, for earlier Disciples, by a practice of discipline we would not want. They barred from the Table a lot of folk (whom God no doubt loves) because they weren't immersed as believers. We don't really want to go back to that kind of fencing of the Table, but we need to find our own ways of saying, "This is special."

KAY: When I make my retreat to Lebh Shomea, I enter the community's discipline of solitude and silence—except for morning Eucharist when we gather together at dawn. The communion bread we receive and share is a handmade bread of whole grain wheat and rye; the crust is brushed with honey. As you put it in your mouth, it is delicious and sweet. But it is also very coarse, and you have to chew it. It is gritty in your mouth—and fragrant. In its midst I feel the love of God. I become aware of the molecules moving in the communion table and the walls of the room surrounding me—the movement of God everywhere—in the midst of the flavor, the grit, and sweet honey of that communion bread. *(moans and smiles)*

JANE: What you just said sums up this book. Life is all those things. My hope for this book is that our readers will reflect on all aspects of life for women in this culture. Women, and all marginalized people, can have communion that is more than just little morsels, but fullness that is gritty and sweet.

BONNIE: I have to be honest that when we talked about having this conversation, I wondered why we were discussing communion. What I have experienced here is that communion is right where our theology comes together. And it is so much a part of the beginning of the Disciples. I have never had a conversation like this before, where I have heard my theology so clearly mirrored in others. As Disciples we think we don't have any theology. *(phone rings for Belva, and we take a break)* As we have worked together and seen people the past few days at this huge academic conference, I have experienced Discipleship with you all as we passed in the halls or in the elevators. I realized tonight that I have a feminist Disciples theology and I share it with you.

BELVA: When I read in the last Forrest-Moss notice that this conversation about communion would take place at this conference, I got so excited. I decided I had to go to Chicago, even though I had not planned to attend this conference. This conversation is the only reason I am here. I came just to be part of this time. Other people asked me what communion had to do with writing a book on feminist theology and I said everything. This is exciting—to make a contribution theologically. *(joyous sounds of "yes!")* I feel grateful to be part of a church that says, yes, you are a part of us. For all of you to invite me to be part of this project is more meaningful than you will ever know. I spend a lot of time trying to figure out where I speak, when I speak, who will be able to hear me, and who will help me get the words right. That's what you all are doing for me. *(laughter, ahs, applause)*

NANCY: Now that I live in Taiwan, so far from home, so far from all of you, so far from all the people I love, communion has become for me a powerful bond that transcends the seemingly impermeable walls of space. Every time we celebrate communion here we know that somehow we are reconnected with our community in the States. At the same time, we have also come to know what it means to be connected to a community that we hardly knew existed a year ago. Here in Taiwan we gather around the Table with people whose literal words we do not understand and yet who speak for us the language of our hearts in the prayers, in the ritual acts, in the sharing of bread and wine. Not only are the walls of space and time penetrated in communion, the walls of culture and language becomes bridges of thanksgiving and praise for the God who calls all people to share the good gifts that have been given to us.

The formal conversation ended, but as illustrated by Nancy's closing comment, which was faxed to the editors for insertion into the text, the conversation continues in new ways. The conversation now reaches not only to Taiwan but also to the readers of this text. Your voices join those above as part of the ongoing conversation around the table as we unset and reset the elements that feed us, bind us to our legacies, and make us a community of remembrance, wholeness, and joy. May the table grow and grow.

Study Guide

A Study Guide
for Using This Book

Belva Brown Jordan

The central focus of this book, *Setting the Table: Women in Theological Conversation*, is how the women's movement—feminism—speaks to the work and theology of the mainline Protestant church. A study guide is included because the authors, and the members of the Forrest-Moss Institute, wish to invite you into this theological conversation. We urge you to bring the passion of your life to bear upon what you read and hear. Form a study group or seek out a conversation partner with whom you can read and discuss. Make your study or conversation time as formal or informal as you like. As you read through each section of the book, use the related part of the study guide to generate, shape, and inform discussions, projects, and daily interactions. Share your opinions, feelings, thoughts, reflections, and insights; be transformed by the renewing of your heart and mind.

As Rita Nakashima Brock notes in the introduction, "any attempt to define feminism for all women who call themselves feminists would leave out a great deal." In our conversations we have only scratched the surface of feminism's implications for Christian thought, the Bible, and the church. Brock reminds us that womanist and mujerista theologians have added their voices to the conversation, offering us new angles for understanding God, faith, sin, redemption, worship, and theological language. As we read, write, and talk with one another concerning these biblical and theological issues, we learn to appreciate and value each other more. Our desire, as participants in the *Setting the Table* project, is to provide an entry for any reader, male or female, into this transforming conversation.

We present these ideas to provoke thought, stimulate conversation, and make room for new knowledge of, and appreciation for, feminist theology. We hope such enlightenment will motivate us all to engage in regular Bible study, theological exploration, and an enlivened Christian life. May we all be so touched and transformed in our daily lives as to go out and proclaim the "good news."

This study guide is divided into four parts. Part one revolves around the **INTRODUCTION**. Here, Brock lays a foundation by addressing the question: "What is a feminist?" She presents five strategies for change, accompanied by corresponding states of consciousness seen within the dominant feminist movement. According to Brock, "the states and strategies indicate how trends in some feminists' thinking developed from the mid-1960s to the 1990s." This foundational piece is referred to throughout the book. The study guide gives opportunities for you to become more familiar with these strategies and states, as you explore how they relate to you and your understanding of feminism.

The second part of the study guide focuses on **THE BIBLE**. This section highlights some biblical interpretation issues that feminist scholars address. These scholars give us "new eyes for reading the Bible and new ears to hear the stories" (Brock). In the introduction to this section, Claudia Camp identifies at least four of these issues. They are: 1) gender issues involved in the translation of biblical text; 2) special perspectives brought to biblical scholarship by feminists; 3) the question of what authority the Bible has for women; and 4) the concern for, and value of, consistency in what the Bible says. The study guide presents some Bible study and interpretation models and suggests Bible passages to study.

Part three deals with **THEOLOGY**. These chapters define and interpret such theological issues as language and liturgy, Christology and Christian community. This section also offers a feminist theological paradigm for the interconnectedness of life. The study guide invites you to stretch your theological muscles as you move through stages of reflection and action.

The fourth part relates to the **CHRISTIAN LIFE** chapters. Here the authors talk about the caregiving and nurturing roles of "mother," the importance and power of prayer, the sensuous and spiritual nature of food, and the centrality of communion in the lives of members of the Christian Church (Disciples of Christ). The study guide invites you to share memories and experiences of those aspects of Christian life that define who we are.

In addition to the study suggestions found here, a glossary of terms has been included. Go beyond the study suggestions and create your own ideas and projects that are relevant to your reading and study situation. Read. Study. Enjoy. Enter the theological conversation with passion. Bring who you are and what you know. Walk away stretched, challenged, informed, and transformed. Dare to laugh and cry as you share this experience with others. Pray alone and with one another. Be refreshed, replenished, and nourished as you help reset and sit at the Table. And then go out and spread the good news, make disciples, and know that God, through Jesus Christ, is with you always, even to the ends of the earth.

PART ONE

What Is a Feminist?
Strategies for Change

Strategies for Change	Transformations of Consciousness	Hunger for...
1. Just Like a Man	"The woman who wasn't there"	The company of other women
2. Add Women and Stir	"Women are equal to and just as capable as men"	Fairness and equality
3. Women as Victims	"The system is unfair and sexist"	Healing and nurture
4. Women-Centered	"Affirming women's lives and valuing what we offer for changing the world"	Affirmation of women
5. Include Everyone	Awareness of "the people who aren't there"	The presence of all who have been left out
6.		

1. Review the Strategies for Change chart, above. As Brock says, "While these strategies loosely describe the development of feminist thinking over the last twenty-five years, they are neither fixed nor permanent." Feminist theology reflects the many varied perspectives women bring to the conversation. Add your voice and your perspective as you discuss these strategies. With which strategy and state of consciousness do you most identify? Do you

identify with more than one? What experiences come to mind as you review the content of this chart?

2. Can you anticipate and name a sixth strategy?

3. What is a feminist? Offer your own definition, based on what you have read and/or experienced. What stereotypes have typically been a part of your understanding of feminists? Share your definition with others. How are the definitions different and/or the same? As you continue to read this book, pause to consider whether your learning reshapes your definition.

4. Create and share a "woman's legacy mobile." First, name the women in your life who have paved the way for you. They may be relatives or other women who have touched and shaped who you are in some significant way. Create a symbol to represent each. Use the symbols and names to make a mobile. A "woman's legacy mobile" can include an image made by each member of your study group or each can make his/her own mobile. As you work, share who these women are with your study group or conversation partner; tell their stories to each other. Hang your mobile in a prominent place, so that each time you walk by, you remember the gifts these women have shared with you.

5. Make a patchwork quilt. Create patches for the women named in the "woman's legacy mobile." Invite women of the congregation—young, middle-aged, and older—to each create a patch. Meet at the church and sew your patches together. If you celebrate "Women's Day" or "Mother's Day" in your congregation, present the quilt to celebrate the gifts women bring, and share it with the church.

6. *Setting the Table* looks at the women's movement in its most visible form, that of white, middle-class women. Seek out the perspectives of other women—African Americans, Asian Americans, Hispanic women, homeless women, and women involved in the civil rights and other liberation movements. Find ways to be in conversation with women who do not fit the dominant group. What are their experiences and thoughts about the Bible, theology, and Christian life? How are their views similar to and different from those presented in this book?

PART TWO

The Bible

1. Bible Helps and Resources. Having a few of these on hand will give you tools to enhance your knowledge and understanding of the Bible.

Harper's Bible Dictionary, edited by Paul Achtemeier. (San Francisco: Harper & Row, 1985). Contains 3700 articles by leading biblical scholars on the books, places, people, and major ideas in the Bible, as well as outlines of all the books of the Bible. Includes color maps and photos.

Harper's Bible Commentary, edited by James L. Mays. (San Francisco: Harper & Row, 1988). A fully illustrated and reliable one-volume commentary that includes introductions and explanatory notes for each book of the Old and New Testaments and the Apocrypha.

The Women's Bible Commentary. (Louisville: Westminster/John Knox, 1992). A new, valuable resource on biblical texts dealing with women and women's scholarship. Includes articles on every book of the Bible and a number of background articles.

A Beginner's Guide to the Books of the Bible, by Diane L. Jacobson and Robert Kysar. (Minneapolis: Augsburg, 1991). Concise, easy-to-understand introductions to each book of the Old and New Testaments.

A Beginner's Guide to Studying the Bible, by Rolf E. Aaseng. (Minneapolis: Augsburg, 1991). Provides basic steps for studying the Bible. Describes helpful resources such as concordances, atlases, and Bible dictionaries.

The Bible Makes Sense, by Walter Brueggemann. (Winona, MN: St. Mary's College Press, 1977). A brief, readable paperback on what the Bible means. A theologian pulls together the seemingly disparate archeological, historical, thematic, and narrative elements of biblical learning to make sense of the Bible.

2. Explore what you know and believe about the Bible. When was it written? How was it formulated? Who wrote it? What is the structure of the Bible? Do some general research with the resources named above. Share with your study group or conversation partner what you have discovered (or rediscovered) about

the Bible. Consult these resources as you study the passages suggested in question 4, below.

3. In the chapter "My Friend the Bible," Marti Steussy identifies some Christian feminist approaches for thinking about biblical authority. This is how Steussy matches them up with Brock's five "strategies for change":

> Just Like a Man — Overarching Theme
> Add Women and Stir — Canon within the Canon
> Women as Victims — Remembrance
> Women-Centered — Women Focused
> Include Everyone — Beyond Self-interest

How does each biblical approach differ from the others? How does each work to transform consciousness? Share which is most helpful for you, and why.

4. We have been taught to think of "truth" and "authority" in concrete and limited ways. Steussy invites us to consider a metaphor that offers a different and perhaps more helpful way to think about biblical truth and authority. The metaphor of looking at the Bible as a "wise and cherished friend" reshapes biblical truth and authority from unconditional and absolute to sensitive in ever-changing human life circumstances.

To some this may suggest we cannot depend on the Bible, because it is not consistent. Steussy believes that the Bible is consistent in the way a human personality is consistent. Influenced and shaped by experience and a variety of cultural variables, it shows generally predictable patterns.

Recall the image of the Bible as a "wise and cherished friend." Consider these "friendship implications" as noted by Steussy in her essay, "My Friend the Bible."

- Friendship takes time to develop.
- The Bible comes from a very different culture.
- The Bible has seen a lot of human experiences.
- The Bible cares and has passion.
- The Bible is flexible.

What other "friendship implications" come to mind for you?

As you think about the Bible as a "wise and cherished friend," discuss the following:

a) Is this an appropriate metaphor for the Bible? Is it blasphemous to regard God's Word with such familiarity?

b) Would you add other friendship characteristics? Does your experience with Bible stories suggest another metaphor to you? Create your own metaphor for thinking about biblical truth and authority, and explain the implications of your image.

5. Elizabeth Lee Thomsen opens a historical door and gives us a behind-the-scenes peek at the women who wrote *The Woman's Bible* with Elizabeth Cady Stanton. The following strengths of *The Woman's Bible* reflect some of their thinking:

- Women's strength of character inspires and encourages contemporary women.

- *The Woman's Bible* underscores the tension between the view of the Bible as historical record and the view of it as literary creation.

- It expresses bold opinions. These women authors named and openly objected to the misogynist judgments and practices reflected in biblical texts.

- They used great latitude in interpretation. Plurality and ambiguity seem to have been positive facts of life that informed their hermeneutics. They encouraged the hearing of many interpretive voices.

- The inclusion of the male voice and experience was important in their work. They strongly believed that the progress or regress of either of the sexes is inextricably tied to that of the other.

These strengths may also be identified as "feminist exegesis" principles. Try to use them as you read (or reread) the parable of the ten maidens, Matthew 25:1–13, and think about the following questions:

a) What elements of the parable make it challenging and dynamic for you?

b) What parts are problematic?

c) How can the bridegroom and the in-group of guests be seen as "successful" when the community is shattered?

d) What essential issues are at stake for you as you push beyond the plot?

e) From your perspective, which states of consciousness relate to the bridesmaids and the parable?

Apply this Bible study method to the reading and analysis of the following passages. (Adapt question c, above, so that it relates to an issue in each story you study and correlates with one or more of the principles named.)

- Judges 11:1–40: The Story of Jephthah and His Daughter
- Numbers 26:33; 27:1–11: The Daughters of Zelophehad
- Acts 9:36–43: The Story of Tabitha

6. Claudia Camp reminds us that the Bible often portrays exceptional women, rather than the lives of ordinary, everyday women. Nancy Claire Pittman shows us how ordinary, everyday women can speak to us through their reading of scripture.

Share the story of one of the women in your legacy mobile, or another ordinary, everyday woman. What is (was) her life like? What occupies (occupied) her time from sunrise to sunset? How much power or authority does (did) she have that does (did) not show up? Did (does) she speak through scripture—did (does) she have a favorite Bible passage, hymn, or part of the liturgy? If so, can you imagine why it was (is) particularly meaningful to her? Is there a Bible passage that reminds you of her? Why?

Answer the first three questions above in light of your own story. Then try to identify Bible passages, hymns, or parts of the liturgy that help you tell your story.

PART THREE

Theology

The authors of the four **Theology** chapters show us how theology is transformed when women's voices and perspectives become a lens through which we examine God, Christ, and the church. Jane McAvoy offers a definition of and reflection on inclusive languages, and invites us to write a communion liturgy with language that "includes everyone." Sondra Stalcup shows us that "feminist Christology" is full of diversity and richness, and invites us to weave our testimonies and interpretations of Christ into the theological tapestry. As Rita Nakashima Brock takes us on a spider's journey to create a "web of life," she teaches us about eco–feminism, which embraces creation as good. Kristine Culp engages us in some reflections on the nature and purpose of Christian community. She calls us to evaluate images and models of Christian community in relation to experience, biblical resources, Christian tradition, and prophetic vision.

1. Take Jane McAvoy up on her invitation. Write a communion liturgy. To begin, examine your Christian community.

   a) How would you describe your Christian community? Use images, metaphors, symbols, Bible stories, to help you define it. Do you have more than one? For what aspects of the community are you the most grateful? What vision do you have for your community(ies)?

   b) Use your description of your community to create a communion liturgy that includes the following parts:

   Invitation to the Lord's Table
   Prayers for the Elements (Bread and Wine)
   Words of Institution
   Prayer of Thanksgiving (to follow partaking of the elements)

   Keep in mind McAvoy's suggestions regarding the naming/renaming of God and the Trinity. Seek words and images that balance the gender and cultural reality of God's presence in the lives of persons in your community. Evaluate/reevaluate your understanding of Christian life and belief. In addition to these guidelines, read Brock's communion liturgy in the chapter "The Greening of the Soul." Additional helpful resources include: *Thankful Praise*, edited by Clark Williamson, and *Table Talk: Resources for the Communion Meal*, edited by Jane McAvoy.

   Share communion with your study group or conversation partner using the communion liturgy you have written. Talk with your pastor and/or worship committee about sharing it with others in a worship service.

2. Have you ever closely examined the construction of a spider's web? If you look very closely, you see a mystery that stimulates the imagination and paints a picture of connectedness between the natural world and human beings. Brock uses the spider's product to illustrate a feminist theological paradigm —"the greening of the soul." What can this "web of life" reveal about our relationship to God, the natural world and one another? Let's take a closer look at the web.

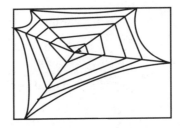

The Web of Life: The power that creates and repairs the great web of life is the love of God. The strands of the web include: the **central knot**, which represents the *"goodness of creation"*; the **radiating strands,** which represent *"affirmation as response"* to creation, embracing the diversities of life with grace and generosity; the **interweaving strands,** which represent *"healing and liberation"*; and the **web's anchor**, which represents the *"covenant with God."*

a) Illustrate a strand of the **"web of life"** by writing or telling a story. How is *"goodness of creation," "affirmation as response," "healing and liberation,"* or *"covenant with God"* operative in the story? Can you identify these strands in stories from your own life? An example might be Ruth's affirmative response to the grace she experienced in her relationship with Naomi. Does a story about one of the women you named for the "woman's legacy mobile" illustrate one of these strands?

b) Where would you place this feminist theological paradigm in the Strategies for Change chart, and why?

c) List as many symbols and/or images as possible that remind you of a web. How are they similar? How are they different? How might components of your symbol/image be analogous to the strands named in the web? One example might be the Native American symbol of the "dream catcher" that is placed over a newborn baby's cradle to catch all good dreams and expel bad ones.

d) Tatting is an almost lost art that resembles the properties of a web. Are there women in your congregation or community who tat? If so, invite them to teach you or show you how tatting is done. Engage in other crafts that employ similar principles of construction, e.g., crocheting, knitting, and macrame.

3. Put your Christian community to the test. Do the images or models you would use to describe your congregation reflect truthfulness? Kristine Culp reminds us that the truthfulness of a model

is relative to its ability "to explain, evoke, and explore ways of living and being Christian community." Use the following questions from Culp's chapter to evaluate your experience of your congregation's true nature:

a) In what way does your congregation respond to the experiences, pressures, and delights of its members' lives?

b) Does life as a part of your congregation ground and direct you in a world filled with violence and compassion, in a world where there is both profound isolation and deep interdependence?

c) To what extent does your congregation draw you toward others and the divine in a world divided by pain and abundance?

d) How does your congregation open up possibilities to experience the merciful abundance of God? Does it also cut them off?

PART FOUR

Christian Life

The **Christian Life** chapters explore how ideas of Christian life are being informed by women's lives and by the thoughts of women who have consciously reflected on their own and other women's experiences. This part of the study guide invites you to do just that—to reflect on your own life and the lives of other women, as you define Christian life. Listed below are five themes that correlate with the five chapters in this section. Review these themes and use them to inform your discussions regarding Christian life. Other themes may occur to you; name them and use them as well.

- Theme One—**Pastoral care from a feminist perspective,** which requires prophetic, transformative challenge to systems of power, authority, and domination that continue to violate, terrorize, and systematically destroy individuals and communities. One strategy mentioned by Bonnie Miller-McLemore is for congregations to engage in public discussion of some of the problems and issues that have been thought of as taboo.

- Theme Two—**Prayerful friendship,** which embodies a prayerful attentiveness to the friend. Kay Bessler Northcutt encourages the use of a balanced strategy that involves the practice of prayer, both in the embodiment of our daily lives and in silence and solitude.

- Theme Three—**Women finding voice to participate in the Protestant tradition,** which places the Word at the center of worship and reflection. One strategy suggested by Mary Donovan Turner is to discover women who have gone before us and courageously carved their own niches in the world of ministry.

- Theme Four—**Food,** which is a spiritual and physical source of nourishment. Nadia Lahutsky shares the strategy used by a large number of women saints from the Middle Ages who deprived themselves of food, sleep, and comfort in order to become closer to God.

- Theme Five—**Communion is relational,** an act of celebration and remembrance by the community. A strategy used by the *Setting the Table* authors was to engage in a conversation on the meaning of communion.

1. Use the stories and experiences of women to explore the nature of Christian life. Read the book *Babette's Feast* by Isak Dinesen, or rent or borrow the movie from your local video store or public library. View the movie with your study group or conversation partner. Discuss the movie, using the themes identified above. What scenes in the book/movie exemplify the themes? Where do these themes show up in your life?

2. Rita Nakashima Brock says, "taking the lives and loves of women and children seriously in reflecting on the responsibilities and promises of Christian life" is central to feminist work in theology. She poses the following theological questions about dimensions of women's lives. Discuss them and their significance for shaping Christian life.

   a) How are we to understand forgiveness and sin in the face of verbal and physical abuse of women and children?

   b) Does having carried another human being inside one's own body, cared passionately about this new life, fed the infant from one's own flesh, and endured sheer exhaustion caring for her/him, affect what we mean when we use the word *love*?

   c) What survival skills and faith are necessary to keep families together under slavery, grinding poverty across generations, racism, and political or class oppression?

   d) What is the shape of hope that helps us through the struggles and joys that come from nurturing a child until it grows up to become a friend, and what is the nature of such friendship?

e) How are we to teach conscience and truth in ways that enhance self-respect and self-knowledge in those for whom we have responsibility?

f) What can we learn about the love of God from our complex, highly charged experiences of intimacy, friendship, and sexuality?

3. Share your experience of Christian life. Create a timeline showing when and where you entered the Christian community. Identify significant experiences along the way and how they helped to shape your undertanding and participation in the Christian life. The following questions may help you identify and feel these shaping experiences:

Do you remember your baptism? How old were you?

Were you ever a part of a "pastor's class"?

What time of year were you baptized?

What is your earliest memory of communion?

Whom do you remember typically serving at the communion table?

Who was your favorite or most memorable Sunday school teacher?

What kind of topics did you discuss in Sunday school?

Did you ever go to church camp?

Share a "mountaintop" faith experience.

What was the graduation gift that you received from your congregation as you went off to college?

How did a faith community participate in your wedding, divorce, anniversary, or remarriage?

Who in the faith community was most present for you when a close family member died?

How did the congregation care for you at this or another time of loss?

Name and discuss other events and rites of passage that you recall in which you experienced the church as being present.

Life Stages as a Woman
"   "   " " Christian
"